CONTESTED COMMUNITIES

Other titles available from The Policy Press include:

Regional government in Britain: an economic solution? by Alan Harding, Richard Evans, Michael Parkinson and Peter Garside ISBN 1 86134 029 X £11.95

Mapping the regions: boundaries, coordination and government by Brian W. Hogwood ISBN 1 86134 030 3 £11.95

Empowerment and estate regeneration: a critical review by Murray Stewart and Marilyn Taylor ISBN 1 86134 001 X £11.95

Community networks in urban regeneration by Chris Skelcher, Angus McCabe and Vivien Lowndes with Philip Nanton ISBN 1 86134 024 9 £11.95

From estate action to estate agreement: regeneration and change on the Bell Farm Estate, York by Ian Cole and Yvonne Smith ISBN 1 86134 022 2 £11.95

Less than equal? Community organisations and estate regeneration partnerships by Annette Hastings, Andrew McArthur and Alan McGregor ISBN 1 86134 019 2 £11.95

[All the above titles are available from The Policy Press, University of Bristol, Rodney Lodge, Grange Road, Bristol BS8 4EA, Telephone 0117 973 8797 Fax 0117 973 7308]

CONTESTED COMMUNITIES
Experiences, struggles, policies

Edited by Paul Hoggett

The POLICY

PRESS

First published in Great Britain in 1997 by

The Policy Press
University of Bristol
Rodney Lodge
Grange Road
Bristol BS8 4EA

Telephone (0117) 973 8797
Fax (0117) 973 7308
e-mail: tpp@bris.ac.uk

British Library Cataloguing in Publication Data
A catalogue record for this book is available from the British Library

ISBN 1 86134 036 2

Paul Hoggett is Professor of Politics and Director of the Centre for Social and Economic Research at the University of the West of England, Bristol.

Cover design: Qube, Bristol.

The Policy Press works to counter discrimination on grounds of gender, race, disability, age and sexuality.

Printed in Great Britain by Hobbs the Printers Ltd, Southampton.

Contents

Acknowledgements

I would like to thank all of the contributors to this book for the way in which they responded swiftly and thoughtfully to my comments on their original papers and my guidance about style, and so on. One often hears that editing a book can be a nightmare as authors studiously ignore editorial guidelines – fortunately this has not been my experience. In part I know that this is due to the tremendous work put in by Chris Hunt here in the Social Sciences Faculty at the University of the West of England – my thanks to Chris for pulling all the scripts together, sorting out formatting irregularities and generally doing all the kind of complex word processing tasks which I never seem to be able to find the time to learn how to do myself.

Notes on contributors

Rob Atkinson is Senior Lecturer in Politics at the University of Portsmouth.

Manmohan Bains is undertaking doctoral research at the University of Central England.

Rick Ball teaches economic geography at the University of Staffordshire.

Neil Barnett is an ESRC Management Teaching Fellow at the Leeds Business School, Leeds Metropolitan University.

Jeremy Brent is a youth worker currently undertaking doctoral research at the University of the West of England.

Jim Chandler is Research Fellow in the Policy Research Centre at the Sheffield Business School.

Harrie Churchill is a researcher with the Social Welfare Research Unit at the University of Northumbria at Newcastle.

Chik Collins is Lecturer in Politics at the University of Paisley.

Stephen Cope is Senior Lecturer in Politics at the University of Portsmouth.

Graham Crow is Senior Lecturer in Sociology at the University of Southampton.

Karen Evans is Senior Research Fellow at the Institute for Social Research at the University of Salford.

Angela Everitt is a researcher with the Social Welfare Research Unit at the University of Northumbria at Newcastle.

Alison Gilchrist is Senior Lecturer in Community Work at the University of the West of England.

Judith Green is a researcher with the Social Welfare Research Unit at the University of Northumbria at Newcastle.

Chris Hart is Senior Lecturer in the School of Information Studies at the University of Central England.

Kathryn Jones is undertaking doctoral research at the University of Central England.

Andrew McCulloch teaches sociology at the University of Northumbria at Newcastle.

Jon Stobart teaches historical geography at the University of Staffordshire.

Marilyn Taylor is Reader in Social Policy at the University of Brighton.

Part One

Introduction

one

Contested communities

Paul Hoggett

Anyone familiar with the outpourings of British policy makers, politicians and journalists in the last few years would have to quickly conclude that the idea of community is one whose popularity conceals a multiplicity of meanings. Nowhere is the idea of community more ubiquitous than in contemporary social and public policy. We hear of care in the community, community policing, community architecture, community development, community mental health and, to add a very contemporary twist to our vocabulary, we now even hear of punishment in the community. A veritable army of professionals operating within the public services now have the term 'community' attached to their job description.

It would be easy to conclude, as Margaret Stacey did long ago in a seminal paper in the late 1960s (Stacey, 1969), that the idea of community has become hopelessly debased as a tool of social analysis. It is not even clear that community means much to the ordinary man or woman in the street these days. Certainly in many urban areas the idea of community in its traditional sense, as something referring to a place or neighbourhood with which one feels some sense of identification, may well be waning. But, if this is the case, what cannot be doubted is the way in which new social groups have begun to appropriate the term and new cultural meanings have gathered around it. For example, gays now speak of the "gay community", christians speak of "communities of faith", activists engaged in local non-monetary trading schemes speak of the creation of a "LETS community", even the new generation of travellers demand "the right to community". So, if the concept has any value today it is clear that it must refer to something far more differentiated than the notion of a Gemeinschaft community based upon ties of blood and soil that Tonnies first introduced into the lexicon of the social sciences towards the end of the last century (Tonnies, 1887).

As an introduction to this book I will try to establish some of the terrain from which contemporary usages of the term have sprung. I will do this by approaching the idea of community from three different perspectives. First, a quick tour through sociological writings on community over the last one hundred years, starting with Tonnies and running through to what might be called post-modernist accounts. Second, and using a shorter historical sweep, I will provide an account of the many ways in which community has been construed within social and public policy since the late 1960s when the Skeffington Report introduced the concept of community into local government practice. Finally, I will turn to the political sphere, where the rise of communitarianism has transcended arcane debates between political theorists to inform the practice of a variety of modernising political parties such as Clinton's democrats and Blair's New Labour Party.

Sociology: community lost and found

Elias (1974) notes how the origin of the sociological concept of 'community' is to be found in Tonnies' (1887) notion of 'Gemeinschaft'. In contrasting Gemeinschaft (community) with Gesellschaft (society) Tonnies sought to provide an analysis of the development of two different forms of social bond – one based upon similarity, the other upon interdependence and exchange – and their vagaries during the process of capitalist modernisation. Elias notes how Durkheim (1893) himself, just six years later, returns to this theme when counterposing mechanical and organic forms of solidarity. Durkheim sees these two forms of social bonding as characteristic of traditional and modern conditions within western European societies. Durkheim clearly knew of Tonnies' work for he had reviewed the latter's book, but in his own text, *The division of labour in society*, he scarcely mentions him. Elias attributes this to the radical difference between the social values of the two men. While Tonnies yearned for "a better world which was lost" Durkheim at that time was still confident about the value of progress in the society he perceived about him. Elias adds:

> ... ever since, the use of the term community has remained to some extent associated with the hope and the wish of reviving once more the closer, warmer, more harmonious type of bonds between people vaguely attributed to past ages. (1974, p xiii)

In passing, however, it is interesting to note something that Elias overlooks. Tonnies, despite his romanticism, provided a far sharper critique of exchange relationships than Durkheim. Whereas for Durkheim the development of organic solidarity is linked to the division of labour and industrialisation, for Tonnies Gesellschaft was virtually synonymous with capitalist society rather than industrial society per se. The target of Tonnies' critique is unequal exchange, a concept almost entirely absent in Durkheim's description of the division of labour.

The power of the concept of community to signify a world of more convivial social relations which had past could be seen in the tradition of 'community studies' which emerged in Britain in the 1950s and 1960s. Borrowing strongly from social anthropology a generation of social scientists went 'native' in a variety of towns and villages in the UK, from Gosforth (Williams, 1956) to Glyceiriog (Frankenberg, 1957) and from Featherstone (Dennis, Henriques and Slaughter, 1969) to Swansea (Rosser and Harris, 1965). The resulting reports were immensely rich in detail but often also deeply flawed. The communities which were revealed were strangely undifferentiated and non-conflictual and somehow or another separate from any wider social context of social change or structural inequality (Crow and Allan, 1994, pp 13-14). As such they were often empirically rich but theoretically barren, a characteristic clearly revealed even in Young and Willmott's justly celebrated study of Bethnal Green (Young and Willmott, 1957). By the late 1960s the concept of community had been sufficiently rehabilitated within the tradition of community studies that the time had arrived once more for it to be killed off. This time the coup de grace was delivered by Stacey (1969) in her article 'The myth of community studies'. Stacey argued that the concept of community not only remained tied to "the obstinate, but still mythical, remnants of the romantic model" but had taken on two more modern meanings neither of which, upon examination, were analytically valid. The first meaning referred to social relations within a defined geographical area, the second to the sense of belonging to a group which community is said to entail. Stacey's method was to demonstrate how the proponents of these meanings were unable to provide any reliable definition of either "the defined geographical area" which was appropriate to the term 'community' or of the boundaries of the group within which the sense of community was said to inhere. In place of the concept of community she proposed the use of the term "local social system".

This seemed to settle things for a while. The concept of community disappeared once more from the sociological lexicon, those such as Seabrook (1984) who did revive it were generally regarded as polemically inspired romanticists. While Stacey's idea of local social systems did not appear to have a direct impact upon the sociological community in the UK the concept of 'locality' as a geographical area profoundly shaped by its role in the spatial division of labour became a key term in the 1980s. As Crow and Allan (1994) note the locality studies which emerged in the late 1980s provided a rich analysis of the local impact of economic restructuring (Cooke, 1989). The problem with the locality approach, however, was that by giving emphasis to the spatial impact of restructuring processes it concealed from view the possibility that the meanings people ascribe to places where they live can often not be simply read off from wider economic and social forces. Moreover the level of analysis of many locality studies tended to be meso rather than micro, the focus tended to be on the city or region rather than the estate, the neighbourhood or the valley.

The demise of studies of community in the decade and a half following Stacey's article was partly a result of the rise of structuralist theories within the social sciences. The point about the idea of community however is that its imaginary dimension is as important as its structural determinants (Anderson, 1991). At the time of writing there are signs that the idea of community is once more making a come-back. A new generation of sociological and geographical researchers appear to have registered the fact that outside of the seminar room the idea of community appears to remain alive and well and people, misguidedly or not, continue to refer to it either as some thing they live in, have lost, have just constructed, find oppressive, use as the basis for struggle, and so on. Speaking of the negotiations between 'locals' and 'incomers' within the Welsh Valleys, Day and Murdoch note,

> In these processes the notion of 'community' plays a central part. As they come to terms with broader structural change, people judge what is occurring in terms of the impact on 'their' community. If social researchers have a responsibility to follow the accounts of those actively involved in social processes, then this would seem to argue for the reinstatement of 'community' as a term at the centre of the study of social space. (1993, p 108)

In his Foreword to Bell and Newby's (1974) collection of essays *The sociology of community* Elias asks if it is possible "to move beyond a condition of community research in which untested conventions and beliefs determine what one perceives as significant" (pp xiv-xv). It seems that this question can be as appropriately applied to those who have persisted in the belief that 'community' has no conceptual significance as it can to those whose analysis of community has been influenced by their implicit assumption of its value. Unfortunately the recoil from the possibility of guilt by association with nostalgic conservativism has for too long prevented a serious encounter with community as a code word "for specific structures of human bonding whose common features change in characteristic manner according to the stage of development of society" (Elias, 1974, p xv). This definition is particularly pertinent given the emergence of the global information society (Castells, 1991) for, as some of the examples given at the very beginning of this introduction suggest, one of the distinctive features of the society towards which we seem to be heading may be the decoupling of the sense of community from the sense of place.

The recent development of what might be called the sociology of identity has played an important role in opening out the conceptual space within which non-place forms of community can be understood. Black and feminist writers in particular have drawn attention to the way in which social identities, derived from one's membership of groups and communities, are both given and constructed (Anthias and Yuval-Davis, 1992; Banks, 1996; Hall, 1990). Even in the most desperately oppressive circumstances people do not just accept the identity they are given. Identities are constantly shifting and mutating as the groups and communities such identities draw from and contribute to change over time. My own research experience in London's East End has shown how, in the space of one decade, the Bangladeshi community has shifted from a primary identification with secular nationalism to an embrace of Islam. But within this overall shift a whole number of other identities have emerged for radicalised young Bangladeshi women and street-wise young males, for example (Jeffers, Hoggett and Harrison, 1996). By linking identity to imagined community contemporary sociology has begun the process of revealing the unseen terrain of 'elective groups' and 'intentional communities' (ranging from cyber-communities to car boot enthusiasts) which seems such a feature of contemporary life. 'Place' now becomes reconceptualised as an identity one chooses as much as one which is accepted as fate, enter the figure of the post-modern Scouser!

Public policy

The idea of community first began to feature strongly in social and public policy in Britain in the late 1960s. The Labour government of the time was faced with a number of interlinked problems. Some were a byproduct of the growth of the welfare state during this period. The massive programmes of public housing, transport and urban renewal disrupted many existing spatial communities. Moreover, enlightened reformers were already becoming aware of the need to involve those affected by such programmes in their design and implementation if they were to meet their objectives (Skeffington Report, 1969). They sought to reverse the process whereby the excluded had simply been enlisted as the grateful objects of urban renewal to include them as subjects who at least were worthy of consultation if not participation in such processes. As a consequence a consensus began to develop which linked the effectiveness of public policy to the need for public participation (Boaden et al, 1982).

By the late 1960s there was also a growing awareness of the persistence of social inequality despite the rapid growth of the welfare state. At first public policy borrowed strongly from the experience of the American War on Poverty. The development of Education Priority Areas and the Seebohm Report (1968) on the future of the social services were both influenced by the idea of cycles of deprivation. In all of these early initiatives the idea of community was linked to assumptions concerning 'system dysfunction' – the problem of community was either seen in terms of the dysfunctional outcome of social and economic progress or in terms of dysfunctional families and social networks.

While this idea that community was something the poor and underprivileged needed has remained a resilient, if at times subterranean, assumption within British public and social policy the ensuing decade brought new concepts of community into the public polity. The 1970s was a decade of heightened social and political conflict throughout much of western Europe as the postwar settlement between capital and labour entered a period of crisis. In Britain the Community Development Projects (CDPs) set up by the Home Office to tackle chronic forms of urban deprivation began to question the earlier dysfunctional models of community by tracing the links between social inequality and social exclusion. In making the link between community and social class the CDPs gave support to growing grassroots forms of community action which gave priority to strategies of conflict rather than participation (CDP, 1977). The 1970s also witnessed the first flowerings of the new social movements built upon identities of gender, race and, later, of sexuality and disability. But in Britain the dominant language of struggle in the 1970s remained the language of class. Thus the idea of community was still strongly spatially oriented and exemplified by the concept of areas of multiple deprivation, for example, Saltley, Batley and North Tyneside.

As community became a resource of resistance and struggle so the state began to develop strategies of incorporation (Cochrane, 1991). As Stewart and Taylor (1995) note, participation became an important strategy for sustaining administrative stability and subduing potentially troublesome elements. This became particularly pertinent after the inner-city riots in Bristol, Brixton and elsewhere in the early 1980s. For a brief period in the early 1980s, as conflicts between leftwing local authorities and central government reached their apotheosis, two entirely different discourses of community vied with each other in public policy. On the one hand local authorities like the Greater London Council

(GLC), Islington and Manchester sought to facilitate the development of oppositional communities via radical decentralisation initiatives and by concentrating support on the new community groups built around gender, race and other identities. But the resources available for such initiatives became dwarfed by those tied to new central government initiatives such as the Urban and Community Programmes. The costs of the growing dependency by community organisations on such programmes in many areas became apparent in the late 1980s as community groups found themselves increasingly involved in a competitive struggle for scarce government resources, a struggle which exacerbated existing lines of tension between communities of difference (Cain and Yuval-Davis, 1990).

Community groups found themselves increasingly entangled in a regime where funding was becoming linked to a narrow range of criteria. The extension of markets and competition within the public sphere, a process which accelerated rapidly after the third Conservative electoral victory in 1987, inaugurated a period in which scarce resources became progressively attached to preset performance criteria rather than need. In the sphere of urban policy this process was exemplified by the City Challenge initiative but a similar approach was adopted by a range of government departments, illustrated for instance by the Department of the Environment's Estate Action Programme. Spatial communities were becoming increasingly drawn into competitive relationships in a way which paralleled emerging relationships between schools, NHS trusts, and so on. Such developments were not simply an outcome of government policy. Broader processes of economic restructuring prompted the emergence of cities and regions as competitive actors in a global market. Civic boosterism was becoming a central aspect of local government strategy in urban areas, the idea of 'community governance' signifying the development of new forms of local corporatism in which community and voluntary organisations competed to be incorporated into the emerging partnerships between local government and the local private sector.

Finally, also noticeable during the period from the mid-1980s onwards, we can see how 'community' became a metaphor for the absence or withdrawal of services by the state. This was most clearly indicated in the area of community mental health where the deinstitutionalisation of mental healthcare was not accompanied by an adequate transfer of resources to the voluntary and local authority organisations who were having to pick up the tab. The fact was that a great many of the mentally ill and elderly people who were in receipt of institutional care were there precisely because of the absence of supportive social networks outside 'in the community' (Hoggett, 1993). In the absence of such networks the function of care was either undertaken by no one or fell upon the shoulders of (usually) female carers who themselves often lacked networks of support.

The point of the previous discussion is to indicate the many different meanings that 'community' has taken on in social and public policy over the last three decades in the UK. As this, admittedly subjective, account indicates the concept of community can signify system dysfunction or social pathology, social instability and threat to the existing order, an imaginary safety net or a form of social capital to be enlisted in the competitive struggle for survival. But if these are just some of the means by which community has been harnessed in the exercise of dominance we have also seen how community can figure in emancipatory politics – as a resource of resistance signifying the commonality of class, the uniqueness of identity or the lost ideal of a more intimate society.

The politics of community: the unhappy revenge of the socially excluded?

For policy makers and street-level bureaucrats within the state the idea of community has nearly always been used as a form of shorthand for the socially excluded. Crudely we could say that whereas the late 1960s saw the rediscovery of social exclusion, and the 1970s and early 1980s was a period of political struggle by the socially excluded, the last decade, in contrast, has witnessed the deepening of social inequalities and the renewed marginalisation of the excluded.

This is not just a question of the political defeat of the socially excluded within an unchanging society. Inequalities have increased and the excluded have become more marginalised as a consequence of the new kind of society which has emerged during the last decade. Until the 1980s social inequality was the product of a particular kind of society governed by what some have termed the Fordist mode of regulation. A society of giant industrial and public bureaucracies, relatively full employment, job security, internal labour markets, a welfare state which at least claimed to be universalistic and the incorporation of organised labour in the post-war settlement – corporatism as it became known within the social sciences. Within western European states there was always a reserve army of labour throughout the post-war period which in Britain tended to underlie the distinction drawn between the 'rough' and 'respectable' working class.

Within a decade much of this landscape had changed. Alongside mass unemployment there is now a new army of the semi-employed, traditional industries have either all but disappeared (mining) or have been restructured out of recognition (printing), job insecurity had increased enormously with the rise of the new flexibilities, a service sector deploying largely low paid and flexible labour has grown enormously. These and other developments have dramatically heightened social inequalities (Joseph Rowntree Foundation, 1995). In inner-city areas, outer-city estates and an increasing number of rural areas, excluded communities are teetering on the point of collapse, their resources of self-organisation and resistance overwhelmed by the sheer scale of economic and social change which they had endured. As the capacity of communities to offer an organised point of resistance to the state has declined so has the need for the state to manage communities by incorporation. In North America, more so than in Britain, the strategy of incorporating excluded communities in the state by involving them in the planning and implementation of government programmes has been replaced a strategy which more closely resembled managed neglect. As Davis (1990) noted in his study of Los Angeles the dispossessed become locked into new forms of spatial apartheid, physically contained within their own areas, kept out of the 'gated communities' of the comfortable classes, the objects of remote surveillance and arbitrary forms of repressive control and subject to the perverse self-regulation of the drugs economy and a constant war of attrition between competing gangs (Hoggett, 1994).

And now to the present day. Mass shootings of infant school children, the murder of a headmaster as he endeavoured to protect one his pupils from a street gang, escalating crime, the drugs economy, neighbours from hell, racial violence, women and old people afraid to go out at night ... the newspaper headlines provide a relentless reportage of the consequences of the collapse of excluded communities. This has important consequences for the shifting significance of community. Perhaps the consequences of heightened social inequality are coming home to roost for the comfortable classes. The idea of community as a nexus of rights and obligations is now seen as crucially important for the well-being of *all* rather than as a something which was primarily a palliative for the poor and dispossessed (something that 'they' needed but 'we', the reformers and planners, did not).

This period of massive social change has also found a reflection in political society. The anti-collectivist ideology of British Conservatism under Thatcher promoted a 'me first' mentality which sank deep into the pores of society. Moreover, with the decline of class, social democracy began to search for a new source of social identity, something beyond 'me' and my happiness – a wider non-class social collectivity. For New Labour 'community' has become what 'class' was for old Labour. But this is a very particular kind of community, and this is where Etzioni's distinctive popularisation of the more arcane debates of North American political philosophers enters the picture (Etzioni, 1995a).

The rise of communitarianism in the last few years has been a remarkable phenomenon. For the communitarians the idea of community, signifying a nexus of rights and obligations embedded within robust social networks, represents both a critique of the under-socialised and individualised self of American liberal political theory and a practical demonstration of the alternative to the fragmentation and anomie of late modernity (Walzer, 1995). While Etzioni is undoubtedly its most well-known proponent, and a moralistic and conservative proponent to boot, it seems that there are already as many varieties of communitarianism as one could dare to choose (Etzioni, 1995b; Frazer and Lacey, 1993; Hughes, 1996). The point however, and it is one well made by Hughes, is that it is Etzioni's brand of "moral authoritarian communitarianism" which has been taken up so enthusiastically by Blair and Straw in the New Labour Party. Etzioni's communitarianism evokes a lost age when neighbourhood ties were strong and families socialised their offspring more effectively than they are held to do today. It was a time when people were more grateful than they are today and when there was more stress upon duty and responsibility rather than upon rights and entitlements.   One sometimes gets the image of the kind of community where no one locked their front door, everyone kept an eye out for the old woman who lived in number 12 and, as one elderly tenant in Stepney once put it to me "the caretaker would come round the estate at 9.00 pm and say to any kids that were still out, 'oi you, in!', and they went".   But of course such communities were also suffocatingly homogenous and intolerant of difference, where nosey-parkers lurked behind the lace curtains and where deference was not only practised to the old and wise but to the educated and clever as well.

Even within local government today there are other variants of communitarianism at large in which 'community' is invoked primarily as part of a strategy to enlist citizens in a new participatory democracy.   Now practised as widely, if not more widely, by Liberal Democrat as Labour activists it seeks solutions to problems of our common welfare neither through the state nor through individuals and their families but through the associations, networks and communities of civil society.   Whether this democratic communitarianism will find a space for the new politics of social diversity so that how we are different is kept in mind as much as what we hold in common remains to be seen.   But surely it is in this direction that a non-authoritarian communitarianism lies.

Contested communities

Community is a fundamentally political concept.   By this I do not mean to refer simply to the use of the term by political parties, what I wish to indicate is the way in which the idea of community is saturated with power.   As such community is a continually contested term.   The chapters in this book, particularly those in Part Two, provide vivid accounts of the many ways in which meanings of community are fought over by different groups – the rough and respectable, cosmopolitans and locals, the state and the people, old and young, men and women, and focus upon the dynamics of community in a number of places around Britain. The level of analysis within the case studies is almost consistently micro – a series of small-area studies within a range of cities such as Glasgow, Newcastle, Salford and Bristol often focusing on housing estates with reputations for notoriety. In the light of what was said earlier about the decoupling of the sense of community from the sense of place this may seem an odd choice. But in a society increasingly prone to polarisation between cosmopolitans and locals (Castells, 1991) perhaps the delocalisation of community applies primarily to the former. As new kinds of non-place communities emerge for some the dispossessed find themselves locked into place more and more.

Although the primary focus of this book is what might be called the neighbourhood, and although at times both insiders and outsiders might refer to such neighbourhoods as communities, what is striking about these studies is the way in which each neighbourhood is a site for a multitude of networks, interests and identities which help determine how people see the place where they live. What comes across, even from the strongly working-class neighbourhoods, is the heterogeneity and complexity of communities. And yet it is this that policy makers and practitioners still seem to be largely unaware of. As Evans notes, in her case study of two neighbourhoods in Salford, if public policies are to be targeted effectively at local areas then an appreciation of the differences within and between them must be the starting point.

A second theme which emerges from this book is the importance of social networks within local residential areas and the importance of women within these networks, not just as neighbours and carers but as activists. McCulloch goes so far as to speak of the triple burden of women – the burdens of household, work and community. And yet many local authorities and other local agencies do not yet appear to have responded to this, their formalised procedures of consultation and the language of policy that they use often means that those who end up 'speaking' for communities are the men.

A third theme concerns the importance of sentiments and emotions in community life. Few, if any, of the case studies convey much of the warm glow that the idea of community is often said to signify. In contrast, fear as a powerful sentiment comes through strongly in both the experience of the elderly in the Benwell and the activists in the Cruddas Park case studies. Anger, jealousy, pride and longing also fuel the process of boundary construction which distinguishes insiders from outsiders, those who can be trusted and those who can not.

Despite years of trying to bridge the gap, government at national and local level still seems to inhabit a separate world from excluded communities. As the chapter by Collins indicates the rhetoric of partnership is often used to disguise crude strategies for engineering consensus. And yet, as the chapter by Hart, Jones and Bains illustrates, where the commitment to sharing power is genuine agencies still face the problem of reversing the accumulated historical experience that many groups have of not being listened to, of being the objects of policies and not co-determining subjects.

The chapters in this book are organised into a number of parts. **Part One** offers an introduction by focusing on an analysis of the concept of community and some of the key social networks which underpin them. **Part Two** provides a series of case studies of community life as experienced by different actors (including those receiving care in the community). **Part Three** focuses upon the way in which successive local government reorganisations have theorised community while **Part Four** considers examples of successful and unsuccessful community mobilisation and the involvement of community groups in the design and delivery of government programmes.

The writers represent almost the full range of social science disciplines, a reflection of the interdisciplinary nature of the conference 'Ideas of Community' held at the University of the West of England, Bristol in September 1995 from which this book is drawn. Although not a conscious criterion in selecting essays for this volume the fact that many of the authors write from the position of 'engaged researchers' is, with hindsight, a unique and valuable feature given the tendency these days for academics to become increasingly distanced from political and social involvement.

two

What do we know about the neighbours? Sociological perspectives on neighbouring and community

Graham Crow

Introduction

The major traditions of sociological inquiry are given less explicit acknowledgement in the field of community than they are in other branches of the discipline. In particular, the community studies tradition has been portrayed as descriptive and atheoretical, although it would be more accurate to characterise this research genre as embodying an implicit functionalism. There are, of course, exceptions to such generalisations. Rex and Moore's (1967) *Race, community and conflict* owes a clear debt to Weberian sociology, while Stacey et al's (1975) re-study of Banbury attempted to move away from the holistic approach and to engage with Marx and other stratification theorists in the analysis of group processes. Pahl's (1984) *Divisions of labour* goes further still in this direction by setting out contrasting Durkheimian, Marxist and Weberian theories of the development of the Isle of Sheppey's social structure (1984, pp 186-8), and no doubt several other instances of community researchers drawing on prominent sociological theorists could be cited. It remains the case, however, that sociology's theoretical traditions sit somewhat uneasily with empirical analyses in the field of community, and the wider significance of their contrasting assumptions is often left unexplored. This chapter aims to discuss some of the implications of this issue in the light of what has been written by sociologists about relations between neighbours.

The study of neighbouring illustrates the need to address theoretical issues and their relationship to empirical evidence. Much of what is written about neighbours turns out to be contentious. For example, Etzioni's case for communitarianism rests in part on the assertion that neighbours have a key role to play in providing for people's welfare, since once individual responsibility has been met, "*The second line of responsibility lies with those closest to the person*, including kin, friends, neighbors, and other community members. They are next in line because they know best what the genuine needs are" (1994, p 144, emphasis in original). Etzioni cites his own experience of neighbourly assistance at a time of crisis in Bethesda, Maryland, and employs this to support a more abstract case about reciprocity, but even communitarians might find such arguments inconclusive; as Durkheim observed, "To illustrate an idea is not to prove it" (1982, p 155). Others have been more sceptical of the capacity and preparedness of neighbours to enter into extensive social relations with each other, and Abrams' study set out from this starting point in search of "An understanding of how and why different sorts of people put different prices on neighbouring" (Bulmer, 1986, pp 9-10). Current political concerns with bad neighbours (Campbell, 1995) and the desirability of creating "a more neighbourly society" (White, 1995) also indicate the importance of the subject of neighbouring.

Sociological perspectives on neighbouring

In the absence of consensus on how many sociological perspectives exist, Collins' (1994) distinction between the conflict, rational/utilitarian, Durkheimian and microinteractionist traditions will be followed, with the addition of a fifth, feminist approach, in order to highlight the competing assumptions which underlie different studies of neighbouring. The simplest approach regards relations between neighbours as unimportant. According to Logan and Molotch, "Within the Marxian framework, neighbourhood is essentially a residual phenomenon" (1987, p 100), neighbourhood processes being determined by the accumulation of capital, and neighbourhood homogeneity being the geographical expression of social polarisation. As Logan and Molotch go on to note, this treatment of neighbourhood as a dependent variable ignores important variations within and between neighbourhoods, and the possibility of analysing these in terms of "the creation and defense of the use values of neighbourhood" (1987, p 99) shows that analysis rooted in Marxist concepts need not be insensitive to the meanings which residents associate with place. Logan and Molotch's view that neighbourly relations involve matters which include informal support, identity (including in particular ethnic identity), security and trust is still broadly within the conflict tradition, emphasising as it does that urban conflicts have micro as well as macro dimensions. In Britain the study closest to this position is probably Rex and Moore's (1967) *Race, community and conflict* in which competition between 'housing classes' for scarce housing resources and disputes relating to the perceived 'respectability' of residents are treated as crucial to the explanation of changing neighbourly relations and their tendency to generate conflict. This study was conducted around the time of the 1964 general election when the potential tension between white and black neighbours was an important local political issue.

Conflict theory highlights the likelihood of conflict between neighbours over scarce resources, both material and cultural. The rational/utilitarian sociological tradition is similar in that it too seeks to explain behaviour in terms of the rational pursuit of interests, but differs in emphasising choice and the scope which exists for mutually beneficial exchange. It also differs in taking individuals rather than groups (such as classes) as its starting point. Within this tradition the exchange theorist Homans' (1951) study of the social disintegration of 'Hilltown' explains the decline in the extent to which community members collaborated by reference to the fact that:

> ... the need for neighbours to work together
> became much less than it had been ... the interests
> of Hilltowners led them to take part in
> organisations ... outside the town rather than
> inside it. (1951, p 359)

The concept of reciprocity plays a prominent role in Homans' perspective, with individuals entering into exchanges with others in a similar position to themselves to their mutual benefit, and avoiding interaction with others who are not their equals and who are not in a position to reciprocate (Collins, 1994). Wallman's (1984) work on resources and networks in inner-city neighbourhoods can be seen to fit into this tradition. So too can Abrams' study of neighbouring, emphasising as it does the reciprocity which characterised the dense interdependencies among kin and neighbours of traditional working-class communities and also the preference to limit involvement in such exchange relationships in 'modern neighbourhoodism'. In Abrams' view, most people "do not choose to make their friends among their neighbours" (Bulmer, 1986, p 98), preferring to limit their social relationships with their neighbours unless compelled to do otherwise by the economic logic of their shared poverty.

Alongside reciprocity, altruism as a basis of neighbouring also figures in Abrams' work, and this thread leads more in the direction of Durkheimian analysis. While it was Abrams' general belief that "neighbourliness and the moral attitudes sustaining it developed in the past in situations where people helped each other because there was no alternative way of surviving" (Bulmer, 1986, p 8), he recognised the perceptiveness of Durkheim's observation that individual interest is an unstable basis on which to build social relationships and that social solidarity requires the restriction of self-interested, instrumental behaviour. Put another way, communities need to be moral orders exercising social control over their members if the pattern of exchanges that takes place between those members is to be sustainable. This theme is explored further in Baumgartner's (1988) *The moral order of a suburb*, which notes that the surface appearance in Hampton's neighbourhoods is one of "An air of harmony, tranquillity, and civility". Baumgartner goes on to argue that while "neighbours experience few open disputes" (1988, p 72), their relations are governed by less direct mechanisms of social control such as avoidance (and, in the extreme, collective boycotting), and making anonymous complaints to official bodies. In working-class communities (which have denser social networks than Hampton) gossip has been reported to be a powerful social sanction against deviance in relation to community norms (Hoggart, 1958; Roberts, 1984), and it was Abrams' view that "The extent of mutual surveillance by neighbours deserves more attention, as does the social significance of gossip" (Bulmer, 1986, p 33). Collins' inclusion of Goffman in the Durkheimian tradition is pertinent here, since gossip as a mechanism of social control relates to individuals being embarrassed by public knowledge of aspects of their lives which they prefer to keep private.

The fourth sociological tradition identified by Collins, that of microinteractionism, explores the dynamic processes within groups which produce different senses of identity. As in the Durkheimian tradition there is an interest in deviance, but with more of a sense of the fluidity of the processes by which normal and deviant behaviour come to be perceived. Elias and Scotson's (1994) *The established and the outsiders* might be considered as an example of what such an approach can achieve in the field of community, for while there is much that is unique about Elias' sociology, the analysis of insider/outsider relations presented by Elias and Scotson hinges on each group's misinterpretation of the other and the subsequent amplification of the outsiders' deviance. The suspicions held by Winston Parva's established population about in-migrants produced a situation in which:

> ... the residents of one area where the 'old families' lived regarded themselves as 'better', as superior in human terms to those who lived in the neighbouring newer part of the community.
> (Elias and Scotson, 1994, p xvi)

This was reinforced by the established group tending "to attribute to its outsider group as a whole the 'bad' characteristics of that group's 'worst' section" (Elias and Scotson, 1994, p xix) while stereotyping themselves in terms of their most exemplary members. The two groups became progressively polarised through the operation of "praise-gossip" and "blame-gossip" (Elias and Scotson, 1994, p xiv), although the newcomers:

> ... who perceived the old residents at first as people like themselves, never quite understood the reasons for their exclusion and stigmatisation.
> (Elias and Scotson, 1994, p xxxix)

The reproduction of social exclusion long after the newcomers' novelty had worn off has a particular bearing on relations between ethnic groups brought together by migration, as Elias and Scotson note in their observations about the social identities embodied in 'us'/'them' distinctions.

Elias and Scotson's approach runs counter to the idea that neighbouring behaviour can be explained as rational when much of what they are describing constitutes "group fantasies" (1994, p xxxvi). They also highlight power imbalances between insiders and outsiders which allow the latter group few opportunities to influence the course of their relationship with the more powerful insiders. These themes echo feminist arguments in which the critique of rationality is developed and the pervasiveness of patriarchal power is emphasised. A further similarity relates to the importance attached to historical analysis, feminist writers having played a leading role in the reconstruction of traditional working-class communities through the use of oral history. Feminist oral historians have highlighted how women were far more central than men to relations between neighbours (Bourke, 1994, ch 5; see also Crow and Allan, 1994, ch 2). Further, Roberts' (1984) work emphasises women's pivotal role in monitoring and maintaining codes of 'respectability' among neighbours. These themes are also present in reports on research into contemporary community life, studies which in addition note the important influence of stage in the life course on neighbouring (Devine, 1992).

Sociological findings on neighbouring

The sociological perspectives outlined above indicate that sociologists have several different theoretical angles on neighbouring. The five approaches are not entirely discrete, as was noted in passing in relation to shared assumptions and foci, but they are sufficiently distinct to direct attention towards different aspects of neighbouring and to suggest different interpretations of what neighbourly relations involve. When it comes to evaluating their respective strengths in relation to empirical evidence, however, two immediate problems present themselves. One is the predictable issue of the shortage of contemporary evidence relating to neighbours, neighbouring being a relatively neglected topic. The second and more serious problem is that the research evidence on neighbouring which is available has not always been collected for the purpose of assessing different theories of neighbouring, and the methods used in the collection of these data are not necessarily sensitive to the points at issue between competing theories. For example, evidence relating to explicit conflicts between neighbours has only a partial bearing on the situation described by Baumgartner in which social control between neighbours "is rarely noticed by anyone who is not directly involved" (1988, p 72), raising all sorts of questions about how outside researchers might come to be aware of it. Similar problems arise in relation to Elias and Scotson's description of the bonds which unite insiders as 'invisible', while conflict between insiders and outsiders may take the form of "silent tugs-of-war hidden between the routine co-operation between the two groups" (1994, pp xxxix, xxxvii). In the light of these problems, it is unsurprising to find that thinking and writing about neighbouring contains a great deal of unconfirmed speculation.

Folk speculation about neighbouring is not hard to come by. The view that semi-detached housing leads to semi-detached lives illustrates how spatial determinism can be used to support a loss of community theme. It is not only common sense thinking which is speculative, however. Several recent examinations have exposed the speculative nature of the view that community life has been undermined by a process of 'privatisation' (Allan and Crow, 1991; Devine, 1992; Pahl and Wallace, 1988; Procter, 1990), but in the absence of more compelling analyses it retains much of its hold on the sociological imagination. The privatisation model characterises the past as a period of extensive neighbourliness and the present as a time of limited neighbourly contact between self-sufficient, home-centred households. Such a contrast has its roots in classic studies like those by Mogey (1956), Young and Willmott (1957), Willmott and Young (1960), and notably Goldthorpe et al (1969) in which the concept of 'privatisation' as a reflection of emerging working-class instrumentalism is developed. While there is much that is unexceptional about arguments that community networks are less dense, less settled and less place-specific than formerly, there are nevertheless several reservations concerning conclusions about neighbourly relations which have been drawn from such arguments.

To begin with, the privatisation model romanticises the past, exaggerating the extent of neighbourly solidarity and playing down the presence of conflicts (Crow and Allan, 1994). It also suggests general acceptance of a norm of communal sociability which simply does not square with the reports of people leading privatised lives long before the advent of mass affluence (Pahl and Wallace, 1988). Sheer physical proximity did not necessarily produce solidarity among neighbours. As Hoggart (1958) noted of traditional working-class community life, "You are bound to be close to people with whom, for example, you share a lavatory in a common yard" (p 81), but it was also the case that neighbours were all too ready to "think that two and two make six" (p 34). In such circumstances, Hoggart argues,

> The insistence on the privacy of home' reflected people's 'knowledge that, though the neighbours are 'your sort' and will rally round in trouble, they are always ready for a gossip and perhaps a mean-minded gossip.... You want good neighbours but a good neighbour is not always 'coming in and out': if she does that, she may have to be 'frozen off'". (1958, pp 81, 34)

Consciousness of the need to establish and police "community's internal boundary" (Crow and Allan, 1995a, p 11) may even have been a more important feature of neighbourly relations in conditions where privacy was at such a premium. Recognition of the reciprocal advantages of respecting neighbours' privacy would also have arisen in situations where neighbours were conscious of "knowing too much about each other's intimate lives", including being able to hear "neighbours talking in bed", a situation which required the development of "distancing devices" (Bourke, 1994, pp 142-3). As a result, for many people, "Friendships with neighbours were considered to be dangerous", and Bourke's more general conclusion is that

> The isolated working-class family living in a predominantly working-class street was not as rare as the 'community' theorists would have us believe. (1994, p 143)

If the privatisation model is guilty of exaggeration with regard to past neighbourliness, it also misrepresents current patterns. Procter's (1990) study of a working-class suburb of Coventry found far more extensive sociability between neighbours than he anticipated on the basis of the privatisation literature, and he concludes that the short-term effects of geographical mobility (which it is agreed can be highly disruptive of community networks) need to be distinguished from purported secular trends towards privatised lifestyles. The passage of time can see the transformation of what Lockwood called "a population of strangers" (1975, p 22) into a settled group in which there are extensive points of contact between neighbours. Saunders (1990) acknowledges in similar fashion that the disruption of social ties accompanying geographical mobility may go at least some way towards explaining the less dense patterns of informal aid between neighbours who are owner-occupiers compared to neighbourhood networks of local authority tenants. His acceptance of the privatisation thesis is further qualified in his consideration of data relating to other aspects of neighbouring such as informal sociability, leading him to conclude that "home owners are if anything less home-centred and less privatised than tenants" (1990, p 288). Also telling is the conclusion, drawn from the re-study two decades on from Goldthorpe et al's (1969) original research, that:

> In opposition to the Luton team's findings ...
> neighbours are often an important source of
> intimate relations and mutual support, especially
> for women in the most demanding stage of the
> family life-cycle. (Devine, 1992, p 91)

In sum, there is little evidence of wholesale privatisation, although it is equally clear that relations between neighbours do vary considerably in relation to key sociological variables.

Willmott's (1986) overview of the literature on neighbours highlights the variation of neighbourly relations according to social class, gender, life-cycle stage, proximity of kin, length of residence and the extent to which an area is socially homogeneous. Similar conclusions are supported by the work of Abrams (Bulmer, 1986), Dickens (1988) and Stacey et al (1975) but, like Willmott, these authors want to say more than that neighbourly relations have greater prominence in the lives of women than men, middle-class than working-class people, long-established residents than newcomers, dependent than independent groups and inhabitants of homogeneous rather than mixed areas. Such an account captures the range of social structural forces influencing neighbourly relations, but it does not convey the dynamic tensions inherent in those relations. Willmott's reference to neighbouring as "A delicate balance" (1986, p 55) echoes Abrams' point that "Good neighbouring could be said to be a matter of finding a point of equilibrium in a highly unstable field of contrary forces" (Bulmer, 1986, p 31). In general terms, neighbouring involves being friendly and helpful towards one's neighbours while at the same time respecting their privacy. In Bulmer's words:

> The complexity and contradiction of neigh-
> bourliness lie precisely in this combination of
> closeness – through passing the time of day,
> visiting, mutual aid, emergency help – with
> distance. (1986, p 86)

Neighbours can and sometimes do become friends, but this simply adds a further dimension to an already complex relationship, and there are good sociological reasons relating to the desire to control the boundary where home and community meet which help to explain why such a development does not occur more frequently. Given the danger that neighbours may "turn out to be inquisitive, over-enthusiastic about entering the homes of others, inclined to gossip, liable to stir up trouble" (Willmott, 1986, p 56), the preference for limiting neighbourly relations is understandable.

Emerging research agendas on neighbouring

The evidence available fails to confirm the view that neighbourly relations are dwindling to a residual phenomenon. On the basis of such evidence Willmott concludes that

> ... in present-day Britain the overwhelming
> majority of people know their neighbours and are
> on reasonably good terms with them, and most
> have sociable contacts, often substantial ones,
> with some of their neighbours. (1986, p 55)

Even if it is granted that there has been a decline in the extent to which neighbours enter into relationships of material interdependence, the privatisation model falls down in its oversimplification of the multi-faceted nature of relations between neighbours. Procter has pointed out how Pahl's data derive from an almost exclusive focus on the extent to which households "call upon the assistance of other households to get their work done", and that the Sheppey study provides us with "virtually no information about 'communal *sociability*' at all" (1990, p 172, emphasis in original). The discrepancy between patterns of mutual aid and sociability found by Saunders (1990) also indicates the dangers of concentrating on only one aspect of relations between neighbours. As Saunders himself observes, "There is a permeable membrane between the household and the wider society, and resources, people and ideas pass constantly between the two" (1990, p 266), and his subsequent exploration of the wide range of factors which have a bearing on relations between neighbours sits rather uneasily alongside his main thesis about the central importance of owner-occupation.   Abrams' argument that "relationships of deep and enduring commitment between neighbours" (Bulmer, 1986, p 99) have become exceptional though choice can in the same way be read as an overstatement of the privatisation perspective (Crow and Allan, 1995b).

A further problem in drawing out the significance for the analysis of neighbouring of Goldthorpe et al's theory of privatisation, Pahl's theory of self-provisioning by households, Saunders' theory of the ontological security brought by owner-occupation and Abrams' view of traditional neighbouring as forced, is that it is difficult to identify what are context-specific influences on their research findings.   Things are significantly different now from the economic context in which the 'Affluent worker' study was undertaken (Devine, 1992), and while Pahl's study was conducted against the background of mass unemployment, we can agree with Byrne that Sheppey is "a rather unusual place" (1989, p 24). Similarly, Abrams' neglect of stable middle-class and upper-class neighbourhoods (Bulmer, 1986, p 47) limits his conclusions' generalisability, while Saunders gives insufficient attention to the point that the meaning of owner-occupation has changed as it has displaced other tenure types to become the most common (Crow, 1989).   Yet for all these reservations, it remains the case that it is in studies such as those undertaken by Goldthorpe et al, Pahl, Saunders and Abrams that the attempt to engage with mainstream sociological theory is most explicitly made, and it is through such engagement that the sociological analysis of neighbouring is most likely to be advanced.

What such developments might involve can only be sketched here.   Abrams' finding that "physical proximity and distance mattered only if something is made of them" (Bulmer, 1986, p 52) highlights the fluidity of the relationship between physical distance and social distance. One possible avenue for the exploration of this issue is to examine the impact which the general move away from terraced to semi-detached and detached properties has on neighbourly relations, in particular on notions of privacy and on where physically and abstractly community's internal boundary is drawn. The instability of this boundary where community and household meet (Crow and Allan, 1995b) points to the need to consider how neighbouring fits into wider patterns of forces which determine the interconnections of public and private spheres. Feminist theory clearly has much to contribute to the analysis of this subject, as do exchange theory (through the suggestion that the very existence of neighbourly relations indicates the presence of some reciprocal arrangements) and the microinteractionist tradition (through its focus on the negotiated character of privacy and of who is classified as a neighbour). The conflict tradition would point more in the direction of following up Saunders' (1990) suggestions about the ways in which owner-occupiers highlight the boundaries of their territory, while Durkheimians would perhaps be more interested in the implications of these changes for the exchange of information and the maintenance of local codes of behaviour. Dickens' observation that "there is very little we can say in general terms about the effect of physical space or design on social life" (1988, p 2) is a further invitation to explore what determines the extent to which the potential for neighbourly assistance (or, in other cases, enmity) is realised.

If the persistence of neighbourly relations despite the move towards greater physical distance between neighbours is one possible line of enquiry to which general sociological theory might contribute, the impact on neighbouring of social class and tenure shifts is another, previous research having concentrated on working-class communities. The social polarisation which Pahl (1984) describes undoubtedly has a broad geographical expression, but polarisation was working to divide neighbours as well as areas on Sheppey. This might suggest a greater likelihood of conflict between neighbours in different social classes, but exchange theory would lead us to expect minimal contact between people with very different resources at their disposal. The interpretation of the Sheppey research findings in terms of the idea that affluence could be associated with 'voluntary' privatisation and poverty with 'obligatory' privatisation may be problematic (Pahl and Wallace, 1988) but it does indicate some scope for analysis in terms of conflict and exchange theories. The further Sheppey finding that unemployed people experienced community as "a prison of jealous eyes" (Wallace and Pahl, 1986, p 118) is more in tune with the theme of surveillance which runs through the Durkheimian and microinteractionist traditions. Likewise, Dickens frames his analysis of social polarisation in terms of "'Community' for Some" (Dickens, 1988) and contrasting positions in civil society (to which Durkheim attached great importance), although he is closer to the feminist tradition in his emphasis on the gender dimension of involvement in relations between neighbours and its implications for what he calls "the politics of locality" (1988, pp 131, 140).

A third research theme which suggests itself is the dynamic nature of community processes such as social inclusion and exclusion. The employment of interactionist ideas in the analysis of the dynamic relationship between 'insiders' and 'outsiders' was noted above, and it may fall to the immediate neighbours of newcomers to act as a bridge with established populations. From an exchange theory perspective Dhooge suggests that the extent to which people are involved in local neighbourhood networks "is partly a matter of personal choice" (1982, p 118), while Homans (1951) explained community disintegration in terms of people's preferences leading to the growth of centrifugal forces while centripetal forces weakened. Interestingly, the concepts of centrifugal and centripetal forces are also employed in Warwick and Littlejohn's (1992) analysis of how social closure is effected in a community context. Their focus on inequality fits more readily into the conflict theory tradition and their emphasis that communities do not necessarily require "a high degree of consensus" (1992, p 12) distances them from Durkheimian assumptions. Other studies like Dempsey's (1990) *Smalltown* suggest that neighbouring is very much influenced by shared norms about what community members should do, although the observation that "most neighbour interaction takes place between members of the same sex" (1990, p 102) offers a clue as to how these common values do not preclude the reproduction of Smalltown's highly-unequal patriarchal system.

Conclusion

By way of a brief conclusion it can be observed that while we may know a considerable amount about neighbours, this remains an area where speculation abounds. Much of our knowledge is open to competing interpretations based on contrasting assumptions about issues such as rationality, choice and social change. Without theoretically informed research it will not be possible to come to a view over whether neighbouring is better understood as rational or emotional, material or symbolic, chosen or forced, short term or long term, declining or persistent. Making the assumptions underlying these competing interpretations more explicit cannot resolve abstract debates between the different sociological traditions, but it should sharpen the focus of researchers in the field. In doing so, it has the potential to contribute to the explanation of why 'community' can be understood and experienced in so many different ways.

Part Two

Community and social diversity

three

"It's all right 'round here if you're a local": community in the inner city[1]

Karen Evans

Introduction

The research for this chapter set out to situate an understanding of the risk from and fear of crime in a comparative, local urban context with a view to understanding how people who live and work in such areas might construct their own responses to 'risk of' and 'fear of' crime.

The areas we chose to study are two local authority wards in the inner city of Salford, both of which are seen as areas of high crime – these wards will be referred to as Oldtown and Bankhill. Both wards display characteristics that are shared with many other impoverished areas of British cities. We would argue that the work we are conducting has given us some insight into the ways in which people live their lives in areas which, in many ways, could be said to be 'in crisis' – exhibiting, as they do, many of the features of decline which are associated with areas of extreme deprivation. These areas are, themselves, situated within a city which, according to a recent University of Bristol 'social deprivation index' (see Forrest and Gordon, 1993) which factors in unemployment, lone parenthood, numbers of single pensioners and long-term illness, is the ninth most deprived urban district in England.

By focusing on a comparative study of two similarly structured areas of the one city we hoped to draw out *the different ways* in which residents and users of these places might respond and adapt to their local situation. These are areas which exhibit peculiarities unique to their own particular history and development but we believe that they also share characteristics with many other parts of Britain. We did not set out to conduct a 'community study', however, Crow and Allen (1994) define a study of community as disclosing "ways in which individuals are embedded into sets of personal relationships which are based outside the household" (1994, p 177).

We are interested in this notion of being 'embedded' in an area, but we argue that other relationships, apart from "sets of personal relationships", come to play an important part in the way individuals feel within their localities, how they behave and how these sentiments and behaviours are expressed in the wider social context.

In this sense then, we are involved in some sort of study of community and how this term resonates at a number of different levels within these inner-city neighbourhoods. The term 'community' must be critically evaluated, not least because it is used with such regularity by those who are involved in the management and control of these areas and the people who live within them but also because this term has been invoked by both national and local government personnel in order to 'make a difference' at a local level.

Community and criminology

The history of the study of community is one which is well rehearsed – from the rejection of the study of community in the 1960s to its replacement with the study of 'locality' during the 1980s, which re-emphasised the importance of 'place'. These studies recognised that:

> People's location within particular places tended to be an important aspect of their lived experience ... and is a major resource drawn upon for many purposes. (Day and Murdoch, 1993, p 84)

Some such studies also argued that a 'locality effect' existed, which meant policy makers and practitioners adopting different policies in different areas to remain sensitive to the effects of local culture and political and social systems (Brownill, 1993; Day and Murdoch, 1993; Savage et al, 1987) but the study of community itself was seen as outdated – with little to offer the contemporary context.

Within criminology the theme of community has remained a recurrent one. Community has been investigated as a way of understanding the existence of criminal activity, explaining crime patterns and, as a result, the appeal to community has also played a major part in crime prevention policies (Hope, 1995). Hope argues that these interventions are informed by differing paradigms informing ideas of community. He charts community-based crime prevention practices, from the Chicago School's Chicago Area Project, established in the 1930s (the disorganised community), through the input of community work up to the 1970s (the disadvantaged community) and the appeal to the community's surveillance of itself (the frightened community), which became fashionable in the 1970s in the US and the 1980s in the UK (through ideas like Neighbourhood Watch).

Despite the different political complexions of these crime prevention paradigms, all these approaches have in common the belief that:

> ... community structure itself shapes local rates of crime – that community crime rates may be the result of something more than the mere aggregation of individual propensities for criminality or victimisation. (Hope, 1995, p 129)

and, as a consequence, those active in the field of community crime prevention have looked to alter, strengthen or enlist existing community organisations and the activities of community members in order to reduce crime in residential neighbourhoods. The setting up of community-based projects for the unemployed and for youth, Neighbourhood Watch schemes, encouraging self-help groups and tenants associations, moving council offices out of the town halls and into neighbourhoods, have all been advocated at one time or another as methods of empowering communities or involving communities in improving their particular conditions.

However, these appeals to community are inadequately explored, theorised or evaluated. Current research understanding tells us that the mobilisation of community around any issues, but certainly in crime prevention practices, has most appeal in the more wealthy areas of predominantly owner-occupied housing which have stable populations and residents with the time and skills to divert to such activity and that they are less successful in low-income, heterogeneous neighbourhoods with more transient population bases and where crime is high (Hope and Shaw, 1988). These are areas where, according to Skogan, residents are:

> ... deeply suspicious of one another, report only a weak sense of community, have low levels of influence on neighbourhood events ... and feel that it is their neighbours whom they must watch carefully. (1988, p 45)

Our work in Salford suggests that this is an oversimplification, that poorer, inner-city neighbourhoods may exhibit very different community structures and patterns of local organisation and networks.

In order to understand fully the play of forces which shape local communities, their responses to local conditions and what prevents or allows effective community organisation itself, there needs to be a greater emphasis on these communities themselves in order to understand more fully, or more adequately, the conditions under which *community crime prevention* or *community safety strategies* might be successful or might fail either in their own terms or in others. We will argue that a significant reason for the failure or limited success of such schemes or strategies is that they have failed to understand the *specific dynamics* operating in the communities in which they have been applied. In order to understand these dynamics we have set out to document and interpret the ways in which people in two inner-city areas of the city of Salford in Greater Manchester, negotiate their safety (and indeed the ways in which they conceive of their own safety or the risks to which they might be exposed), noting that this may occur in ways which might not perhaps be fully understood by those whose business it is to make and implement policy locally and nationally.

The Salford areas – Oldtown and Bankhill

The two wards have similar economic profiles. From 1991 Census returns we can see that both wards had unemployment rates of

22.5% of the economically active population at that time – the figure for Salford as a whole was 13.4%. Youth unemployment was high – 32.4% in Oldtown and 37.5% in Bankhill. Of the economically inactive in the wards around 42% were retired and 20% were long-term sick. Nevertheless both wards appeared to us to be responding to these structural factors in very different ways.

Oldtown

The ward of Oldtown is characterised as Salford's most well-known 'trouble-spot', but it also contains a redeveloped dock-side area, an area of council housing which is managed by a local estate management organisation – encouraged by government housing policy since 1988 Housing Act – and further areas containing redeveloped former local authority flats which are now in the hands of owner-occupiers. The estate is known for having erupted into violent confrontation with the police in 1992, action which culminated in the razing to the ground of a Carpetworld warehouse, which was situated on a retail estate facing the ward's 'problem housing area'. The estate and its residents will, perhaps, be long tainted with the fallout from that episode. Housing within the ward area is predominantly local authority owned (61%) and much of it has already undergone renovation as a result of central government funding under Estates Action and Urban Programme schemes which will eventually give the whole area a much-needed 'face-lift'.

The homogenous character of housing tenure in much of the ward, especially within what is known as the 'Oldtown triangle', seems to have contributed to a sense of stability in the area which its residents often alluded to. This stability appears to us to be fragile and tenuous, but nevertheless a characteristic of the area. There is little movement into or out of the council area. The ward is perceived as a 'high crime area' and, according to our reading of local crime statistics, most recorded crime appears to be directed against businesses or to be crime involving stolen or vandalised cars.

Bankhill

Bankhill was involved in similar disturbances to those which occurred in Oldtown in 1992, but these were on a smaller scale and less publicised throughout the media. They seem already to have passed from the collective memory of that place. This ward has areas within it where property crime is high, vandalism and graffiti widespread and many residents are taking the option of 'flight' from the area. Many houses are boarded up and many others seem much neglected. The image is of a once proud area 'going rapidly downhill'.

Within the ward there are some quite different areas, and this is the main characteristic of the ward – it is a mixed, disparate, heterogeneous neighbourhood. Within this ward it is possible to *see* the difference – areas of council houses, high-rise blocks, working-class terraces and affluent, almost suburban, housing share the same ward. Sikh and Pakistani settlement of the area is the highest in Salford and there is an area of seven or eight streets which is almost exclusively settled by orthodox Jewish families. There are visible reminders of their presence in this part of the ward – not only is the orthodox Jewish style of clothing very different to the mainstream, but Jewish bakeries, food and clothes shops, businesses and schools are also found here. It is also an area with a great deal of private rented accommodation and student houses – giving the area an air of transience, rather than permanence – as in Oldtown.

Community feeling in Bankhill and Oldtown

So what resonance does the term 'community' have for local residents of these areas? During a survey of householders which we conducted in each ward we asked respondents whether their area had a 'community feel'. Out of 296 respondents in Oldtown 47 said 'yes it did' (about 16%) and 34 out of 302 respondents in Bankhill said that their area had a community feel (about 11%). Similar numbers responded positively to the statement that the 'best thing about living here is the community'. However, this only tells us about the response to our suggestion that community may or may not exist and as yet tells us very little about *what is actually meant* by an affirmative or a negative response to this suggestion.

We recorded, on the questionnaire, any comments respondents made about 'community' during the course of the interview. The following are a sample of those comments:

"It's beginning to get a community feel" (Oldtown, Canalside)

"No community spirits, some people are friendly, people move in and out very quickly" (Bankhill)

"Everybody knows me but it's not a community thing" (Bankhill)

The comments made reveal a number of things about 'community'; perhaps most of all they reveal a *lack of consensus* about what community is. Community may relate to a particular area for some, for others it relates to who you know. The loss of community is significant for many older residents who recall a time when it used to exist but who remain unclear about what the term actually meant. Overall, residents tend to talk about localness or 'being local' or 'neighbourly' rather than making overt use of the term 'community'.

Where the term community *was* used by local residents or professionals working within the area its use can be categorised as follows:

- as place, geographically defined;
- as social networks;
- as a symbolic construct;
- as denoting shared characteristics, such as ethnicity or social group;
- as a motor for collective action.

The term 'community' was also used by professionals working in the area, as a management issue. We cannot explore every usage of the term among professionals in this paper but we *do* consider the utilisation of community in the management of crime.

Community as place

During the course of our research Salford was often described to us as a city where its residents are strongly attached to their local area and as 'fiercely territorial'. A number of people we interviewed suggested that this strong sense of attachment to local area might stem from the working practices of the docks. The docks were an important local source of employment. Different 'docker gangs' operated the loading and unloading of the ships and membership of this gang and therefore an avenue to employment, was often based on place of residence, where kinship and neighbourhood ties were strong.

Whatever the reason, this sense of territory pervades down to a very local level. The following are some examples of how this sense of territory could limit access to facilities within the wards of Oldtown and Bankhill:

- At the time of our initial round of interviews, Salford's Jobshop was situated in the heart of Oldtown and continually found it could not attract users from other areas. Bankhill was therefore to have its own Jobshop but it was thought that it would not be used by many of the ward's residents because it was to be situated 'in the wrong place' to the West of the ward, in a place which is seen as student dominated and peripheral to the majority of the ward's residents.

- A youth justice worker told us that he was surprised by one young girl's insistence that there was no chip shop which she could use in Bankhill – when he pointed out a nearby shop he was told "it's not in my area".

- An activist from a local estate management body in South Oldtown which serves a few hundred houses on the southern tip of the Oldtown triangle, described the local youth as 'tribal', explaining that local people do not expect to see people on their side of the estate who are not from their 'patch'. If they are seen they are immediately identified as possible 'trouble-makers'.

These allegiances work at a level much smaller than the ward. Professionals operating in these two areas drew up maps of the different areas of allegiance. They produced what can only be described as a 'patchwork quilt' of localities, dividing the ward of Bankhill with approximately 10,000 residents into 13 distinct areas and Oldtown's approximately 7,000 residents into eight areas. Some of these divisions were based on *existing boundaries*, for example, major and minor roads which intersect the areas, and some around the *planned and built environment*, for example, rows of older terraced housing or a single block of flats, limiting the concept of community to very small areas indeed.

Community as social networks

Within the two wards we found there existed a considerable number of quite varied social groupings – from sequence dancing and scrabble clubs to local history societies and church groups. One bowling club had been founded in 1933 and was still providing 'The teaching of bowling and a social gathering' to 30 members three times a week in the summer and twice a week in the winter. Furthermore when we invited numbers of people to focus group discussions we often found that the people we had invited were part of the same social networks, or had been in the past. If people did not actually know one another they often recognised faces and knew where other participants 'were from'.

Sometimes social networks and place of residence combined as occurred in a permanent caravan site situated in one ward, we were told by one of its residents, "This community here is very close, has never changed, won't let anyone do any damage, only mix with each other." More often, however, the networks were based around particular interests, age-groups or social needs, for example, mother and toddler groups.

Community as a symbolic construct

Where this idea of community was employed notions of belonging and exclusion were more readily invoked. There were more examples of community used in this way in Oldtown where both the homogeneity of the ward's social composition and the relative stability of residence within the area meant that a shared knowledge of local myths and the operation of boundaries could be more easily sustained. In some respects even to acknowledge that you are from Oldtown automatically acts as a symbol of 'Old Salfordian', 'hard young man', 'loyal to a troubled estate' and so on, because of the symbolic role which this estate plays within Salford as a whole.

'Canalside' in Oldtown offered a symbolic boundary. Local businesses and residents often use Canalside in their address, to denote their allegiance to a certain type of vision for the future of the area, or simply that they are 'Not Oldtown', and to distance themselves from the troubled nature of the place.

Within Oldtown the park serves to separate 'honest' Oldtown from 'disordered' Oldtown, as with the local management organisation to the south of the Triangle's insistence that their young people are not like those "from the other side of the Park".

This use of community does not sit so easily in Bankhill. In that ward local connections can lead to knowledge of which areas are considered unsafe – due to high rates of property crime – and those where you can live more safely, but this is a street by street assessment and says little about community and neighbourhood links.

Community as shared characteristics

Within Bankhill ethnic identity plays an important part in constructing community. Probably the most noticeable example of community constructed around ethnic groupings comes from that of the Jewish community in Bankhill. Jewish respondents *did* refer to community as in "it is different in our community". But there is also a smaller Sikh area and the Islamic mosque in a neighbouring ward acts as a meeting point for many of the Pakistani residents of Bankhill.

In Oldtown being seen as a 'local' appeared the overriding definition of shared characteristic and could become a method of negotiating individual and collective "ontological security" (Giddens, 1991), for example, one middle-aged male told us:

> "I think ... [Oldtown] is a great area if you are a member of the community [went to the local school, grew up with the local villains, etc] but terrible if you're an outsider."

Community as collective action

Within Bankhill we found a number of organisations which had grown up around a collective concern and had based their action around a particular residential base. One area had set itself up as a conservation area, another neighbouring area wished to follow suit and both had independent organisations working to secure these interests. A group of Salford council tenants had joined with a neighbouring city's tenants to work for improvements to their estate. Other organisations had come together to try to deal with high rates of property crime – one had been successful in obtaining European funds to 'target-harden' all housing in the immediate environs. At one time or another 28 Neighbourhood Watch schemes had operated within the ward.

In Oldtown we found examples of collective organisation but these were more likely to have been initially set up by professionals working within the ward, rather than arising independently and as a result of resident action. As exceptions to this, however, were a long-standing tenant management co-operative as well as the local management organisation in South Oldtown. The latter had developed out of independent resident action. In order to respond to what they saw as rising crime and incivilities within one particular part of the Oldtown estate, as well as perceived police inaction, residents had formed a 'telephone tree'. So, for example, if any resident who was part of this communication network saw a stolen car brought into the area, the telephone tree would go into operation and they were assured that someone would go out to deal with the incident. It is also true that some residents find expression of community in their membership of, or links with the local criminal network or 'Firm' which operates around the Oldtown Triangle and elsewhere within the city.

Community in high crime areas

In the wards of Bankhill and Oldtown, vandalism and crime were both high on residents' agendas, although these concerns were more often cited in Bankhill than Oldtown. We asked residents which, of a possible list of problems faced in the local area, was the biggest, lack of a play area for children was cited most often in Oldtown, crime was the biggest problem for residents in Bankhill.

For 'urban managers' (the planners, police and other professionals working in the areas) crime was a primary concern – the council's Community Strategy, developed late in 1994, focused on crime as an issue requiring urgent attention in many parts of the city and community strategy officers have set up meetings and forums which have provided local residents with an opportunity to express their concerns. However, in some instances it can become accepted that these forums exist mainly to address 'the crime problem'. These forums operate locally and meet in the local area, therefore it has become accepted lore that community as a *place* is where responsibility for doing something about crime is best sited.

However, there are some very important differences between Oldtown and Bankhill in the ways that crime is experienced and negotiated.

Oldtown

As we have previously outlined, the crime which takes place within Oldtown appears to be directed principally against businesses or involves stolen cars. In addition, many of the stolen cars which are brought onto the estate and driven around subsequent to being dumped or burnt out will not belong to estate residents. So, although residents may see crime taking place they are less often directly the victims of it themselves. The existence of the Salford Firm (a kind of meeting of anarchist politics and local 'villainy') also influences the collective local consciousness, and this is also acknowledged by the local police. It is believed that the 'Firm' operates it's own moral code, protecting Oldtown residents from much petty crime. So we were told:

> "People don't take off their own – businesses are more likely to be hit by crime."

> "Criminals live here and rob elsewhere."

> "Locals think they're Robin Hood."

> "Burglaries in this area are rare but some people are involved in robbery elsewhere."

> "You have to be known as living in this area and then they'll protect you."

Furthermore, while conducting our survey in Oldtown last summer, we soon noticed a tendency among many estate residents to communicate to the interviewer that many of the questions we were asking about feelings of safety in the home and around in the local area did not apply, because, simply, "you're all right if you're a local", or, as one respondent put it "you're regular round here". For example, people told us:

> "I've lived round here all my life and feel safe. What goes on here is a way of life. You have to stick up for yourself and teach kids to do the same."

> "It's safe for locals but not strangers in the area."

> "I've no real problems because I know the people and the area and grew up with the local villains and know local youths."

> "If your face doesn't fit here you'll have problems, otherwise you're okay."

Because such beliefs were expressed so frequently and with little variation in content, we concluded that they amounted to what might be termed 'neighbourhood dogma'. That is to say, they were not views formed in the isolated moment of the interview but had a shared local currency beyond that moment (this point is further explored in Evans, Fraser and Walklate, 1995). This perceived immunity to crime and at times, active protection by 'the villains' in the area seems to be one of the most significant expressions of community on the Oldtown estate. But how does someone qualify for this status? Is it through length of residence or through active participation in communal activities? We interviewed a self-styled spokesperson for the Salford Firm and asked him how a newcomer might come to be seen as part of the community, he told us:

> "It's how they act – react – to the community, to the new area – I mean if they're on the phone 'the fucking kids are always playing ball against the wall' you know what I mean, then they're going to get stick, you know, they're not going to be acceptable, you know, so people break into their house and smash their windows and they become a real nuisance to them, you know, so that they clear off ... and this is what happens."

In order to achieve this *immunity* or *protection*, therefore, you are required to obey certain rules as well as to simply 'be known' – most significant of which seems to be the code of not grassing to the police (or indeed to anyone in 'authority').

This dogma is *transmitted* or *publicly displayed* in important ways and the physical configuration and sparse amenities as well as the close network of kinship relations on the estate facilitate this transmission. The one health centre, library, post office, book-makers, chemist and two of the estate's three pubs are all located within yards of each other in the heart of the estate – providing ideal conditions for daily public encounters between people and a display area for public shaming rituals. Graffiti announcing that so and so is a grass or merely the word 'grass' or 'informer' is regularly plastered over these public buildings and because large numbers of residents will come into daily contact with these sites, such messages are a clear warning to everyone about the consequences an individual can expect if they should break the code.

So a number of people living in the area believed that if they accepted the rights of the alternative structures of control over the estate then they could possess a sense of confidence in their area. They believed that they could remain largely free of crime against their property and against their person. In such an environment conventional 'crime prevention' practices are perceived, for genuine reasons, to be inapplicable. What we should be careful about at this stage, is overstating either the prevalence of the depth of this confidence. Residents will accept that this code operates and appreciate the personal advantage that it affords them but may nevertheless worry deeply about their children growing up in such an environment. Certainly those who, for whatever reason, do not fit in with this system of beliefs or are regarded as 'outsiders', can expect to suffer certain consequences. Throughout the ward women expressed significantly higher levels of fear of crime than did men – suggesting that this sense of security may be heavily gendered.

A detailed analysis of one month's local recorded police crime and incident data showed reported crime on the estate to be highly patterned: in the heart of the estate there were very few reports of property crime, but in adjoining areas (eg, a part of the redeveloped estate that has been sold off to private owner-occupiers and housing associations and had largely more recent tenants and residents living there) reports of property crime and of stolen and vandalised vehicles were higher. Those incidents which are reported as taking place in the 'heart' of the estate tended to be interpersonal disputes between neighbours, or incidents of domestic violence as well as reports of dumped cars.

Bankhill

We soon realised that there was no equivalent to this shared dogma operating in Bankhill. At no point did a survey respondent express with such confidence, the belief that if you were 'a local' you would not be harmed. For some feelings of safety or security *were* linked with length of residence in the area, for example, one resident told us: "I always feel safe as I've always lived here", but this belief was not expressed with the same regularity as in Oldtown and did not include the idea that added protection would be afforded to a person who subscribed to particular neighbourhood codes of conduct.

One of the most significant differences between the wards was how *outsiders* were regarded. For many residents of Bankhill, outsiders posed a considerable threat in terms of community stability and identity. There is a strong belief that it is tenants who have been moved into the area at various stages during slum clearance programmes of the 1970s and after, who are responsible for much of the crime and the general instability of the area. For example people said:

> "This avenue was very quiet until a rough family moved in – they're on drugs and petrol bombs are thrown."

> "The street has a bad reputation because Irwell Valley [HA] moved people in."

> "The locals are very friendly but young troublemakers have come into the area."

> "The area's less safe than it used to be because Oldtown families have moved here."

And there seemed to be the feeling that even those newcomers who were not directly involved in criminal activities could be held in some way accountable, or to blame for the area's problems; for by moving into the area they have added to its instability and created the conditions under which crime could flourish. For example, we were told:

> "It's going downhill fast. New people moving in and bringing problems with them."

> "People have moved into the area that don't care."

> "It's not as friendly or safe as it used to be – a moving population."

So crime was perceived as caused by people moving into the area who had no sense of community and no sense of the area's particular development and its worth.   Certainly in Bankhill residents can also be "deeply suspicious of one another" (Skogan, 1988, p 45).   In one particularly vulnerable small area in the heart of the ward, residents set up a covert community group.   They felt a lack of trust even in their own street and worried about being targets for crime from others who lived in this small area if they were seen to be actively engaged in attempting to stand up against criminal activity.   Interestingly, the families which they regarded as responsible for the high rates of property crime in the area had lived very locally for at least two generations – but in the eyes of these community members they could still be classed as outsiders because their family's heritage lay elsewhere.   These families were described as 'tinkers' or gypsies, rather than originally from Bankhill, or even Salford.   Furthermore, these families had been seen as 'trouble-makers' since moving into the area, and as having never conformed to the aspirations of most residents in the area who wanted to keep its reputation as 'a nice area to live'.   They were instead perceived as always having been involved in petty crime, anti-social behaviour and vandalism of the local streets.

The management of communities

As we outlined above, the received wisdom tells us that lack of social control within inner city areas is likely to arise as a result of weak communities, a lack of social networks and a lack of concern about an area, neighbourhood as a collection of disparate persons living in close proximity but not caring for community values. Thus, interventions into such areas aim to resurrect ideas of community, for example, local people are exhorted to watch out for one another, care for neighbours, work collectively for change and to liaise with and accept the input of professionals, whether police or local authorities.   However, our work challenges the assumption that lack of community feeling or weak social bonds are the key determinants of social disorder within these areas.

Within both areas, we have argued, community works on a number of different levels.   Many local people whom we spoke to were closely linked to their local areas and recognised the importance of sustaining such links in order to maintain their own 'ontological security'. In Bankhill many community activists struggled to maintain community cohesion against incredible odds.

In Oldtown the close ties which exist in the area mean that the organised criminal gang can claim to control the area and sustain levels of intimidation and fear. As one local community activist told us:

> "Everyone knows who this group is and what they are into at any particular time. This creates the fear – nothing is kept secret really and the grapevine is very active. The gang's exploits are known throughout the estate very quickly after any incident has occurred. People then become wary of walking past this gang – they may be challenged as – because everyone knows what is happening – then everyone is a potential grass."

Rather than a lack of surveillance and control within this ward there is maintained a surveillance of local people by those involved in the criminal network, mainly young men, who maintain a vigilant gaze over the central part of the estate.

Looking at the experience of crime helps us to see how people *use* their sense of community and of neighbourhood and how this can differ from place to place. Within the two wards in which we conducted this research very different strategies emerged. In Oldtown your place in relation to crime places you in a community of belonging and exclusion; in Bankhill there is an absence even of this ordering. In Oldtown there exists a strong sense of community which competes with the professional definition and application of community; in Bankhill there is an absence of trust beyond that shared by a few residents within very small areas or within social networks which have been built up over many years. Where trust is so limited that which *is* found can work to exclude individuals who are not party to a social scene or do not conform to certain expectations and roles. Given these differences and difficulties the question must be asked; what does community safety, community crime prevention or indeed community anything actually mean? Yet policy makers and practitioners still invoke the notion of 'community' without reference to how the different dimensions are actually experienced, intersect with one another and play a part in shaping local people's beliefs and behaviour.

However, it is a matter of importance and in need of some reflection that, despite the problems faced within both these wards local residents opened their doors to our team of researchers and discussed, on their doorsteps, or in their homes, issues of significance to their own lives which touched on extremely sensitive points of local social relations. This suggests that these areas are not the disordered and frightened maelstroms of some media, government and academic opinion but are areas where the residents must find ways of coping with day-to-day issues of community, neighbourhood and local problems and that they will reach out to others in an effort to find solutions.

Note

[1] This research was funded under the Economic and Social Research Council's Crime and Social Order Initiative, award no L210 25 2036. Karen Evans of the University of Salford and Sandra Walklate of Keele University were grant holders.

four

"You've fucked up the estate and now you're carrying a briefcase!"*

Andrew McCulloch

Introduction

The title was overheard in a fish and chip shop in the West End of the city of Newcastle upon Tyne in 1991. The female speaker had rebuked a male community activist who was about to move out of the Cruddas Park/Loadman Street Estate on which they both lived. He had become employed through his experience of activism and his marriage had broken down.

Gender is a major issue in community activism and raises certain questions. Why did certain groups of people come to 'represent' this white, working-class estate during a recent attempt at economic and social regeneration? Why are there so few community activists in total and why are most of them usually women?

The Cruddas Park/Loadman Street Estate

The boundaries of the Estate are marked on the north and south by major routes into the city centre, two miles away. The boundary to the east is a wide road and to the west lines have been

---

* I would like to thank Sheila Livingstone and John McLauchlin for their help in preparing this paper.

drawn by skirmishes between the young of the adjoining estates. The area contained at the time of the research (August 1990-December 1991) approximately 1,400 people and about 850 households living in local authority-owned housing. The west part has low-rise two- and four-storey family housing with deck access (Loadman Street) and the east, eight fifteen-storey tower blocks (Cruddas Park). In the north-east corner of the estate is a covered shopping centre. This shopping complex, surmounted by another residential tower block, also included a local library, a community centre, a local authority housing office, a branch of the Citizen's Advice Bureau, a community cafe (for older people), a training outpost of the local computer firm Mari, a social services office, a health clinic and the Community Enterprise and Employment Centre. This centre was the physical base for the community regeneration project. The commercial premises included a cafe, a chemist's shop with pharmacy, a full range of food shops, a supermarket, a newsagent's with post office services, a public house, a hardware shop and hairdressing salons. On the south side of the complex, outside the enclosed area, is the fish and chip shop, a betting shop, an off licence, and a cooperatively run launderette, a community business. Some people rarely need to go into the town centre.

In 1956 there had been wholesale clearance of the 19th-century terraced housing. The replacements, three- and five-storey blocks of flats with no lifts and heated by coal fires, acquired a miserable reputation (Benwell Community Development Project (CDP), 1981; Davies, 1972, p 51). Rightly demolished in 1978 to make way for the present buildings, a significant proportion of these in Loadman Street were themselves demolished during 1991-92. Some clearance has continued.

Notwithstanding extensive recent refurbishment through a succession of Urban Programmes and the personal visits of the Prince of Wales, the area has a male unemployment rate of nearly 60%, high numbers of children on the 'at-risk' register, significantly above average numbers of long-term sick and many ex-mental hospital patients. Around 20% of the households are single old age pensioners, and the area has the lowest rates of car ownership and possession of household telephones in the city. At least one third of the properties were untenanted and many households did not stay long in the area at any one time. (There is a good deal of circulatory movement.) Out of 1,000 dwellings in the free-standing tower blocks, 462 (46.2%) had no elector in October, 1990.

In the nearby working-class areas to the west there has been much less wholesale redevelopment. Among the pain, violence, crime and drugs, many say that some sense of order and structure has been retained. However, there is in Cruddas Park a bleakness which is the province of the permanently disappointed young who have nothing to lose. People tend to throw anything out of the tower block windows including on occasion, it must be said, themselves.

The project

In *Initiatives beyond charity* (1988) the Confederation of British Industry (CBI) called for an effective urban partnership between national and local government and the private sector (see Lawless, 1989, p 132). Northern members of the CBI were the key to setting up the Newcastle Initiative, which, after an approach to the City Council, agreed as part of its mission to support the special challenge of working in Cruddas Park/Loadman Street. The centre-piece of this example of partnership was the Employment and Enterprise Centre, opened in October, 1989. A privately funded coordinator (official title, executive director) of the project worked in concert with two Department of Employment officials, a local authority funded community worker and administrator, a Training and Enterprise Council (TEC) funded outreach worker and a business development worker funded by the European Development Fund through Entrust. One of three community businesses, Design 2 Print, also ran from this office. Another business, Overall Clothing, not located in the project area, had a relatively brief and troubled life and only the launderette, heavily supported by volunteer labour, proved a long-term asset. The major representative structure was a community council and this had, as its executive arm and owner of the real assets, a community trust.

Community activists

Community development, as it is understood here, is a service provided by (mostly white male) middle-class professionals for poor working-class (black or white) people living in working-class districts which have declined economically. These professionals must solicit the appearance of and work with people known as community activists. The professionals may once have belonged to the latter category themselves.

A total of 80 people had attended *at least one* of the project's meetings or sub-groups during January to September 1991. Of this number, moving away (24), present inactivity (7), 2 cases of illness and 7 refusals resulted in 40, 12 men and 28 women, consenting to be interviewed in October and November of 1991, although one questionnaire was barely completed. As it turned out, the refusals were largely prompted by a proper modesty (five were not very active), but if they had been included, they would not have altered the distributions by gender or age significantly.

These 40, with the exception of 2 older female refusals, actually constituted the whole core of activists. The members of this core, with very few exceptions, fell into three distinct groups (see Table 1) which, with startling originality, will be named here as the 'young women', the 'older women', and the 'activist men'.

Table 1: The involvement of individuals in community groups

	Number of groups				
Numbers in each category	0	1	2	3	4+
Young women	0	6	5	2	0
Old women	0	8	3	3	0
Activist men	2	2	1	5	2

The core of community activists is almost always relatively small. Forty is the maximum figure for activists mentioned by Buchanan (1986), in his survey of community businesses in Scotland. In 9 neighbourhood care projects Abrams and his team identified about

250 helpers in all (Abrams et al, 1989, p 39). They also discovered 87% of those engaged in a large variety of neighbourhood care schemes were female (p 39), as were 70% of the activists in this study. This is a commonplace of the community activist literature. Barke and Turnbull remark of a powerful Tyneside tenants' initiative in South Meadowell Estate that, "As with many such groups, the origin was to be found with the actions of a few strong-minded women" (Barke and Turnbull, 1992, p 137). And similarly, Donnison rather patronisingly comments that, "Women often play leading roles in the early heroic days of the community projects, but then hierarchies, formality and bureaucracy reassert themselves and the men take over" (Donnison, 1988, p 13). In this formulation, the usurpation apparently has little to do with men themselves.

The men who did actively participate in Cruddas Park were distinctive in that the majority (8 out of 12) were members of the Thursday Club, a gay support group. Three of the other men from the local community who did participate were, nonetheless, somewhat isolated from their male peers, as two of them willingly acknowledged, and all three were distinctive in either their political attitudes and/or their values, although not homosexual. The remaining male participated almost exclusively by supporting his female partner. With the exception of one straight male, the men were incomers, although the majority were from the West End of Newcastle.

The older female activists belong to a recognisable group valiantly preserving the neighbourhood traditions of the 'respectable' working class. In their multi-storey block of flats, they clean the common hallway and place a homely mat outside their flat door. They have been in the area since at least when it was last comprehensively redeveloped. Their husbands were in skilled work and their small, stable families were the centre of their lives. They longingly hark back to the days when they believe crime in Cruddas Park/Loadman Street was less frequent and less violent. They also lament that, "You cannot say anything to anybody's children these days without getting a mouthful of cheek!" (see Ross, 1983, p 13).

Most of the males were between 20 and 30 years of age. The distribution of the women by age was bi-modular: nearly 70% of the women under 45 years were in the 30 to 40 years of age bracket, and over 70% of the women more than 45 years of age were in a group whose ages ranged from 55 to 64 years. This is a rather startling coincidence with the age distribution of Abrams et al's mostly female helpers (Abrams et al, 1989, p 39).

Important groups did not participate in Cruddas Park/Loadman Street community activism. Missing were women below the age of 30, and women in the intervening years of 40-55 years. Crucially, there is no evidence that the average working-class white heterosexual male, young or old, employed or unemployed, who lived in Cruddas Park or the surrounding area, showed any inclination to involve themselves in the project. This is graphically illustrated by the failure of the project to make any meaningful links to the local working men's club. The club's chronic financial problems culminated in a catastrophic fire. Indeed, for all effective purposes this group of males disappears, along with the club, from this analysis.

Male and female activist households

There are interesting variations between and among the different groups of activists if employment, unemployment and household structure are examined. Six of the 12 men, all of them gay, lived alone. Six were employed full-time (three of them gay), four were on Income Support and two were on sick benefit.

Of the older women, a bare majority lived alone, although one had been very recently widowed. Only a couple of the women were in paid employment. It was possible to notice, however, that friendships formed between some of the single older women and the single activist men. The activist men, nevertheless, were much more isolated than the young women.

Of the 13 young women, only three lived without a partner. Two of these were single mothers employed part-time. The only young woman who lived alone was also unemployed and spoken of in pitying tones by the others. The largest single category among these young women active in the project was of employed women who lived in households in which there were two earners. All of the male partners of these six women worked full-time, and half of the women worked full-time and half worked part-time. The six households fell into three equal blocks of two households with four children, two with two children and two with none. Part- or full-time working did not appear to be influenced by whether or not there were children in the household, or by how many children there were, except perhaps in one case. There was also one household with four children in which the male worked full-time and the female partner did not have paid employment.

Working or not, full-time or not, was apparently determined for these women with school-age children by particular combinations of work availability, work proximity and necessity, not choice. Nevertheless, that women with jobs and children could also find the time to become involved in work in their community speaks of a remarkable level of commitment and energy and, perhaps, a distinctively powerful set of values.

Membership of community groups

The project set up 12 different specialist sub-groups. The most popular groups for the young women were the Community Council and the Launderette Group (a community business cooperative). With minor exceptions, the old women focused their attentions on individual tenants' groups. For the men the pattern was different: most of them claimed to be active in three or more groups. Eight of the men (two of them not gay) were on the Community Council and five (two of them not gay) of these were also members of the Community Trust. Thus, the activist men were disproportionately involved, compared to the women, in the central community organisations of the project, the council and the trust. It should also be noted that two of the men, one gay and one straight, claimed to be active while not involved in any groups at all. This could not be said of the two older women who were refusals.

Over the two years ending in December 1991, the records show that 25 men and 31 women attended the Community Council at least once, but the residents who were committed *over a period* are disproportionately female: only two males (one gay) and six females regularly and continuously attended over this whole time.

The decline of working-class community

The sinews that bound the male-dominated working-class community together – the trade union, the friendly society, the working men's club, the cooperative society (Thompson, 1970) – have declined severely. The organisationally fertile working class of the past did not need community development: it had its politics (Macintyre, 1980a; 1980b).

Almost 20 years ago, Clarke observed that there had been a "decline of working-class involvement in local forms of political representation and a reduction in the legitimacy attributed to them." Clarke suggested that schools, housing authorities and the police have also suffered from an evacuation of working-class civic commitment: "hence community work, community schools, community liaison, community development and so on" (Clarke, 1981, pp 42-3). Abrams wrote more recently of "a world turned up-side down" for "today it is more accurate to speak of middle-class than of working-class neighbourliness" (Abrams et al, 1989, p 133).

Community development is not an indicator of buoyant activism and strong community bonds but of their absence. Although politicians and programme managers of urban regeneration initiatives often make inflated claims, their real achievements are often the limited ones of "containing disadvantage; [and] ameliorating the effects of disadvantage – making it more bearable" (Fordham, 1995, p 8). This still means that without help areas like Cruddas Park/Loadman Street would be worse. Equally, there is little evidence that they will get significantly, rather than cosmetically, better (see Power and Tunstall, 1995). If there are ever signs of that happening the predictable response of local and national government, faced with other competing patches of urgent deprivation, will be: "Clearly, Area X has now had its turn (of funds, support, etc)" (Kelly, 1995). Limited success, in this kind of climate, can only bring eventual funding failure. If that is the case then the sane question would perhaps be not to ask why men in the relevant areas are absent, but why women are, or anybody is, present in a supportive capacity at all.

Community development, gender and professionalism

Community development necessarily involves the symbiotic relationship of paid workers and unpaid volunteers. This usually maps directly onto gender distinctions with paid men confronting unpaid women. Thus, the issues of professional domination and patriarchy are inextricably linked and these inequalities lead to conflicts in themselves. They contrast oddly with overt commitments to empowerment by professionals.

The Cruddas Park Project had begun in 1989 with the 'parachuting' into the area of an all-male professional team. They paid a nucleus of locals to conduct a local skills and community survey (Wood et al, 1989). Who was paid and by how much caused some friction. Three of this original group became full-time paid workers on the project. Although only three posts were in contention, a majority of women activists saw only one of their number employed. The rest of the nucleus resigned or left the area, an ominous symmetry.

An inner group of people came to 'own' the project (see Abrams and McCulloch, 1976). This largely male core of activists and workers (both gay and straight) did not all agree, but they had a common history. It was said on more than one occasion, particularly in time of internal conflict, "We always said that ...", which was often accompanied by confirmatory nods from the remaining members of the inner group. The meetings also covered a bewildering range of topics for those on the periphery. The Community Council discussed an average of 18 topics per meeting, with one meeting covering 30 different topics. For newcomers, this range of material made the meetings almost impenetrable. Equally, the more focused participation of the women meant that much of the business seemed irrelevant.

Discussions, which were often dominated by the members of the highly articulate and forceful inner group, excluded formal voting. It was the opinion of the project director, that, "If we get to the point where we are a committee voting on things, we have lost it" (Community Council, 13 June, 1991). Dissent was smothered. Even when, in July 1990, a local member presented to the Community Trust his formal paper entitled, 'The Cruddas Park/Loadman Street Initiative, are we really in control?', which raised issues over which six months later he resigned, no vote was called for or taken.

The Cruddas Park Community Council was to represent the local inhabitants and the Community Trust was to be its executive arm. In practice the relationship was reversed. The trust meetings were dominated by the business professionals from outside, most of whom were male. Decisions made by the trust were largely accepted without question by the Community Council, for those on the trust formed a bloc on the council.

The view of the city employment development officer, a woman, was that the local community was weak: "there was not a strong base of local people. The partnership was always going to be unequal." The project director/coordinator believed that he could have controlled and dominated more because, on many occasions, he had deliberately held himself back (a view which many of his critics felt was patronising). This view of the locals meant that resignations over matters of principle, and there were several key ones, were interpreted as signs of political immaturity.

Not surprisingly, only two men and seven women from the activists believed that their contributions at meetings made a difference. Moreover, when they were asked if the locals were in control of the project only three men and three women said that they were. The effects of this were palpable: there were constant complaints that the early concerns with the social issues of community pride, housing, childcare and crime had retreated before a central concern with economic regeneration. Female concerns became refracted through this economic prism.

Gender and patterns of community activism

Among the 40 activists were a married couple and one woman reported that her partner, although inactive, was nevertheless very supportive. These two couples were exceptions. One unemployed husband's animosity temporarily reduced when he became employed and his wife, from being an activist, became employed by the project. (As her career progressed the marriage broke down, as have others among female activists.) It was the majority experience for women to find that their male partners resented their involvement outside the home in community activity (see Gittins, 1985; Hartmann, 1987).

The women as a whole were very much more likely than the men to live near (next door or a few doors away) their best friend and, equally importantly, *not to think of their partner as their best friend*. The older the woman, the more likely the friend lived very close by. In contrast, the men either lived with their best friend or that friend lived outside the West End of Newcastle. Female friendship also seemed more intense than male friendship. No man claimed to see his best friend (who was not a partner) more than once or twice a week. Just over half of all the women saw their best friends *at least* three times a week. The conclusion can only be that for these groups of women, being a friend was also being a neighbour and a member of a community, much more than was the case for the men. Indeed, for the activist men, both gay and straight, friendship and community/neighbourhood relationships in Cruddas Park/Loadman Street seemed to be distinctly different sets of activities.

Less than a third of the women but two thirds of the male Cruddas Park activists had worked away from the area, a difference between the genders which is to be expected. None of the activist men said that they would *never* leave the area, although four of the younger women and five of the older women were certain they never would. The most important positive reason for leaving the area would be to improve the respondent's housing. Only among the men was there a bare majority who would leave the area for better employment. The most important negative reason for leaving the area was crime and harassment. Eighteen (8 men and 10 women) out of those 27 responding to this question would have left the area because of crime. However, the women activists, both young and old, saw themselves as much more resistant to harassment. This perhaps reflects the greater commitment of women to their communities and the reality of their geographical immobility. Most of the men were incomers and most of the women were not. When things get difficult men can nearly always leave, and they do. Clearly, this difference in potentiality significantly affects how men and women relate to local community activity.

Men and women and paid work

Some of the schemes that Abrams et al (1989) examined used paid helpers. Payment did not encourage men to become carers and, "There were no men involved in these projects due to their being unemployed" (Abrams et al, 1989, p 40). Equally, only two women who were looking for jobs participated as volunteer carers.

According to Abrams et al, there was a whole swathe of working-class women with the right capacities for and experience of caring but the women who became involved in formal schemes for caring did so because "they were recruited from that small proportion of working class women who could either afford to stay out of the labour market or could not find a way into it." (1989, p 27). This contrasts with the significant but small group of young, activist women in Cruddas Park/Loadman Street who did domestic labour, community work and also found their way into the labour market.

But an obvious question is, why did *men* who could not find a way into the labour market fail to be recruited into volunteer caring? The easy answer is that men are not attracted by the mundane, domestic labour, paid or not, that caring requires (even though Abrams tells us, somewhat hypocritically, that it is "unalienated labour"). It is the exception when female caring is rewarded and perhaps it was the case that the payment for caring, even though men would not do it for money, made the caring by the women acceptable. The conflict many women experience with 'their' men when they do something for nothing is reduced when some payment is made and the activity thereby justified. On the other hand, when slivers of work were rewarded with cash payment in Cruddas Park, there was great jealousy, particularly among the women.

Doing good, altruism and generalised reciprocity

Altruism is frequently given as an ultimate justification for community activity (Abrams et al, 1989, p 38; Bulmer, 1986, p 103; McCulloch, 1994, p 30). Although people often claimed to be doing helpful things because "it is the kind of person that I am", they almost always in practice qualify this claim by itemising some rewards or satisfactions they receive because they help others (Bulmer, 1986, p 111; McCulloch, 1994, p 30). What looks like beneficence or altruism is in reality part of a generalised reciprocity.

Abrams' central claim is that, given certain conditions, "debts can be suspended in time, carried to other, comparable relationships through the life cycle. And as a result reciprocity can look like beneficence at the moment it is enacted. Exchanges over time can replace exchanges now; giving to third parties can replace a direct return to a beneficiary one is unable to help directly" (Bulmer, 1986, p 112). The conditions are "trust and certainty" which

> ... permit the postponement of debts – just as they ensure their eventual repayment. Communities in which high levels of trust and predictability are diffused among members will also be communities with high levels of generalised reciprocity, that is, of apparent altruism. (Bulmer, 1986, p 113).

Abrams identified three factors which enhance the possibilities of caring taking place. One of these was a sense of personal competence in concretely helping others. Training is relevant but Abrams remarks in an aside that, "Once again it seems that mothers can do just as effective a job as [trained] colleagues" (Bulmer, 1986, p 114). This must be because the archetypal and most common form of generalised reciprocity is (adequate to good) mothering.

In a famous paper Ross (1983) floated the now well-received idea that working-class women in poor areas of London before the First World War created an informal inter-household economy which, to some degree, compensated for the deficiencies of the waged economy as experienced by their fathers, husbands and brothers.

> Aid in emergencies such as major illnesses and evictions were routinised in women's culture, as were some forms of resistance – protecting their streets from authorities, for example, or harassing court officials during evictions. (Ross, 1983, p 5)

Ross comments further that, in the straightened circumstances of the London poor,

> The bulk of women's day-to-day sharing was exchange; in theory, at least, reciprocity was the rule. 'You always got it [what you lent] back,' one woman recalled. To be thought of as untrustworthy as a borrower was one of the worst

> accusations that could be brought by a
> neighbourhood gossip against a woman,
> threatening an important part of their livelihood.
> (1983, p 11)

Generalised reciprocity and community activism rooted in trust are thus longstanding components of female working-class experience.

When asked whether people turned to them for help more than they turned for aid to others, nearly half of the old women agreed. The young women were slightly but importantly different: despite their frequent claims that they had no confidence, most regarded themselves as 'strong women' upon whom people depended. Only 2 of the 12 young women said they turned to others more than others turned to them. The older women can cash in their communal credit; the younger are building their reserves.

Abrams' argument about generalised reciprocity is really about female people, female communities, female traditions, female reciprocity. Insofar as female working-class communities and traditions have persisted, they have done so because they were part of an informal, social economy that existed outside the market. Payment for community activity excited jealousy in Cruddas Park because although it facilitated them in the short term, it corroded these non-market exchanges in the long term. On the other hand, working-class men's traditions and communities depended on the market in their labour and their traditions have been dislocated by the collapse in the demand for certain skills. Without the continuity offered by tradition – which although rooted in the past is actually a commitment to the future and requires trust and predictability – the conditions for generalised reciprocity cannot exist for either men or women.

The breakdown of trust and predictability

The most popular explanation by Cruddas Park residents for the failure of a local Neighbourhood Watch scheme was the blunt conclusion that the residents themselves were criminals. It is senseless to rely on the vigilance of neighbours if they are seen as the source of the problem. Almost equally popular was the view that people who did join such a scheme would suffer reprisals and/or victimisation. (An extreme case was described in a local paper, *Newcastle Journal*, 16 October, 1992.) Harassment and intimidation are a fundamental condition of existence of much of the petty criminality that does exist. Indeed, crime and harassment are *not* separate problems. Harassment is itself a crime. In these areas there is ample evidence of the sanctions which are central to what might be called the culture of the 'grass', or the informer. Everywhere there are graffiti, "Jackie is a grass", or more ominously, "This is a grass house".

It may even be the case that the financial gains for those who do steal and are part of this culture are paltry because there is no strict economic rationale being applied. Theft, harassment and car crime are the exercise of power and the display of masculinity by young males primarily for their own sakes against their own communities (Campbell, 1993).

It is important to remember that this is an area with high unemployment with many people at home during the day. Nevertheless, a police crime survey centred on Cruddas Park/Loadman Street found that 84% of the illegal entries to houses were via the ground floor, either through windows or doors. The most common form of entry, if via a door, was through the front door. In *only one third* of the burglaries were the normal occupants *out of the house* at the time of the offence. This is brazen theft in which often the thieves make little attempt to disguise their work. They count on the reluctant complicity of those around them to ignore their activities. If they are challenged, the response can be violence or the threat of violence.

It is a tragic irony that families whose sources of income have been traditionally criminally generated find it easier to maintain their structure and their control over the younger generation. Indeed, criminal families of longstanding in areas like Cruddas Park despise the unemployed young members of the 'street culture' who steal cars and wreck them for kicks. Evans et al (1995) argue that, in a Salford estate they call 'Oldtown', traditional ideas still prevailed: local criminals had a moral code and did not rob their neighbours. The existence of these beliefs "is perhaps one of the most significant expressions of community on the Oldtown estate" (Evans et al, 1995, p 13; see also Chapter 3).

Unfortunately, one of the problems (which exasperates Campbell, 1993) is that young male violence depends upon, commands and uses, female support, household work and female networks. Most young men, particularly the members of the street culture, do not cook, clean, shop, sew, iron, and so on. They depend upon females for these necessary services, and they can get those services, even if they cannot offer anything much in return. The young men, it seems, are beneficiaries of the female practice of generalised reciprocity. The same values which make working-class women more likely to be community activists are more commonly expressed in practical support for the men who are the chief immediate danger to community stability, trust and predictability. However, no one should underestimate the dilemma of these women. One of the activist young women consciously decided to concentrate on saving her three youngest children when, to her horror, her eldest son enthusiastically joined the 'street culture'. All her truly remarkable capacities and threats could not save him from his fate: he is currently charged with murder.

These areas are not poor because they have crime. They only become worse because of the forms it has taken. Their original problems derive from the continual restructuring of the labour market which is intrinsically part of capitalism. Trust and predictability are fragile but significant achievements in fundamental opposition to the basic features of modern societies.

Conclusion

What this analysis underscores is the very significant difference between the genders on almost every dimension of community life. Working-class men and women live in sharply different social worlds, and their commitment to their communities and localities is therefore very different. Community work is largely performed by women in their own areas because they are, through tradition and circumstance, committed to them.

The bi-modal distribution by age of Abrams' helpers and the Cruddas Park activists is not a coincidence. Mothering is the paradigmatic example of generalised reciprocity and it is women in their early 30s with children who constitute one of the major groups of activists. Despite the difficulties of juggling children and sometimes work, the appeal of generalised reciprocity and its occasional emergence in community activism is at its strongest for these mothers. For older women generalised reciprocity is reinforced by the maintained traditions of earlier working-class life.

Many women bear an increasing double burden: work in the household and in waged work. Providing creches for women to go out to work is supposed to make this waged work more possible for women with children. The active young women discussed here often bear a triple burden: of household, community and work (see Dominelli, 1990, p 94). Thus, whereas women are increasingly stretched in areas like Cruddas Park, men seem to contribute less and less positively to their households and community and through their work. When men do take up community activism they often mop up any paid work. It should be no surprise that a man, after "fucking up the estate" and who was now leaving it "carrying a brief case", can seem so irksome to a woman. Such outbursts are, however, rare.

five

Community without unity[*]
Jeremy Brent

'Community without unity' is a catchphrase that has caught my imagination as a way of describing and understanding everyday practices and theoretical discussions of community. In this chapter I want to explore the ideas this phrase seems to encapsulate, to see if the words have use as more than a soundbite.

The phrase is the title of an interesting, slightly idiosyncratic book by Corlett (1989). That book lies within the wide field of academic writing on community. However, discussions about, and practices of, community take place on many other stages. The theatre which I am investigating is that of Southmead, an area of Bristol, where the question 'What is community?' has been running around for years, continually exhausting itself, but never dying.

It may be unfair to single out Southmead, a large outer-city housing estate, as a laboratory of community, a fate that it shares with many other poor areas of Britain. Residents there hate being researched. In fact, community is invoked as a defence against researchers poking their noses into local lives, and used as a strength to counter that interference. There was a short-term radio station set up in the area in 1994, Radio Southmead, its activating principles based very much within the discourse of

[*] I would like to thank Richard Johnson, Meg Lovelock, Jeffrey Weeks, John Bird and Paul Hoggett for their valuable comments, and acknowledge the financial support given to this research project by the Kingswood Foundation Ltd.

community, as expressed both locally and nationally. On one of its programmes a local 'community activist', when asked about Radio Southmead, gave this view:

> "This is the first time we've had the media speaking out from Southmead in the 40 years that I've been here, and doing a good job of it. For years and years we've had people coming in from outside to find out what's wrong with us, how we live, and what makes us so criminal." (Les Palmer on Radio Southmead, 12 August 1994)

My research focuses on Southmead because I am implicated in local constructions of community (I was, for example, one of the organisers of Radio Southmead) and my interrogation is as much about my own practice as it is an outsider's dissection of how other people live. I am interested in community being as much a representation and tool of social policy that is imposed from outside, as being some kind of 'authentic' and self-generated local manifestation of identity. I am *not* finding out 'what's wrong with' Southmead and certainly do not label its residents as criminal, though crime is a major ingredient of the discourse of community and its perceived breakdown, locally, nationally and internationally (Brown, 1995; Hope and Shaw, 1988; Safe Neighbourhoods Unit, 1991).

I have not disguised the area behind a pseudonym, for three reasons. First, pseudonyms can slip so easily: the 'Upfield' of earlier research in the area (Spencer, Tuxford and Dennis, 1964; Wilson, 1963) is a mask that fails to disguise. Second, local people do publicly speak and write about the area, for example: Radio Southmead; the Southmead Community Play, *Lifelines* (1994); books of poetry (Bristol Broadsides, 1980; 1986); community magazines; 'people's history' (Truman and Brent, 1995). To ignore or disguise these cultural productions would be insulting to their authors and contributors. Third, community is an idea, practice, discourse, notion, that is used in context, not an ungrounded theory or hypothesis. Naming the context grounds the salience of the debate. I am not, however, arguing from some kind of realist position that, on the one hand there is a domain of ideas and, on the other a domain of reality, against which ideas should be tested, but from a position that ideas and discourses are very much part of the 'reality' of everyday life. Theories of community occur in everyday conversation, and affect people's perceptions and actions.

Naming Southmead does have the disadvantage of publicly reifying it and turning it into a spectacle, a place that attracts *voyeurs* investigating if 'community' does or does not 'exist'. Southmead already possesses a certain historical and symbolic significance as a "Difficult Housing Estate" (Wilson, 1963), a significance which is both constitutive of the area, and heavy to carry.

These observations are not simply the soul-searching of a researcher, struggling with the guilt that the research process can engender. They hint already at the problem of seeing community as a unity, as they start to sketch the fact of there being two (at least) versions of community, one from what is seen as 'outside', the other from 'inside', maybe in relationship with each other, but not identical. Even what is envisaged as 'inside' and 'outside' is not amenable to simple definition, but depends on contested boundaries, drawn differently as both Southmead and community are imagined in a multitude of ways by different social actors. Southmead is not one definable community, but the locus of more than one idea of community, and more than one set of community practices.

Community as unity

Many writers have identified the ideas of oneness and wholeness that pervade much of the writing on community. Corlett, who provided my starting point, writes of: "the shared oneness at the center of recent communitarian thinking" (Corlett, 1989, p 4). In the introduction to a collection of essays on the community debate Avineri and de-Shalit underscore the point: "The 'communitarian' community is more than mere association; it is a unity in which the individuals are members." (1992, p 4). The same theme is noted by Bhabha, though from a different perspective, in an essay about nationalism and the nation:

> We may begin by questioning that progressive
> metaphor of modern social cohesion – the many
> as one – shared by organic theories of the holism

of culture and community. (Bhabha, 1990, p 294)

Community as an ingredient of 'progressive' (and not so progressive) social policy has been a fixture in virtually all thinking about Southmead since it was first built as a poor copy of a garden city, with visions of semi-rural bliss as an answer to the social problems of inner-city slums. That dream did not, however, materialise, and there have been a number of reports since (the major ones being the Bristol Social Project in the 1950s (Wilson, 1963; Spencer, Tuxford and Dennis, 1964) and the Safe Neighbourhoods Unit survey of 1991) that try to come up with new ways of realising community as a social policy objective to overcome the perceived problems of delinquency and anti-social behaviour. The 'problems' are remarkably consistent, though the early, post-war work associates them with people not being able to cope with an increased standard of living, while the more modern ones cite their poverty! The history of the original design of the estate, and of the various reports since, demonstrates the persistence of the idea of community as some kind of sublime, if elusive, answer to social division and stress.

The reports also have their own community effects, as their recommendations are turned into practices. For example, the Bristol Social Project recommended a new type of professional, the community organiser, the precursor of today's community worker, of which there are now, years later, a number in the area.

"Out of many one" as a founding dictum (Bhabha, 1990, p 294) also informs vernacular communitarianism. In Southmead much effort was put into the production of a community play, *Lifelines*. This play, performed in December 1994, in which some 150 people took part, was a history of the estate from when the first tenants were moved there in the 1930s to the present day, devised from locally told stories. The narrative structure of the play had the effect of presenting Southmead as a unified historical subject, with a continuity and identity over time: it established a heritage. The conflicts that were portrayed in the play were either with outsider misinterpretations and misunderstandings of life in Southmead, or were staged as familial rows that are a shared experience. The history of internal conflicts is used to show a closeness – what Anderson, in writing of a similar process in national histories, rather dramatically calls "the reassurance of fratricide" (Anderson, 1991, p 199).

The motivation to stage *Lifelines* (which was a major undertaking) was deeply informed by the desire to bring people together – to create community. Ivy Baker was the chair of its committee. In an interview on Radio Southmead she summed up the project:

> "... the community play that I'm in now ... is about Southmead. For the people of Southmead. Bringing people in Southmead together. The division. Making people work as one together. People who had never talked to each other or even share conversation, is working now in a play."

> "I love Southmead, I love the people.... And they need bringing together as a community." (Ivy Baker, Radio Southmead, 10 August 1994)

This is an attractive vision. If one is living on a large housing estate in material decline in this era of rampant individualist economics (local poverty is well documented – Avon County Planning Department, 1991; Bristol City Council, 1994), damaged by racism, and perceived as "a problem estate where crime, lawlessness and anti-social behaviour are rife" (Safer Neighbourhoods Unit, 1991, p 7), community as unity offers a promise of hope.

However, this hoped for unity of any community is deeply problematic, and I suggest that any attempt to claim or impose unity can of itself lead to strife. It certainly did in the case of the community play, which created furious, even frightening, antagonism between people. The public unity hid massive conflict, with a strong faction being antagonistic to even staging the play, seeing it as totally irrelevant to local needs and antithetic to local aspirations for economic improvement. It would be impossible to write a definitive history of this conflict, partly because so much went on out of the public eye, but, more importantly, because the writing of any but the blandest of accounts would itself be a controversial act, creating further suspicion, division, conflict and history. The play itself was a 'safe', unifying story of Southmead, closing with an anthem of praise to the area and its people. The history of the production of the play is still a 'risky' story, full of unresolved conflict and fragmentation (see Johnson, nd).

While there is a powerful and seductive strand of 'unitarianism' within communitarianism, this appears as a history of unrealised hopes, both for communitarian social policy, and for locally generated dreams of community. Community is maybe, as Bauman describes it, a postulate rather than a fact of life and to postulate the existence of any community, in this case in Southmead, would be, to him, plainly contentious (1993, p 44).

The postulate may, however, be the idea of community as *unity*, rather than other possibilities of community. I want now to work through a four-part argument on the possibilities of community *without* unity:

- Community is multi-dimensional, not reducible to a unitary phenomenon.

- Exclusion and splitting, rather than union, is constitutive of community.

- The splitting is not a simple insider/outsider division, but is internal to community.

- Conflict is inherent within community as a concept, so community is always an ambivalent practice.

Multi-dimensional community

The problem of lack of unity meaning disunity is a theme which dominates many meetings within Southmead.   At one such meeting, which was becoming overwhelmed by the problems affecting the area, one participant summed up the general feeling: "The need is for professionals and residents to pull together". The meeting went on to discuss the existence of so many different community groups in the area.   First this was posed as being a problem, a block to effective collective action.   However, when someone said that there were 28 such groups, and that he had a list of them all, there seemed to be a perceptible shift towards pride that this was an area that contained so much vitality (field notes, October 1994).

In her work on the East Village of Manhattan, Abu-Lughod (1994) criticises those past studies that assume and search for singularity in the construction of community and instead develops an approach that incorporates diversity. So, for example, within her study area she has identified 10 socially diverse groups of residents. It is this very diversity, not unity, that constitutes East Village as a modern space of community relationships and forms the community politics of the area. For not only is the area diverse, it is also full of controversy. One of her recommendations for studying community is, interestingly, not to look for unity, but to focus on community controversies as these erupt (1994, p 195). Importantly, she does not want to impose a unity by the way she portrays the area, but, "accepted the fact that there was no single 'authorial' [authoritative] image of the neighbourhood." (p 195) so the research was carried out by several people, each one researching a different perspective to capture a range of visions.

Southmead, on the surface, does not appear to be as diverse, certainly not as cosmopolitan, as that New York neighbourhood, partly because of the seeming uniformity imposed by municipal architecture. However, one-dimensional thinking about Southmead is locally resented: a constant local complaint about research and press representations of the area is that they perpetuate a stereotype that flattens – into statistics, into the single image of 'trouble'. To contest this there is a strand of community activity that is about asserting the wealth and breadth of local life.

This was one clear motivation behind a large open-air rock concert held in the area in July 1993. The concert was organised to raise money in memory of two local people who had died of cystic fibrosis, and some 500 people paid to attend. However, there was also a propaganda reason for the concert. Much effort was put into obtaining media coverage and making public statements to display the fullness and humanity of Southmead:

> With six of the bands from tonight's line-up either still living in Southmead or retaining family links, it is indicative of the talent and goodwill that abounds in the area. (Brian and Maria Chappell, Rock Show '93 Souvenir Programme)

One of the highlights of the evening was when a local Rastafarian gave an unscheduled a cappella performance. The immense applause he received as the mainly white audience sang along with him was indicative of a strand of generosity, and inclusion of difference, that can at certain moments exist within community.

There is much writing on community that stresses the diversity and complexity within community (Cohen, 1985), and there are communitarian writers who certainly do not insist on unity. Sandel, a major contributor to the communitarian debate, writes that there is: "no single 'ultimate' community whose pre-eminence just goes without argument or further description." (1982, p 146).

However, assertions of the multi-dimensionality of community can be seen as an attempt to incorporate difference into unity, without seeing that community formation is intrinsically about creating difference. So while at the rock concert there could be a warm feeling of self-congratulation at the acceptance of the Rastafarian, that can be contrasted with the suspicion, animosity and violence that he and his friends had suffered when they first, defiantly, grew their dreadlocks in the early 1980s, and were virtually expelled from the area – a different moment in community life. Many different voices may be heard within community, but this should not blind us to the fact that it is a site of division.

Community as division

Much has been written about community formation being based on boundary drawing. One justification for studying community in the modern age, against arguments privileging globalisation, or massification, or individualisation, is that people continually draw collective boundaries to differentiate themselves from others, to create a sense of their own identities (the main theme of the essays in Cohen [1986], not dissimilar to Maffesoli's [1996] argument on the formation of neo-tribes). And it is almost a commonplace to say that this boundary construction of 'self' (collectively or individually) is built on the construction and rejection of 'others'.

There is a problem, as a researcher, in discovering why certain people, or categories, are constructed as other. For example, when I ask why it is at times so important to fight people from Henbury (an adjoining estate), I am told: "Of course you can't understand. You're an outsider." I immediately make myself an 'other' by even asking the question, and my lack of understanding strengthens the closeness of those who do understand. There are plenty of signs in Southmead of boundary drawing. In late 1994, two of the local pubs sported notices reading:

Sorry

No Travellers

or Gypsy's

Welcome here

justified as necessary by the fights 'they' caused.

In a local discussion about racial harassment, community was posed as a solution to the isolation of those who were harassed, partly by the formation of a local multi-cultural association, described as a 'big family, lovely, united'. This was generally accepted, until the topic of Asian women was mentioned, when the mood changed as 'they' were criticised for not mixing with 'us', typified by not joining in local social events. Living in the area (Southmead being an assertion of a spatial definition of identity) was not enough and was a difference too far, for at least some people, to be contained in even a multi-dimensional community (field notes, November 1994).

Boundaries are drawn to create a sense of unity 'inside', through conflict with 'outside'. However, Zizek, from Slovenia, who maybe has a heightened awareness of the effect of boundaries, argues that the very process of boundary drawing finally makes any unity impossible:

> ... every boundary proves itself a limit: apropos of every identity, we are sooner or later bound to experience how its condition of possibility (the boundary that delimits its conditions) is simultaneously its condition of impossibility. (Zizek, 1991, p 110)

That rather dense quote sums up the deflation that some felt at the end of the meeting on racial harassment. We had reached the limit of the progressive unity of community in diversity and were realising that there is a greater constitutive force of community, division, that made that hope impossible. Community cannot, because of that boundary which is a necessary constituent of its existence, create an all-inclusive unity. The boundary that separates 'us' from 'them' is the limit that shows that community has no possibility of encompassing all people, of being an ever-uniting force. Zizek's argument continues: "every Whole is founded on a constitutive Exception: ... the very gesture of completion entails exclusion." (Zizek, 1991, p 111).

Any 'complete' community either excludes, or is based upon exclusion of some sort, whether that exclusion be *of* certain groups, or whether the whole area itself suffers exclusion *by* its poverty and reputation.   One of the main drives for much community activity in Southmead is fed by a reaction to the exclusion that the area suffers.   Community, as a concept that aspires to inclusion and unity, but based on exclusion and division, seems to exemplify Zizek's assertion of the "impossible accordance of the object with its Notion" (p 69).   This is not because of a mismatch between an ideal and its always incomplete realisation, but because the ideal bears the split *within itself*.   Ideal communities are themselves based on division.   It is not just practical difficulties that prevent unity – even in ideal terms unity is unachievable.

In everyday life there are notions of Southmead as a community, but there is no single object which accords to these notions.   However, the situation is more complex than that outlined by Zizek, because there is no *single* exception, no intrusive not-Southmead, making unity impossible, but a whole series of these exceptions.   Both Southmead-as-place and Southmead-as-community are unstable definitions, because they are based on a shifting multitude of boundaries, many of them permeable (the Rastafarian as insider or outsider?).

Boundary drawing is a major problem for those social surveys that pride themselves upon their objectivity, as there are no agreed or de facto boundaries. The three surveys of the early 1990s that include Southmead as a social and geographical entity each delineate it with completely different boundaries.   But without those boundaries there would be no Southmead at all, however unstable, even to be able to discuss.

It is a danger of community studies that they only research those constituted as 'within' community, not those excluded, so by omission emphasise unity.   It was only by chance that I met an Iranian who, with his family, was suffering such intense harassment in Southmead from local people because of their 'difference' (including his house being burgled and rammed by a joyrider and his wife and children being abused as 'Pakis' in the street) that they were driven from the area, thus giving me an outsider's perspective on certain practices of community and division in operation (field notes, October 1994).

The split community

There are developed psychoanalytic theories on splitting. The knowledge of their complexity makes me nervous about the potential naivety of my next argument – that as community is based on division, it is not only an unattainable unity, but an internally and irretrievably split one as well (see Klein, 1986, p 181 for a similar argument about the structure of the ego). The greater the pressure for unity, the more pronounced the external divisions, so there is an increased prevalence of internal splits, as different sections are anathematised in the search for an ultimately unrealisable uniform and pure community.

One major theme of Southmead, creating it as an object of study, policing and social concern, has been its depiction as disreputable and low. Even those community manifestations that contest that depiction cannot escape it, this press item on the Community Play being representative:

> Southmead is often in the news for the wrong reasons, *but* now more than 150 people have come together to show there is still a strong, positive community spirit. (*Bristol Observer*, 24 November, 1994 – my emphasis)

This creation of Southmead as a problem area does have a reassuring effect on those who carry out this labelling – the risks and fears of modern city living are spatialised as existing in Southmead, which, with the various other low places of Bristol, takes on a symbolic importance (see Stallybrass and White, 1986 for the psychic role of low places). Southmead is split off as a disreputable community from outside, by those who construct themselves as safe and respectable.

But this splitting continues inside. There are streets thought of as reputable, and streets powerfully imagined as low, within Southmead. And what is most striking, in this situation, is how widely young people have the weight of disreputableness loaded onto them. They are created as the outsiders within, the constitutive 'other' of community, through the association of young people with crime.

Young people are, in spatial terms, indisputably part of Southmead. Southmead has a significantly higher proportion of young people than Bristol as a whole (Bristol City Council, 1994, p 38), and they depend more than adults on their immediate neighbourhood for their social life – so in some ways they are more of the community than are adults. They should be central to community, but are instead commonly seen as the destroyers of community. In the 1991 Southmead Survey: "There was almost universal agreement that those largely responsible for crime in Southmead are young people." (Safe Neighbourhoods Unit, 1991, p 46).

In fact, so closely allied were young people with crime that under-18-year-olds were the only section of the population to be asked, in a special section of that survey, whether they had been involved in crime (and if they drank alcohol or took drugs – other projections onto young people) (p 57). Crime was seen as a major problem in the area by 74% of adults (p 33), who were not, of course, asked about any of their own criminal activities and substance use, and 'gangs' of young people were identified as a problem six times in the report. Young people and gangs were also a major preoccupation of the Bristol Social Project whose research was undertaken 35 years earlier: "Juvenile delinquency was the original problem and starting point for the project" (Spencer, Tuxford and Dennis, 1964, p 24).

Brown has conducted a more detailed survey, in Middlesborough, of the relationship between constructions of juvenile crime and community (Brown 1995). In this she found a persistent linkage in adult's perceptions between crime, young people and the disintegration of community, despite her evidence that young people suffer more from crime by adults than they are perpetrators of crime against adults. Because of this association with crime, young people were seen as "both symptom and cause of the collapse of the moral universe." (Brown, 1995, p 36).

In response to this fear of young people, Brown finds that "'community' becomes defined as middle aged and elderly residents of a locality." (p 47), and leads to community practices that are exclusive and oppressive of young people. Adults project their own uncertainties onto young people, creating them as the outsiders of their hoped for safe community. It is striking how blatantly this internal division between people who are, whatever their age, all residents of the area, turns into calls for exclusion. One of the recommendations of the Southmead Survey was that the City Council, through its housing allocation policy, should "reduce the very high density of children on the estate" (Safe Neighbourhoods Unit, 1991, p 65). A section of the population to be 'reduced' as a community practice?

I have highlighted the position of young people within the internal splitting of Southmead, partly because of the publicly available data and partly due to my work as a youth worker. This should not blind us to other areas of splitting – gender relations, sexuality, race, and the not so hidden injuries of poverty and class. Gender as a major factor in dividing community is the principal theme of Campbell's (1993) *Goliath – Britain's dangerous places*, though in her book it is again *young* men that are the destroyers of community. Communities are not oases of equality where major issues of power magically stop at the boundary. And community activity is not just about uniting against an outside world, but also about dividing off, even denying, what are seen as the unacceptable parts within, the parts that create doubt and ambivalence.

Community as ambivalence

Ambivalence is a word that is heavily used as a description of the condition of existence in late or post-modernity, but I can think of no better word, nor can I invent a suitable neologism to describe the feelings that I have about community, and those that I hear around me. My own ambivalence revolves around the concept of community offering marginalised people a strength to act as agents, but also being used as a way to control those very same people – it is ironic that in most of the literature on Southmead, community is seen as something that should be done to people, not what they do themselves.

Membership of community itself can be ambivalent – many people living in what is generally geographically defined as Southmead do not want to be associated with its low reputation, and repudiate membership, even refusing to take part in a local survey (Safe Neighbourhood Unit, 1991, p 27).

In July 1995 the local Scouts called a public meeting to discuss the future of its operation and that of its building situated in the 'heart' of Southmead. The building has been subjected to so much vandalism that the Scout leaders were feeling on the brink of defeat, and wanted outside support. To gain this they told a whole range of stories about events and people to the meeting, an evocative and effective technique to describe the situation and, importantly, their feelings about it. These stories, both separately, and collectively, were heavy with ambivalence. There were stories of decline and despair, coupled with stories of loyalty and pride – how the roof was destroyed by 'them', how 'we' repaired it, "though none of us are roofers". There were stories of attachment to the area, pride that they all live locally (the stories were prefaced with "I live in ____ Road"), together with fearful tales of drugs and poverty.

From all these stories emerged new stories, of collective action to improve their building, of reviving the Scout band to play a full part in local events, of becoming active in an oppressive situation. All too human stories of despair and hope leading on to a creative, but still uncertain, story of community. The problem comes when this story of community becomes what Corlett calls a politics of reassurance: "a desire for foundations; a desire to escape the play of the world and stay at home for the night." (Corlett, 1989, p 67).

Corlett understands this need for reassurance, but wants to supplement it with a politics of extravagance, of community being more than a municipal provision of safety (pp 209 ff). Community needs to move beyond trying to provide safe stories into the tension of exploring risky ones. This again seems like a great slogan, but how can it be incorporated into the everyday practice that people are searching for? I want to end with just a few pointers, though no tidy solution, for which I need to rely heavily on the work and words of other writers.

In place of unity, the French sociologist Maffesoli introduces, or 'disinters', the idea of unicity. As he puts it, in discussing complex societies, "lack of *unity* does not mean the absence of a certain *unicity*", which term he explains in a footnote:

> While unity expresses a closed condition, the medieval notion of *unicity* summons up a more open and heterogeneous situation. (Maffesoli, 1991, p 12)

Unicity maintains the idea of uniqueness, without which any Southmead or any community would be nothing, but without imposing the purity and closure of unity. A 'unicity' can be a locale for action, without demanding or forcing an unattainable harmony and uniformity.

Following from this, the idea of, or hope for, community as a singular phenomenon is misplaced. In unicity there has to be an acknowledgement of multiplicity and diversity. There is no single, true, absolute Southmead, as: "unidimensionality of thought is unsuitable for understanding the polydimensionality of lived experience." (Maffesoli, 1989, p 4).

The dangers of disunity and disintegration brought by this polydimensionality are offset by its potential energy. The more differentiated the collective 'we-experience', so the more vivid it is (Volosinov, 1973, p 88).

Communities do not resolve conflicts – in fact we have seen how desire for unity in Southmead even creates conflict, and how part of community construction is through having, or creating, both outsiders and insiders with whom the community is in conflict. We can not overcome the *aporias* (unbridgeable chasms) that are the fate of modern society (Bauman, 1993, p 8) through some simple idea of community, but we are in active relationship with them through our various collective identities.

Ambivalence can not be driven out or repressed – it is both an inherent and incurable part of community, as seen above, for:

> ... ambivalence resides at the heart of the 'primary
> scene' of human face-to-face.... All subsequent
> social arrangements ... deploy that ambivalence as
> their building material. (Bauman, 1993, p 10)

Community is too often used rhetorically as a positive and unambivalent word to weigh against the negatives of disintegration by writers and policy makers across the political spectrum, without an understanding that any formation of community brings with it a whole range of further questions, difficulties and struggles. Community is not a term suitable for use as a unequivocal slogan of redemption.

Finally, it is the very struggles around the idea of community and around my chosen location, Southmead, that give meaning to these terms. This need for conflict to create living meaning is well captured in a work attributed to the Russian, Volosinov, writing about linguistic signs, with an idea equally applicable to social forms and places:

> A sign that has been withdrawn from the pressure of the social struggle ... inevitably loses force, degenerating into allegory and becoming the object not of live social intelligibility but of philological comprehension. (1973, p 23)

Southmead and community are live relationships that are part of the social struggle. If they were outside of the struggle, they would be redundant as spatial and social formations, as locales for social action. Their very complexity ensures their meaningfulness and the continual struggle for meaning that both induces and feeds their existence. Creating unity and simplicity in the hope of fixing meaning and informing action in these contexts would result in both the death of their significance, and the impossibility of any subsequent community action.

Community is as much about struggle as it is about unity. It is this contradiction, this disunity within the term, that makes it such a resonant and pertinent inspiration of social action.

six

The dialogics of 'community': language and identity in a housing scheme in the West of Scotland*

Chik Collins

The language of 'community' has a long history in contests over processes of social change. In current contests this language displays a continuing, perhaps even surprising, vitality. The language of community has to be contested because, it seems, it cannot safely be conceded (Collins, 1996a). In practice such contests always take place in contexts which are historical and concrete. Often they are also distinctly local. It is in this light that this paper seeks to make its contribution. It provides a case study of a contest over the identity of a working-class 'community' in Ferguslie Park, a housing scheme in the town of Paisley in the west of Scotland. In doing so it attempts to address a set of related questions which might well be applied more broadly. Who gets to define and redefine what 'community' means and what goes to make up the social and political identities of actual communities,

* Some of the material in this paper was rehearsed at a seminar involving members of the Department of Applied Social Studies, University of Paisley, in February 1995. I would like to thank those who participated in the session. John Foster, Mike Turner, Joan Kelly Hall and Mike Huspek offered useful comments on an earlier draft, as did participants at the 'Ideas of Community' Conference at UWE in September 1995. Thanks are also due to Jim Lister whose collaboration on related work has been of much assistance in developing the argument of this paper.

in specific contexts? How is this achieved? How does this influence the ongoing process of social change and the contests over this? Answering these questions involves grappling with complex relations between language, social identities and the local and national contexts in which contests over community take place. This means that the study must be theoretically tooled. In turn, if the presentation of the study is to be clear, then the nature of the theoretical tool must be explained. This is the purpose of the following brief discussion.

Theoretical framework

A useful theoretical framework with which to approach the above questions is provided in a recent article by Hall (Hall, 1995; see also Collins 1996b). Hall emphasises the ways in which our uses of language work to "(re)create our world" – our relationships, identities, ideologies and ultimately our language itself. This, she recognises, is not a novel idea (Hymes, 1974; Halliday, 1978). However, she suggests that insufficient attention has been paid to the ways in which our use of language is constrained by the histories attached to, first, different language resources and second, the social identities of the speakers who use them. She examines these twin issues of language resources and social identity in turn.

In the first connection she draws on the works of the Bakhtin circle (Bakhtin, 1981; 1986; Gardiner, 1992; Volosinov, 1986a; 1986b). For Bakhtin, our use of language involves deploying historically developed, conventional meanings to create spoken meanings which are specific to the concrete conditions of the social interaction taking place. The conventional meanings are crystallised in particular 'speech genres' associated with typical contexts of language use. As we use them in contextual utterances we infuse them with our own personal senses and evaluative tenor, and in so doing fashion our own unique 'meanings'. However, as Hall points out, the meanings of the words which we use are "differently weighted" in terms of the scope which is available to any individual to modify or transform them in the actual moment of their use. Conventional meanings are not innocents in contests over social change. They are the products of past utterances of other people. They bear the marks of a history in which they have been developed and sustained, to different degrees, as valid and authoritative meanings by sociopolitical actors with sociopolitical interests.   So they are neither socially neutral, nor uniformly plastic.   In extreme cases conventional meanings can seem quite impregnable to the particular senses and evaluation of the speaker, and appear to have no history and embody no particular intentions.   The 'given' use can appear entirely unquestionable and authoritative.   More commonly, however, different speakers contest the 'tenure' of linguistic resources – the right to semantically occupy them with their own point of view deriving from their own experience.

However, for Hall, the scope to do this is also affected by the social identity of the speaker: "the freedom to use language is tied to how 'who we are' is sociohistorically constructed" (1995, p 207).   Our talk is mediated by our assessments of the social groups to which we and our interactants belong.   These assessments go to make up the social identities of the participants within the interaction.   Different sociohistorical identities with different levels of power attached to them typically carry with them different beliefs about the prerogatives people have in making use of the available linguistic resources.   Thus, the more power attached to the social identity of a speaker, the more scope they have to "define, use, and manipulate the resources available to their own ends", and evaluate whether the uses of other speakers are "appropriate and valid", or should be defined as "resistant, inappropriate or wrong" (Hall, 1995, pp 216-17).

So for Hall, contests over language and identity can only be grasped from a 'sociohistorical' perspective.   She distinguishes this from both formal and sociocultural perspectives.   In the formal approach the focus is on linguistic resources abstracted from their actual use.   In the sociocultural perspective the focus is on use, but the above detailed constraints are largely ignored.   The sociohistorian's primary interest, on the other hand, is in examining:

> ... the locally situated contests between the conventional meanings of the resources brought to any particular moment and the ways in which people maintain or transform these meanings as they go about (re)creating their everyday worlds. (Hall, 1995, p 211)

Thus Hall's article provides a theoretical framework designed to facilitate the study of local contests over language and identity, and in this light it seems a promising framework within which to present an analytical account of a 'contested community'.

Ferguslie Park

Ferguslie Park was built as a public sector housing estate between the 1920s and the 1960s. The majority of the housing was built in the late 1930s, at which point the population grew to 10,000 – around a tenth of Paisley's people. This housing consisted of tenemental flats built for those being cleared from the town's slums. The latter were generally the families of unskilled manual workers in low-paid and irregular employment. They lived in extreme poverty and were often regarded as a feckless and dangerous social element requiring supervision and control. Perhaps symptomatically, the scheme was located between two railway lines which virtually sealed it off from the rest of the town. It duly became known as the longest dead-end in Scotland. In 1942 part of the scheme was set aside for supervised housing for 'anti-social tenants' (Worker's Educational Association [WEA]/ Ferguslie Elderly Forum, 1992).

Henceforth, Ferguslie's reputation has borne the stigma associated with these origins. But the stigma has intensified. When, in the 1960s, industrial decline brought increasing poverty and unemployment to Paisley, the combination of the scheme's blue-collar history, its 'undesirable' reputation and the operation of the council's allocations policy meant that the victims were disproportionately located in Ferguslie (William Roe Associates, 1994). Since then further economic decline, poor management, low investment, failed experiments and the myriad of social problems associated have deepened the problems of the estate. In turn a savage media have propagated the 'notoriety' of the scheme throughout Britain as a whole.[1]

A major factor fuelling this notoriety has been the high profile given to it by a stream of urban policy projects and experiments. From 1972-77 it was one of 12 areas designated under central government's Community Development Project (CDP). In 1979 the local authorities designated Ferguslie an Area of Priority Treatment. And, from 1984-88 the local authorities together with the Scottish Office Urban Renewal Unit collaborated on a 'corporate attack on deprivation' under the name of an Area Initiative. In terms of their ostensible remit – tackling deprivation and reversing the decline of the area – these projects were failures. In the mid-1960s Ferguslie had around 13,500 people living in some 3,500 units of housing. By the late 1980s the population had more than halved and 1,000 units of housing had been cleared and demolished. Unemployment, poverty, housing problems and the wider stigmatisation of the area had all become substantially worse. In 1988, 75% of all households in the estate had an income of less than £5,000 per annum; 35% had less than £2,500 (Gaster et al, 1995).

The partnership approach

In 1988 Ferguslie Park was singled out for yet another urban policy project. The broader context of this designation is important. In 1987 Margaret Thatcher had been returned for her third term as Prime Minister. This was the beginning of her most 'triumphalist' period. Yet, on election night she declared: "tomorrow we've got a big job ahead of us in those inner cities" (Robson, 1989). Voters in the English inner cities were continuing to reject the Tories' vision of Britain. But in Scotland the situation was worse. Here the Conservatives had been reduced from 21 to 10 MPs (out of a possible 72). How could it be that, in the land of Adam Smith, Thatcher's free-market message fared so badly? The Scottish Office's response was that Scottish society had a 'dependency culture' (see Mitchell, 1990). Rehabilitating the Conservative Party in Scotland would require that this be broken and replaced by an 'enterprise culture' – demoting the public sector to an 'enabling role' and allowing a dynamic private sector to take the leading role in redefining Scottish society. Thus, Scottish society found itself facing a substantially new and concerted policy agenda – in housing, urban policy, economic development and training (Kemp, 1993). This was to be known as the 'partnership' agenda.

   In Scotland the worst examples of the 'dependency culture' were seen to be, not the inner cities, but the public sector estates on the peripheries of the major towns and cities (Scottish Office, 1988). On this basis the 'partnership approach' was to be applied first to these areas. Four high-profile estate-based initiatives were announced in 1988.[2] The Scottish Office were to lead the initiatives and direct the involvement of the various quangos. They were to have a duration of some 10 years, and would serve to establish the new policy framework. This would then be generalised, supplanting existing approaches (Scottish Office, 1990a; 1990b; 1991; 1993; 1995). The four areas were carefully chosen for their potential to demonstrate the viability of the approach. In the case of Ferguslie Park the attraction lay primarily in its location (Collins, 1991a; Cunning Young and Partners, 1988). It was one mile from Glasgow Airport, with almost immediate access to the M8 motorway and only six miles from the centre of Glasgow. It was also immediately adjacent to one of the largest property developments in Scotland (the Tilbury Group's 'Phoenix' development on the site of the old Chrysler car plant at Linwood), and had developable land both within the estate and in its immediate environs. To the Scottish Office it seemed that, in a situation where parts of the economy were booming and even overheating, this potential might be harnessed to a long-term strategy to change the face of Ferguslie and its environs once and for all (see Massey, 1988). Tenure patterns could be transformed using the private sector, housing associations and cooperatives. More affluent socioeconomic groups would be attracted in and, statistically, the deprivation figures would be transformed. In 10 years the Conservatives and the private sector would achieve what 20 years of Labour-inspired public sector solutions had failed to do – the transformation of Ferguslie Park.

But in the wake of the election results the problem of legitimacy remained. In fact, given the intention of demoting the Labour-controlled local authorities it became more acute. It was in this context that the distinctive rhetoric of partnership was developed by the Scottish Office (Scottish Office, 1988). The Scottish Office, the private sector, the quangos, the voluntary sector, the local authorities and the local communities concerned would come together as 'partners' in pursuit of the noble aim of tackling urban problems once and for all. The initiatives would actually be called 'partnerships'. The local authorities would be junior partners, of course, but partners nonetheless. Any deficit on the side of representative democracy would be made up on the side of participatory democracy. Here the Scottish Office drew on the critique of the public sector which had been developed by working-class tenants themselves over a period of some 20 years. This critique had become crystallised in a discourse of community action. Partly inspired by the New Left of the 1960s, its major theme was an attack on bureaucratic and centralised public authority and the demand for the devolution of real power to working class communities themselves. But the broader discourse of partnership was not to be an argument for enhancing political democracy. Rather the discourse of community action was contained (Fairclough, 1989) within a broader, anti-collectivist discourse. Its thematics were those of choice, privatism and enterprise ("Ending the monopoly of municipal housing estates"), and it pointed towards a model of democracy based on free-market economics. Thus the government, while implementing the poll tax, was simultaneously telling the unemployed tenants' leaders in Ferguslie that they wanted "to help ordinary people to take more control over their own lives"; that their "full involvement" and "participation" was the most important factor in the whole project; and that "local needs and aspirations" must be "the central force in the regeneration process" (Scottish Office, 1988; 1989; Robertson, 1990). Their feelings on encountering this are probably well encapsulated in the words of a tenant from another of the pilot areas: "I'm being deprived of something, but I can't say what. I'm being out-argued, but I know I'm right." (Castlemilk tenant, quoted in *The Herald*, 19 February, 1992).

The partnership and the community

The Ferguslie Park Partnership was formally established in June 1988. Membership was decided by the Scottish Office, as was the make up of the partnership board. The Scottish Office took the chair and a further three seats, including one for a secondee in the role of chief executive heading the local implementation team. Also represented were the Scottish Development Agency and the Training Agency (soon to be merged in Scottish Enterprise), the Housing Corporation in Scotland (soon to be incorporated in the new Scottish Homes), the Department of Employment, the local Health Board, and the local Enterprise Trust. A senior official represented each of the local authorities (Renfrew District Council and Strathclyde Regional Council). In May 1989 two members of a newly formed Business Support Group – including the deputy chair of the Tilbury Group – joined the board. The partnership finalised its strategy by Christmas 1988, and published it in January 1989 (Scottish Office, 1989). Detailed implementation was devolved to five thematic sub-groups. In turn these were serviced by an implementation team, led by the Scottish Office, who moved into purpose built offices in the heart of the estate. The key principle of implementation was that: "the Partners should act in harmony and should be seen to be doing so" (Scottish Office, 1989).

The community was represented at board level by four members of the Ferguslie League of Action Groups (FLAG). FLAG formed in the latter stages of the CDP as an umbrella for the local tenants' associations and other action groups. In the period after the CDP its identity was that of a combatative and resourceful organ of community action. FLAG's banner tells us something about how this local community saw itself. It proclaimed their demands for jobs, peace and social justice, and bore the following motto:

> May the people awake
>
> To the recognition of their rights
>
> Have the fortitude to demand them
>
> The fortune to obtain them
>
> And henceforth sufficient wisdom and vigour to defend them.

In this post-CDP period FLAG earned a reputation for mobilising large numbers of tenants into confrontations with authority through well-publicised direct action (McGregor et al, 1992; William Roe Associates, 1994).

The Area Initiative of 1984-88 was in large measure a response to the ensuing crisis in the local relations of authority. At this point FLAG entered into a significantly new set of social relations through which its identity was subtly reconstituted. Here the local councillors played a key role in negotiating a re-alignment of the organisation to achieve effective collaboration with the local authorities (Ferguslie Park Strategy Group, 1988). FLAG's shift was based on the perception that their voice and concerns were now being heard and accorded legitimacy by the local authorities, and that the Area Initiative reflected this –

particularly in its focus on poverty and the promotion of community development. Now the organisation became somewhat 'Janus-like' – "at once both staunch and vociferous defender of community interests and responsible manager of local programmes" (William Roe Associates, 1994, p 10). However, as the overall level of active campaigning declined, so too did recruitment of new activists. And as existing activists left, the work of the organisation steadily devolved to a diminishing core. Nevertheless FLAG never forgot their historic identity. They no longer sought to 'batter doors down', but only because they felt they did not have to. If the need arose, this approach could be used again. For the partnership this posed a problem, for the whole legitimacy of the model was based on the idea of a harmonious participatory democracy. Thus the possibility that FLAG might resort to their historic methods was one which the partnership was acutely aware of, and which it worked assiduously to prevent.

Yet, the Scottish Office did not have the local knowledge or authority to achieve this by themselves. Here the partnership needed some local operators.[3] A leading FLAG activist who was heavily involved in the negotiations around the formation of the partnership, and was one of the original FLAG representatives on the partnership board, was recruited to the partnership as its community development executive (CDE). With this he entered into a highly ambiguous position. In the days of the Area Initiative he had been seen, as another activist put it, as "the voice ae the people" in the relationship with the local authorities. In his new role he continued to live in the area, and as such was a member of the local community, but now he was also a paid official of the partnership. FLAG took the view that he could no longer be part of the FLAG executive, or be considered as a representative of the community. Yet, he retained a significant degree of authority in the eyes of many, both within FLAG and also in the wider community. The partnership played on this ambiguity, and sought to portray the CDE as a legitimate community representative for purposes of consultation and participation.

The Scottish Office also seem to have reached an understanding with the area's local councillors. Initially, and much to their chagrin, excluded from the partnership board, the local regional councillor (RC) and one of the district councillors were soon given seats – also as 'community representatives'. In particular the RC, who had a long history of involvement with FLAG, proved very sympathetic to the aims of the partnership. He, like them, was keen to see that the progress of the project was not delayed by the possible reversion of FLAG to public campaigning. But, compared to the Scottish Office, he, together with the CDE (a close associate), was in a better position to ensure that it was not.

In due course this position was tested. By late 1990 the active core of FLAG had been reduced to between six and eight people. They had seen the plans of the partnership unfold for some 2 years. Poverty initiatives were increasingly sidelined (Gaster et al, 1995) and high-profile property developments by private firms and housing associations were much to the fore (Scottish Homes, 1990; Scottish Office, 1991). Opposition had been either ignored or marginalised. The day-to-day business of the partnership was also conducted in such a way that the tenants got a clear message that they were not equal partners, never mind the 'central force in the regeneration process'. In the words of one activist, FLAG had "been over-run by what the Scottish Office says we need". When FLAG raised these objections they were told that they were being "obstructive", that they were being manipulated by "politically motivated community workers", and that they were "losing their credibility".

What made the situation even more difficult was the fact that they were being told this, not just by Scottish Office, but also by the CDE and the RC. This was symptomatic of a crucial realignment which had taken place, and which had important implications for FLAG. FLAG's identity since the mid-1980s had been redefined by a new relation with the local authorities and FLAG's prerogative in making use of language in exercising their voice was tied closely to this. Now that relationship had changed and the key figures who had cemented it – the CDE and the RC – were closely aligned with the partnership. This left the other activists both trying to cope with the loss of an important leader and trying to exercise their voice in the context of a new social alignment which made that task much less easy.

Thinking about all of this in terms of Hall's sociohistorical perspective on linguistic contests, we would be inclined to conclude the following. In Ferguslie, wider economic, political and ideological forces have ensured that the most salient identity of the community is one that has been stigmatised and often despised. This identity has been both a product of their lack of sociohistorical power and a major factor blocking their attempt to contest degrees of that power, and its effects, with other groups. One way in which they had contested this power in the 1970s and early 1980s was through the linguistic and paralinguistic practices of community action. Here the ideas of struggle and resistance became a focal point around which the community could construct an alternative identity for themselves. In the mid-1980s this identity and discourse were realigned in a new relation with the local authorities in the Area Initiative. Now the identity of the local community became much more ambiguous – still an organ of community action, but also working cooperatively with the local powers. Yet, here, the local community felt that for the first time in many years, they could exercise their own voice in public fora. However, the advent of the partnership brought a shift in the relations with the local authorities which had made this possible. And, at the same time, much of the language of community action had been appropriated by the Scottish Office and subjected to a process of containment within a broader Thatcherite discourse of 'partnership'. All of this placed FLAG at a strategic disadvantage in the interactions which were determining the future of their community. The wider sociohistorical and political forces residing in both the identities of the interactants and in the meanings of the linguistic resources most available to them, meant that their attempts to use the available resources in their own way could simply be declared inappropriate and silly.

Eight or ten years earlier FLAG may have responded to this situation by mobilising the local tenants into some kind of direct action. But their cooption to the strategy of the Area Initiative had seen their capacity to do this decline. The ideas of struggle and resistance had become much less central to the identity of the organisation. Now Ferguslie's tenants had begun to identify FLAG with the various institutions which had continually failed to deliver on promises of better days. One option might have been to undermine the legitimacy of the partnership by withdrawing their participation (as tenants in the Castlemilk Partnership had done). However, it was clear (as we will see) that life would be made very difficult for anyone proposing this course of action. If it was done without carefully building local support – and this would be a hard fought battle which would take time – then FLAG could be portrayed as holding back progress and be discredited as a result.

So the FLAG leaders found themselves in a position where they could neither sustain their own voice in the partnership, nor apply any of their historic methods to remedying the situation. What made the situation even more daunting was that their limited attempts to make their case led, not to a review of the workings of the partnership, but, more ominously, to a review of the workings of FLAG itself.

Contesting community

FLAG's response was to seek to counter this review with a report which would put their own perspective on the partnership and which they hoped would help them in their attempt to sustain their own voice. In this they were acknowledging the problems which they faced in the contest over the deployment of the available linguistic resources. They were also recognising that this was a contest which they could not opt out of – for that would be to concede the contested ground to their opponents. Instead they tried to bolster the authority of their own voice by having it recorded and reported in written form and reinserted into the debate. At the end of 1990 FLAG approached the author of this chapter with a request for the preparation of such a report. As a worker with a local tenants' housing cooperative I was already known to FLAG. It was also known to them, via a local community worker, that I had an academic background and interests, and that I might be interested in conducting research on community participation in the partnership. FLAG offered to co-operate with this research if I provided them with a report for their own purposes. The 'brief', agreed during discussions, was to detail the problems which FLAG had been experiencing and the grievances which they felt, take an overview of the current situation, and provide recommendations about how to address it. Through my university affiliation I obtained access to other members of the partnership – notably its chief executive, the CDE, and the RC.

The fieldwork for the report was conducted in the early part of 1991. It consisted primarily of interviews with seven of the core activists who had been most heavily involved with the partnership. It was made clear that statements made in these interviews would not be attributed to individuals. What emerged in the interviews was a thoroughgoing critique of the operation of the partnership and its relations with the community. FLAG was excluded from many of the most important planning meetings of the partnership. The partnership referred to these as 'in-house' meetings. When FLAG got irate over this, one was 'pulled aside' and asked what the problem was:[4]

> "... n ah said tae them well they want tae know, where aw these fancy CARS are goin tae the partnership n what MEETINS are goin on, an if theres meetins goin on we waant tae know tae be involved in thum. an ah wis totally bawled an shouted et n says, weel do what we want an there no bloody way thit we tell youse when weer goin tae meetins." (Interviewee 1)

At meetings which FLAG did attend, minutes taken by partnership employees failed to record any dissent or questioning from FLAG representatives (Interviewee 2). Such questioning or disagreement was defined by the partnership as being 'obstructive' or 'negative':

> "... n then if we ask too many questions weer NEGATIVE, THEY MIGHT THINK weer negative bit weer positive fae oor side, because weev gotae get the VOICE iv ferguslie park across weer HELD, at the end up weer held solely tae the PEOPLE iv ferguslie park, weer no held tae the partnership, the partnership are NO GONNAE DICTATE TAE US." (Interviewee 3)

Yet, resisting these labels was not easy. Thus, the FLAG representatives felt that unwanted contributions would lead to them being 'shown up':

> "... ah hiv been shown up QUITE A FEW TIMES ... they aw sit n LAUGH AT YE, ah mean its very degradin ... n yeev git aw these BIG WIGS sittin roon a table n ye feel THAT SIZE [indicating small size with finger and thumb]." (Interviewee 4)

In this light it is not surprising that this same activist described the community as the 'lowerarchy' of the partnership. Another

activist contrasted this state of affairs with the relations under the
Area Initiative:

> "... ah hink the consiltation then wis better,
> THEN, thin it is NOO, eh, because noo eh,
> theyve git a they cim up wi a PLAN, n the
> consiltation is 'this is whit yir GETTIN'. ehm.
> maself PERSONally, wi workin wi aw the
> different groups, as well, its no consultation. its
> more or less sayin well weer gaun tae dae this
> here. eh although theyll say tae ye its only a
> DRAFT ye cin CHANGE it n different hings. bit
> BASICALLY theyve goat the idear in their heid
> before they come tae ye." (Interviewee 5)

It also emerged that FLAG's activists were attending up to 30
meetings a week. The combination of this workload, the speed at
which decisions were forced through, and the lack of information
and support available, meant that: "the consultation process is oot
the windae" (Interviewee 6). FLAG felt pressured:

> "... tae make the decisions fur the people in
> ferguslie, withoot the time tae sit n DIGEST aw
> the infurmation thit weev goat n then make an
> INFORMED decision which is whit we waant tae
> dae, weev no git the time tae do it ... weev jist
> been over run by, what the scottish office say we
> need ... ah mean in the strategy document ah
> think its quoted ehm, to enable the people iv
> ferguslie park tae take a better con, ehm, more
> control ae their life. THATS CRAP. ah mean it
> really is. (Interviewee 2)

It also transpired that the partnership were working hard to ensure
that the Ferguslie tenants did not share their experiences with
tenants from the other three pilot areas.

> "... they always told us thit we were the best, we
> were WAY AHEAD ... ye know this is the patter
> ye get off thum we were way ahead iv all the
> other ones, ehm, ye dont REALLY want tae go n
> see whit wester hailes n whitfield n castlemilk ur
> doin do ye? ... n they wur gettin told the exact

> same   things   bi   THEIR   PARTNERSHIP."
> (Interviewee 4)

It was this type of manipulation which earned the partnership the name of "the pattership" (Interviewee 3).

Perhaps even more significantly, it emerged that FLAG's contributions to public events relating to the partnership were being scripted for them.   One such event was a high-profile conference organised by the Scottish Office in Glasgow in May 1990.

> "... we were all DRESSED UP, our speeches WRITTEN FUR US, and sent along tae stay in this BIG PLUSH HOTEL ... fur THREE DAYS, all at the expense iv the partnership. ye know its if its ALRIGHT when it suits them the partnership need us tae be there." (Interviewee 4)

Here the chief executive:

> "... physically wrote the speeches thit we gave ... the activists thimselves recognise that we selt the jerseys that day." (Interviewee 6)

Another individual who was due to speak at a different event was handed a set of cue cards with a preprepared speech – including jokes (Interviewee 7).   Finally several activists alluded to the technique of 'taking people out individually'. "The minute youre branded a trouble maker they close ranks and close doors on you." (Interviewee 6).

One such individual set about organising an anti-poll tax demonstration to coincide with a visit by the Scottish Secretary of State to the area:

> "... the chief executive ae the partnership, he fun oot aboot it ... the next MORNIN he phoned me OWER ... n ee asked me whit ah KNEW aboot it an ah told im ahd ORGANISED it. he says, aw ye cannae dae that he says, youre wan ae the as he put it wan i the sorta LEADIN LIGHTS in the community is fawr is the partnerships concerned, yeev git a loat tae cintribute tae ferguslie park, bit yir gonnae hiv tae puhll yir REINS IN. an when ah refused tae cancel the anti poll tax

deminstration, he actually THREATENED ME.
he said theyve git ways a removin people fae the
BIG PICTURE, ye know n that wis, his words tae
me." (Interviewee 7)

By the time of the interview this individual was no longer actively
involved with either the partnership or with FLAG itself.

When these types of concerns were put to the partnership's
chief executive he said that the problems were of FLAG's making.
While he would not speak on tape, the following phrases were
transcribed verbatim from one notable outburst:

> "... people with a background of problems ... with
> a knack of misunderstanding things ... difficult to
> deal with themselves ... If you had to sit through
> some of the nonsense yourself ... often this is
> because someone has wound them up ... see
> intimidation and cheating as a way of life ...
> inbuilt antagonism to authority ... full of
> suspicion ... they have no stability in their lives,
> how can you expect them to have it in their
> dealings with us."

What was happening was this. The Scottish Office needed the
'local community' to be seen to be participating fully and
harmoniously in the partnership. Yet the task of fulfilling their
strategic objectives meant that in practice this would not actually
be allowed to happen. The continuing fear of the partnership was
that FLAG's historic identity as a campaigning and action group
might be reasserted. The particular danger was that the discourse
of community action might be wrenched free from its containment
within the broader discourse of partnership and used to pose very
dangerous and very leading questions. The language and the
identity would then be mutually reinforcing in their growth and
development.

As the research progressed it became clear that this process
was already taking place. The FLAG activists' experience was
leading them to the conclusion that what they and the Scottish
Office meant by words like partnership, community participation
and community development were very different indeed.
Different "evaluative accents" (Voloshinov, 1986a) belonging to
different voices with different histories were contesting, albeit in a
muted way, the tenure of these linguistic resources – what they

were to mean and what their effects would be. Increasingly 'partnership' itself became a dirty word in the mouths of the tenants. It was almost as if all the grievances which they felt were distilled and expressed in the intonation of this one word (Volosinov, 1986b). On this basis some activists were speaking explicitly about resurrecting the old FLAG. This process was already well under way by early 1991, but FLAG's commissioning of the research report seemed to catalyse it further. It seemed that their participation in the research obliged them to confront the problematic gap between rhetoric and experience explicitly, and to formulate their own positions in relation to it more systematically (Collins and Lister, 1996a; see Freire, 1972).

For the partnership, such a radicalisation of the Ferguslie community had to be prevented. And the fact that it was beginning to take shape had not escaped their notice. It was in this connection that the review of FLAG had earlier been instigated. What was at stake was the broader identity of what, for the purposes of the partnership, was to count as 'the community' in Ferguslie Park, and the terms in which they were going to talk about the processes affecting their lives. Here, the partnership decided that a restructuring was the only safe option. The task of effecting it was left to their local operators – the RC and the CDE (Strathclyde Regional Council, 1991). In the CDE's words, they embarked on some 'social engineering' to remove FLAG as the representative body for the community and replace it with something more suited to their purposes. Initially FLAG would be reconstituted. Only tenants' associations (TAs) would be members. Thus FLAG would cease to be a broad umbrella organisation. Subsequently a 'community forum' was to be created as the new umbrella organisation. FLAG would be affiliated to this, but it would be just one lobby among others. The other lobbies were to include fishing, fitness, knitting and dressmaking clubs (Strathclyde Regional Council, 1991). In this way a new cohort of inexperienced groups and individuals with no explicit political interests or agenda, and no previous knowledge of the operation of the partnership, would be drawn into the partnership process. They would meet as a 'forum' rather than an 'action group', and would be tightly controlled by the Scottish Office's chosen local operators. They would replace FLAG, with its historic identity of resistance and struggle, and would count, for the purposes of the partnership, as 'the community'.

(Re)creating 'community'

This is what actually came to pass, but in the face of the processes taking place within FLAG the partnership felt forced to implement the first stage of its plan immediately.

The report which FLAG had requested was completed in July 1991. It conveyed FLAG's case in extensive verbatim extracts (unattributed) from the interviews with the activists. It juxtaposed these with the interviews of those on the partnership side – expressing their attitude to FLAG and their intention to replace it with a more docile community forum. It recommended that FLAG should urgently seek to rebuild its relations with the local tenants' associations and the wider community, that it should explain their position to them, and that on this basis they should propose withdrawing community support from the partnership. The report was passed to FLAG and an oral presentation of the findings was arranged for the 25 July. But it was passed to the partnership in advance and they moved to take pre-emptive action.

The CDE called a meeting of selected community members for the 24 July – on the theme of 'Participation in the partnership and the way forward'. Most of those attending were only invited on the day of the meeting itself. Twenty-four people attended, of whom the great majority had no direct experience of working with the partnership. Some of the most critical voices from within FLAG were not invited and others who were seem to have become significantly less critical. The report from this meeting makes fascinating reading (McIntyre, 1991). The tenants listened as the problems of participation were blamed on 'various weaknesses' in FLAG. Then "The meeting was informed that FLAG had taken a critical look at themselves and improvements were promised."

The next stage was to resubordinate the rhetoric of community action to the needs of the Scottish Office. So, first: "It was agreed that FLAG should go back to its grass roots as an activist association of tenants associations that got things done." But then, it was argued that this would require that "the structure of FLAG was looked at" And it was looked at there and then. Seventeen of those present voted for the CDE's proposal that FLAG should restrict its membership to TAs, thus relinquishing its role as the umbrella organisation for the estate. Then:

> "The meeting agreed that there had been a good debate and it could now be reported to the

> Community Development Committee that the
> Tenants Associations had fully been consulted."
> (McIntyre, 1991)

This decision was to be "taken back to tenants for endorsement" (not discussion or consideration).

It is perhaps understandable how the more inexperienced tenants could allow all of this to go unchallenged. What is harder to understand is why the FLAG activists who were present, who had all been very critical of the partnership in the recent past, and who had been seeking to make their criticisms more effective, did not voice dissent. It may be that they were pondering something else which had been put on the table that evening. This was the option to:

> "Pay local people to get fully involved to enable
> the influencing of decisions at the outset and a
> better flow of information to and from the
> Partnership." (McIntyre, 1991)

The small group of FLAG activists were faced with the choice of going along with all of this (with the possibility that they may benefit personally), of standing out against it and being subjected to personal attacks and vilification, or of just walking away. Of the seven who were most heavily involved and who had participated in the preparation of the report, four took the first option. These four were present at the meeting, and are all now employed with community organisations in Ferguslie. One took the second option, and two took the third. Two of the latter three have since left Ferguslie altogether.

On 11 September the FLAG Annual General Meeting duly changed its constitution. At the same time the CDE moved his desk out of the partnership offices and into the FLAG premises. FLAG, while it was no longer an umbrella organisation, continued to function as the community's representative organ while the community forum was developed. The fact that this latter task was not completed until the summer of 1993 seems to support the idea that in the summer of 1991 the partnership had been forced to act before it was fully prepared. When the forum was established the partnership's CDE was re-employed as its chief executive.

Of course, the meeting of the 24 July was an ad hoc meeting which had, democratically speaking, no authority to make any decisions for FLAG or for the wider community. But the partnership, working through their local operators, were able to use their power to ensure that in practice the meeting *did* exercise this authority. It was this which was ultimately to determine the basic shape of what was in practice to count as 'the community' in Ferguslie Park in the period ahead – and the ideas of struggle and resistance which were part of that community's historic identity were duly suppressed. In the same way the Scottish Office, insofar as they were able to marginalise or neutralise the most dissenting voices within FLAG, resubjected the language of community action to its previous containment within the broader discourse of partnership.

Conclusion

This is not to suggest that ideas of struggle and resistance which were part of the historic identity of the community in Ferguslie, and which threatened to re-emerge in 1991, have forever been expunged. Nor is it to argue that the language of community action can safely and forever be contained within the broader discourse of 'partnership'. Yet the contest which took place during that year, and which the partnership managed to win quite decisively, has meant that the Scottish Office has managed to pursue its objectives in the area with much less resistance from community organisations than might have been the case.[5] In that contest different social groups struggled over the way in which words were going to be deployed in the (re)creation of the world which they inhabited. But the scope which these different groups had to use the language for their own purposes in this process was crucially constrained by the sociohistorical and political forces present in the linguistic resources which they used. It was also constrained by the degrees of sociohistorical power attached to the identities of the groups using them. But these constraints were not mechanical determinants of the eventual outcome. They made the contest a rather unequal one in which a certain outcome was more likely than others which were conceivable. But there was nothing inevitable about the outcome. It could have been different. In grasping this we also grasp that the ideas of community which really count in our changing world are neither abstract nor arbitrary. They are, rather, historical, concrete and contestable.

Notes

[1] This perception has generally been shared by the town's 'respectable' working class. As a grammar school boy in the 1950s, the young Andrew Neil (erstwhile Editor of the *Sunday Times*) already saw Ferguslie as a 'no-go area'. He now regards the area as a pernicious 'disease' which is infecting the rest of the town (Neil, quoted in *The Scotsman*, 19 April 1995, p 14). For a sample of the treatment of the estate by the Scottish and national press, see the coverage surrounding the Ferguslie Community Business Security Limited controversy (especially week beginning 17 April 1995).

[2] The other areas chosen were: Castlemilk in Glasgow, Wester Hailes in Edinburgh and Whitfield in Dundee.

[3] Martin Davidson, a director of Windex Developments and previously an employee of Glasgow District Council, the Scottish Development Agency and Tyne and Wear Development Corporation, offered the following advice to those intent on the partnership approach: "It is vital to secure community goodwill. Local authorities are often the best vehicle to do this, not only because they have built up community contacts over the many years but also because they are wonderful sources of information on the informal way in which an area really works" (Scottish Business in the Community, 1990, p 45).

[4] Note on transcription. The transcription seeks to preserve the voice of the interviewees by conveying the grammar, dialect and pronunciation they used. Capitals are used to convey a word which is stressed. A comma indicates a short pause, and a full stop a longer pause. A series of full stops indicates that a section of the utterance has been omitted.

[5] However, for a view of the broader impact of the partnership's restructuring of community organisation on the broader dynamics of the locality – and especially the growth of particularly resistant, but also highly anti-social organisation within it – see Collins and Lister (1996b).

seven

Taken away from community: older people and sheltered housing

Harrie Churchill, Angela Everitt and Judith Green

Researching in the community

The Social Welfare Research Unit, set up in the early 1990s in the University of Northumbria at Newcastle, when it was a polytechnic, undertakes research, evaluation and development with public sector organisations with the explicit purpose to promote social welfare and contribute to the social regeneration of our region. 'Social welfare' is used in the justice, equality, well-being sense of the term. This approach to research for change necessarily involves us in critical social research methodologies, engaging in research to generate and share understandings of social and economic change and the impact of policy, and to contribute to changing policies and practices. The research programme of the Unit is eclectic in its methods, analysing data both quantitatively and qualitatively, drawing upon feminist methodologies and upon the contribution to research methodology made by new social movements such as disability research (eg, Barnes, 1991; Oliver, 1992). Particularly important in the research programme is a vast number of small pieces of research undertaken collaboratively with small voluntary projects, usually with funds secured by the project from local charitable sources. The research presented in this chapter was undertaken with one such project, the Search Project, in Benwell, a ward in the West End of Newcastle.

The northern region has the highest proportion of low income households in England and Wales (Central Statistical Office, 1993). The inner west wards of Newcastle (Benwell, Elswick, Scotswood and West City) include some of the worst concentrations of deprivation, with one of these, West City, in terms of key indicators of deprivation, ranking top in 1991 out of the 678 wards comprising the Northern Region (Phillimore, Beattie and Townsend, 1994).

Benwell lies a couple of miles to the west of Newcastle city centre on the steep banks above the Tyne. Developed in the 19th century and formerly an area of industrial vibrancy, throughout this century the area has experienced rapid economic decline. More recently, Benwell has received media attention as the 'Neighbourhood from hell' (Campbell, 1995), a label actively resisted by community workers and activists trying to achieve something better. Opposite, on the other side of the Tyne, is the MetroCentre, one of the success stories of Thatcherism, a shopping mall to which people come in coaches from far and wide, a symbolic temple of consumption which people in Benwell may gaze upon across the Tyne but from which most are financially excluded. For three decades, the deprivation of Benwell has received official recognition through a series of anti-poverty, inner city and urban redevelopment initiatives. The Home Office Community Development Project (CDP) was set up in 1968 and now Benwell is a beneficiary of City Challenge, lying at the heart of one of the largest City Challenge areas.

Economic decline is clearly a factor, but at the same time social change in the locality is more complex than a direct result of industrial change. The Benwell CDP pointed out that:

> ... the actual historical relationship between the two is mediated through other systems (in particular, the housing market and State intervention) which interact with the underlying economic changes to produce the specific local outcomes. (Green, 1995b, p 4)

This chapter focuses on such interactions as they affect the daily lives of older people living in Benwell. The proportion of older residents in the West Newcastle wards has remained relatively stable over the last 20 years at approximately 17%. However, this masks considerable variation at a more local level. The 1991

Census shows that, in the area just north of the central shopping street in Benwell, 27.9% of the population was over retirement age compared with 8.1% in the south of the ward (Newcastle Westend Partnership with the Research Section, Newcastle City Council, 1994).

The area which local people talk of as Benwell is not the same as the Benwell delineated by ward boundaries or by funding and policy initiatives. Broadly defined, it is an area that stretches from the West Road, a major road with shops, public services and facilities linking Newcastle with the prosperous rural and commuter belt of the Northumberland Tyne valley, down to the Scotswood Road running alongside the River Tyne. The Benwell terraces, terraced houses and Tyneside flats built to look like houses, used to stretch north–south across this area, their status declining as they sloped down towards the river. The clearance programme in the 1960s and early 1970s started with the old, lower quality housing in the south and turned the Scotswood Road from a lively street of factories, shops, pubs and churches into a lifeless thoroughfare. Here, in what is known as Low Benwell, the new housing to replace the terraces is older, of poorer quality from that in the northern part of the area, and distant from shops and facilities down the steep bank of the side of the Tyne. The shopping street, known as the Terrace, runs east–west in the north part of Benwell to the south of and parallel with the West Road. This area, once described as "the 'respectable' stable working-class residential area of Benwell" (Davies, 1972), is still remembered by local people and workers alike as a popular area to live with a stable and cohesive community of older people. Between what is known as Benwell in the north and Low Benwell in the south is a large tract of land that has largely remained derelict. While drainage systems and roads were laid for planned housing developments, including a local authority–housing association sheltered housing scheme, these all became caught in the Heseltine moratorium on council house building in the 1970s. Since then, despite many building plans and encouragements to private developers, the area remained largely a wilderness comprising a small nature park and play facilities, and now a sheltered housing scheme.

The sheltered housing, a scheme of a national housing association for older people, looms large from this otherwise near-barren area providing 40 self-contained flatlets, single and double, in a three-story building. It rose quickly when City Challenge arrived in the area in 1993. Lighting upon an already designed scheme, it was quickly able to notch up an output. The scheme met all the criteria: job creation; the redevelopment of derelict land and, with private contractors engaged to build it, a public, private, voluntary development. To local people, community workers and residents, the sheltered housing development was a surprise. Their knowledge and experience generated a scepticism of the viability of such a project. The uncharted mine shafts beneath the imposing development, which in the past had been a disincentive to developers allowing only for low density build, together with the reputation of Low Benwell, made them think that no one would want to live there. There is talk of it becoming a difficult-to-let estate.

The Search Project, a long-established voluntary project set up in the 1970s originally under the wing of Age Concern to increase the take-up of benefits by pensioners, occupies a small shop-front on the Terrace in Benwell. Its neighbours are a small branch of Presto's, the supermarket chain, a small amusement arcade housing a cafe, a shoe repairer and a number of small hardware, grocery and greengrocers shops. Further along the street a 1960s concrete shopping centre which rapidly became a white elephant has recently been demolished to make way for a prestigious health resource centre. It is a shopping street struggling to survive, significant to the people of Benwell although rarely visited by those living outside of the locality. In the 1970s, opposite the Search Project, the Benwell CDP provided a vibrant centre for community action and action research. But this, along with other local authority community provision, disappeared in the late 1970s and 1980s leaving only a few small voluntary organisations, including the Search Project, which have struggled to survive year by year. Now though, in the mid-1990s, community development workers are much in evidence again, spawned by City Challenge and initiatives funded through the Single Regeneration Budget (SRB).

An early and continuing emphasis of the Search Project is to carry out or encourage research into the situation of older people in west Newcastle and the problems they face. Towards the late 1970s, with funding through the Job Creation Programme and later the Urban Programme, the project gained financial independence from Age Concern and extended into campaigning and organising work. The influence of new social movements such as the women's movement and black self-organisation was important together with ideas of empowerment and collective action from Grey Power in the United States. In particular, the Search Project keyed into trade union pensioner organisation developments and focused its efforts in the late 1970s on building a pensioners' organisation, equivalent to a trade union. The North East Pensioners Association, launched in 1977 by 500 people in Newcastle's Tyne Theatre, has a West End branch which continues to be supported by the Project.

The main funders of the Search Project are now the local authority social services department, the health authority and the lotteries board supplemented by a number of small one-off grants from a range of charitable trusts. The Project now employs four full-time practitioners and an administrative worker together with sessional workers. As well as work with the Pensioners Association, the Project provides an advice and welfare rights desk with outreach work and a health promotion programme with groups such as keep fit, tai chi and a walking group (Carter and Everitt, forthcoming). It has linked with the Social Welfare Research Unit in an historical and evaluative account of its work (Green, 1995c), an ongoing evaluation of its health promotion work (Carter, 1993) and an evaluation of its welfare rights and advice work. The evaluations have been supplemented by a series of very small research projects, each focusing on an issue arising through the evaluations and designed to inform policies and practices of the project itself and of related agencies. The first piece of research was concerned to explore and enhance older people's access to leisure provision (Gibson, 1992). Following this, and recognising the importance of friends for participation in social activities, the second research study explored older people's friendships (Sugden, 1994). The third piece of research was undertaken with older people who had recently moved into the new sheltered housing scheme to explore with them their social relations and activities (Churchill and Everitt, 1996). This chapter draws particularly on the sheltered housing research and on interviews with older people living in Benwell undertaken for the evaluations.

Community taken away

The title 'sheltered housing' has been traced back to the 1944 Ministry of Health Housing Manual which discusses the need for choosing a 'sheltered site' when building housing specially designed for older people (Butler, Oldman and Greve, 1983). As time passed the concept of sheltering from the weather has grown and changed to encompass being protected and looked after in all aspects of life (Parry and Thompson, 1993). With the move away from institutional care, increasing emphasis has been placed on this form of housing so much so that it is now the major form of new and revitalised local authority–housing association developments in West Newcastle, as elsewhere (Fletcher, 1991). Townsend argued that sheltered housing would avoid the many drawbacks of institutional care, respecting privacy and independence (Townsend, 1962). However, the most comprehensive study of sheltered housing since then, carried out in the late 1970s, raised a number of issues concerning the uncritical emphasis on sheltered housing, the implicit assumptions about the 'special needs' of older people and the lack of alternative options (Butler, Oldman and Greve, 1983). There is now an acknowledged lack of clarity about sheltered housing (Fletcher, 1991), probably because policy guidance has focused on design features, neglecting who sheltered housing is for and what needs it is trying to meet. Housing and physical and social needs interact, and policy responses based on separate housing solutions for older people have diverted attention away from the diversity of their needs, the underlying causes of housing problems, and from housing problems experienced by others.

There are ageist implications in sheltered housing policy and practice where age, like sex or colour, is used to provide explanations for problems that have to do more with social and economic processes and the structure of society in which we live (Butler, Oldman and Greve, 1983; Phillipson and Walker, 1986). The result of housing and urban redevelopment policy and funding regimes in west Newcastle is age-segregated housing, with enclaves of developments, made so secure as to be prison-like to keep people out, in areas of dereliction, vandalism and burglary. Set against the 1990s concept of sheltered housing as a community for the tenants and as a community resource in the broader network of welfare services in the locality, this generates some tensions for older people and for those assuming responsibilities for enhancing their social relations, such as wardens and the Search Project workers.

Sheltered housing is both part of but separate from the local community. This is how it is experienced by older people. Studies have shown that sheltered housing is popular with tenants and valuable in providing a sheltered place to live, away from fear of break-ins and vandalism, with adequate heating and no repair problems, near to family and friends (Clapham and Munro, 1988). Similar stories were told by older people who had recently moved into sheltered housing in Benwell. At the same time, a common theme in interviews with older people was the sense of loss for the home and community that they had to leave in order to feel secure. The overwhelming reason for moving into the sheltered housing scheme in Benwell was to be taken away from experiences and fear of crime. Perhaps the most distressing aspect of the social decline of the West End of Newcastle has been the rise in crime and disorder, especially since the late 1980s. The 1991 'riots' were a particularly stark form of what had by then become an everyday experience of crime and intimidation for residents in many parts of the area. For many older people, harassment and fear have become part of everyday life.

Many older people have commented with sadness on how unemployment, poverty and lack of opportunity have taken their toll on the local community:

> "This area is deprived in a lot of senses.... It's a dodgy area now. People are going nowhere now. They've just got this attitude of 'There's no future'."

One man, who has lived in the same house for 40 years, commented:

> "The deterioration has been terrific. It was a wonderful estate ... a really nice estate with lovely people on it, but it has deteriorated."

Another said she liked her flat, but the area as a whole had deteriorated enormously, especially in the last five years. She described shops closing, buildings falling down, joyriding, mass flight of population and older people afraid to go out. Another, who has lived in the West End all his life said that, although he was still committed to living there, the worst thing is:

> "Seeing the deprivation around the West End.
> Some parts are an utter nightmare and horrific.
> The worst thing is people having to live in these
> situations. It's horrific you know."

A number of people have commented with particular shock on the serious decline of the North Benwell terraces, now seen as one of the most dangerous and dilapidated parts of the West End despite formerly being known as a 'class area'. It is not surprising therefore that many older people, particularly women, are concerned about issues of personal safety. A number had experienced actual and attempted break-ins themselves and this was one of their greatest fears. There is also a common feeling that the police have 'given up' on the area and people feel unprotected. Many older people are afraid to go out, fearing that their houses would be burgled or burnt while they were out and also fearful about their own safety when out of the house. One woman, who had been a staunch local activist for many years, said that she did not go to meetings any more as she was worried about being mugged.

It would be a mistake to paint a uniformly negative picture of gloom and decay. The picture that emerges overall is of significant fragmentation of the local community but not complete disintegration. Most older people interviewed in our studies have lived in the West End of Newcastle all their lives. A significant number has moved around the area through successive waves of housing clearance and renewal but had obviously chosen each time to be rehoused in the local area.

The sheltered housing development offered yet another choice. All the older people interviewed, who had moved in when it opened a year before, had been living in the immediate surrounding locality. They spoke of their reasons for moving having to do with crime or fear of crime, either on their own part or on the part of their sons or daughters. The decision to move in was often one shared with or taken by relatives and/or professionals. For one woman, the decision was made by relatives while she was in hospital after a fall in her flat where she lived alone. For 24 years, she had lived with her husband, a school caretaker, in the school-house attached to the local primary school. On his retirement, they moved to a small estate built in the 1960s just yards from the Terrace. As she reflected: "they vetted us then for those flats, but now they can't rent them and let anybody in". For her, the experience of having been taken away from home and community was stark:

> "My daughter came over and sorted things out. Now I can't find things that I knew I had. She rings me once a fortnight and I have a list ready: 'where's this? 'where's that?'. She says: 'Mam, you didn't need them so I threw them out or gave them away'. She gave all my gardening tools away. I can't find the things I want. I had little notes with addresses on and telephone numbers and they thought I wouldn't need any of these so they just threw them out and that was it."

Her feelings of powerlessness and loss were more than exacerbated through encounters with professionals on the hospital ward:

> "When I first went into hospital the doctor asked me who I lived with. I said I lived on my own. He said: 'Oh, don't be a silly girl. Nobody lives on their own.' I said: 'Well, I do. I'm a widow'. Later, the doctor asked me where I lived. I said 'I don't really know'. He turned to the nurses and said: 'This girl, she has no-body to live with and she doesn't know where she's living'. And when they said I could come out of hospital I was in tears and the sister came and she said: 'what on earth's the matter with you now?' I said: 'I have nowhere to go'. She said: 'what d'you mean you've got nowhere to go?' I said: 'well, my son came the other day and said, "do you want the good news or the bad news?"' I said, 'we'll have good news first'. He said, 'well I've given your house up. I've put the keys in. You're paid up, your rent is seen to. No more trouble up there, you're finished absolutely'. So I knew I couldn't go home. So I thought when the doctor asked me where I lived, I didn't really know. And he said she doesn't know where she lives. Well, I felt like a little orphan Annie. But it was a fact you know.

> I had nobody to live with and I didn't know
> where I lived."

She is now thankful at not having to deal with burglaries and
intruders described to her by her former neighbour who visits her
twice every week. She appreciates the friendship of the sheltered
housing scheme: "All the people here are really friendly.
Everybody speaks to everybody. They are really nice people." At
the same time, experiencing contradictory feelings, she misses her
own home:

> "I loved my own home. In fact, they put me in
> an ambulance one day to go to the blood clinic.
> The driver came in and he had a sheet of paper
> with him. He said 'Margaret Brown'. I said
> 'that's me' and he said 'where do you want to
> go?' I said 'Cochrane Court' and he said 'that's
> not on my list'. I said 'well, you asked me where
> I wanted to go and that's where I would like to
> go'. It was my house you see. That was where I
> used to live. I loved my house."

Another woman spoke thus:

> "We've been in about a year. We come from
> Benwell and have lived in Benwell all our lives.
> We've come from Cochrane Court. I liked my
> house but there were that many break-ins we
> were getting frightened. The family said,
> 'mother, dad's getting on, he's 87 this year,
> you're 72, it's time you thought about going in
> here'."

Cochrane Court, a small 1960s local authority estate just to the
north of the Terrace, comprising two-bedroomed houses with
small front gardens, would seem ideal for older people. From
these it is a short walk to the shops, the clubs and pubs, the bus-
stops and the Search Project. But available policy and funding
regimes make constructing secure communities for some through
sheltered housing a more viable option that enhancing security in
traditional communities.

Very clearly, for older people in Benwell, sheltered housing
was a way of meeting their needs for security and peace of mind.
The scheme provides shelter from vandalism, harassment and

burglaries. With extensive security and an office look-out at the main door, it offers older people security, locking the community out in which they have lived for many years and, for many, where their families still live. As one woman said:

> "It was the fear of break-ins that made me move in here. We wouldn't have been in sheltered 'cause I like my own front door to tell you the truth. I'm not used to, I like going out me own front door, you know."

Another from the same estate told a similar story, reflecting on both how frightening the area had become but also the loss in having been taken away from her community:

> "I was frightened with it being a low-down flat. Burglaries round about. The woman was burgled next door to us. Since we left, there's been about 18 burglaries. All my friends are up there and they say how much they miss me. We have a right gossip. My friend, she's never been the same since I moved 'cause I was always chatting to her. We had a cup of tea and that, it was great."

Some certainly experienced the move as a wrench from the community in which they had worked and created their own home. For working-class older people who had scrimped and saved, their sense of loss at having to part with their own homes and furnishings and the loss of community which once had been respected and a well-regarded place to live was evident.

> "I'm a person that likes to mix with people but coming out of my own front door. It's taken me a long time to get used to it in here. My family, I've got five, and they all think, 'mother, you're safe and it's great'. But it's still not my own door."

> "My daughter says 'you've got your own front door. You go out, mother, when you like', but I say 'but it doesn't feel like me own front door, it's the long corridors'. They cannot understand that I cannot get used to it. I love me grandkids, I

> love kids. I'll never be happy here, till I get a
> place of my own."

> "I must have lived in Benwell for almost 30 years.
> It was a beautiful place, you can take it from me.
> And the street where I lived, everybody's garden
> was lovely. Now it's ramshackled."

One woman, who had only moved about 250 yards from north of
the Terrace to the sheltered housing scheme spoke thus:

> "I've heard they're going to build on Benwell. He
> [nodding to her husband] says 'you're dying to
> get back to Benwell'. 'Yes', I say, 'I'd like to go
> back. They're building little flats or bungalows.
> I'm hoping to get on their lists, but I don't
> know."

Becoming excluded from community

Important in any analysis of community is the need to recognise
that:

> ... contemporary community life, with its
> interlocking networks of differentiated relation-
> ships, is as much about division and exclusion as
> it is about integration and inclusion. (Crow and
> Allan, 1994, p 176)

The undervalued and marginal status of older people is seen by
pensioners' associations as deriving from their position outside the
labour market through enforced retirement, in the words of one of
the founder members of the local branch of the association "cast
out into the geriatric wilderness". A more detailed analysis of
older people's economic status in the community, however, leads
us to question the use of the term economic exclusion as only
meaning excluded from paid employment.

Urban regeneration policies such as City Challenge, concerned
with economic regeneration, pay minimal attention to the needs of
people who have no place in the labour market. As we have seen,
older people only become included in such programmes by
chance, as tenants of the sheltered housing scheme. Meeting their

needs is not valued. City Challenge outputs are more in terms of the marginal increase in jobs generated in the building of the sheltered housing and in its maintenance; the use of formerly derelict land; and the balance of private, statutory and voluntary sectors.

Being categorised as economically 'spent' rather than excluded, older people, while blown about in the changing winds of social policies for urban regeneration, are never the specific focus or subjects of such policies. Their place is within the National Health and community care legislation. They are either clients or patients depending on their own health and social status and the caring capacities of their daughters and wives. In social policy, older people are 'welfarised', a process which ignores their involvement in local community (Arber and Ginn, 1991b; Estes, Swan and Gerrard, 1982). In fact, community care, being not institutional care, fails to take account of the importance of community to older people's involvement in creating and sustaining communities.

To understand the meaning of older people's economic exclusion a number of important points need to be addressed. First, their exclusion from paid work is the result of economic and employment policies and not necessarily the result of their own abilities and desires. With early retirement and redundancies people are becoming excluded from opportunities of paid work, never to enter the labour market again, at increasingly earlier ages, so much so that the Search Project is now offering its advice and advocacy services to people in their 40s. It is acknowledged that as people become older, they experience a decline in social class in relation to economy. As working-class people become older, their economic status becomes even more precarious.

Second, although older people are not in paid employment, they are nevertheless economically active as consumers. Benwell, the Terrace, depends upon local people for its sustenance. The Terrace was meaningful for older people in our study and they are meaningful for the local shops. One woman living in the sheltered housing left each day as early as possible to return at the end of the day, spending all the time on the Terrace, going from one shop to another and in the amusement arcade cafe, chatting with friends, both customers and local shopkeepers.

Living in the locality also meant going to local clubs, the bingo, the pubs, all of which are important to the local economy.

Moving into sheltered housing involved moving out of this local community although many of those interviewed continued to make great efforts to go out, some to stay out as long as possible. One 85-year-old woman went three times a week to the sequence dancing club in the church hall on the Terrace, along with 40-50 others of a similar age. Membership of this dancing community included dancing weeks away in Scarborough and visits to other dance clubs in the region. For some, these efforts to continue to be active in social activities meant overcoming the problems of a disabling environment to walk from the scheme to the Terrace, helping each other to walk the steep bank in the windswept area above the Tyne:

> "When I go out I go with Mary. She is nearly blind, has very, very bad eyesight. She can't see very well and I can't walk very fast so we go together. We help each other. She says she can hear the traffic but doesn't know which way it's coming. I'm terrified she will get run over. I am really, my conscience wouldn't let her go on her own. She knocks at my door. 'Jean, do you think we could walk on the Terrace?' And I'm limping and she's hanging on to my arm to see that I don't fall down and I have to watch her for the road. It's really difficult sometimes though. It's so often so very windy and we struggle from lamp-post to lamp-post, clinging on to them like a couple of drunks."

For others, the problems were too great to continue to visit the club:

> "I really like going up to the club. They make me very welcome there. But I am wholly dependent on my daughter for taking me up. She handles the wheelchair and you've got to be careful and that. But transport, that's a big problem. Getting anybody to take me out is a problem. She's on holiday next week."

Transport, always a major problem for the Search Project in ensuring that people can take part in its activities, was clearly articulated as a problem for older people in the sheltered housing scheme. Not everyone was able to use public transport. For some the difficulties or embarrassment at not being able quickly to board the high step of the bus, or handle the money for the fare, was too much to cope with. For others the fear of stumbling prevented their participation in activities that before would have been straightforward. For those able to use public transport, it was easier to go into town from the bus-stop outside the scheme than to visit local shops and pubs. It was also easier to use public transport than the care bus, a transport scheme designed to meet the needs of older and disabled people.

Third, the experience of paid employment is a meaningful one for older people. To deny them this experience is to fail to acknowledge their lives. All except one of the older people in our study, men and women, were in paid work throughout their lives. One woman of 85, not in this study, attends once a month a seminar for retired employees of a National Health hospital. She is able to maintain interests and social relations developed while she was in work and to contribute to debates about changing health needs and services. Such opportunities to make links between work and retirement have been both the focus and the impetus of pensioners' associations. However, to maintain links with former employment that no longer exists, that is now knocked down, that always was fragmented poses difficulties. The men interviewed and the husbands of widows worked as postmen, school caretakers and in building. Women worked locally on the West Road, as shop assistants, as cleaners in the General Hospital, about a mile's walk from Benwell, in catering at the University in the centre of town, at Vickers on the Scotswood Road and in a local pickle factory. At the same time, it is significant that none of these women received pensions from their work and none of them had had opportunities of post-school education and training through their work.

Fourth, the one exception, the woman who had not been in paid work during her married life but had depended on her husband's income, had nevertheless worked all her life to enable others to work: as a mother so that her husband could work and as a grandmother so that her daughter could work.

The work of older people in supporting the employment of their sons and daughters, or rather daughters and daughters-in-law is well recognised. Their unpaid care of children in many families takes the place of pre-school and after-school provision more available to working parents in other European countries. The move of older people, particularly older women, into sheltered accommodation made this form of older people's economic activity more difficult, sometimes impossible. The size of the sheltered accommodation flats, the corridors taking the place of streets and the communal garden designed for easy lawn-mowing and car parking made the care of grandchildren no longer feasible.

> "And my grandchildren, they say 'Ah Nana, go back to your house where we could play in your garden', little Rosie and little Tom, they say 'we don't like it here Nana'. I used to see them regularly, but now I don't see them as much 'cause they say 'there's no where to run Nana or play'. I had a little spare room and they all used to go in there and play."

The relationship between economic exclusion and social exclusion is well-documented for those of working age in long-term unemployment. The resulting paucity of material resources is compounded by experiences of lack of worth, respect and self-esteem, all contributing to exclusion from social activity and relations and to little control over your own life. For older people the dynamics of economic and social exclusion are complex. The interpretation of economic exclusion as not active in the labour force is ageist. It denies the economic activity of those deemed ineligible, through employment legislation, for paid work. For older people, their exclusion from economic activity, from being consumers at local shops, from being regarded as former employees, from supporting the paid work of others, also brings with it social exclusion. It denies them meaningful ways in which older people engage with others in worthwhile and valued activities.

Conclusion

In this chapter, we have covered only some aspects of older people's lives, community and processes of inclusion and exclusion. We have focused on urban policy and change in a working-class area of economic decline. We have explored ways in which policies and change shape older people's experiences of local community. Their experiences of sheltered housing as community and processes of inclusion and exclusion within the scheme through gender, race, disability and respectability, is the subject of a further research paper.

In talking to us, older people living in Benwell have challenged many ageist assumptions which underpin so much of sheltered housing, community care and urban regeneration policies. First, older people cannot be considered a homogeneous group. Their life experiences, interests, aspirations and needs vary in relation to their social location. For older people in Benwell, social class and economic status are major determinants in access to resources for independent living in communities of their choosing. Their reasons for moving into sheltered housing; their place in decision making about moving made even more complex by their own contradictory feelings; losing their homes and belongings carefully gathered over many years to finally be given away by others; all these demonstrate a complex interaction of lack of resources and being old which requires an analysis combining a political economy of ageing with an understanding of the routine lives of older people in communities and ways in which these are shaped through policies and practices.

Older people are often constructed as a burden on the family, the community and the state. Our interviews with older people have shown vividly that older people are a significant resource to the local community, having productive and resourceful roles and involvement in local social and economic systems: as grandparents; as shoppers and clubbers; in voluntary, cultural and political activities; as 'commodities' for service providers such as the housing association and health and welfare services; as consumers of local goods and services. The danger is that by ignoring these strengths and resources of older people, social and economic policies at community level have the effect of undermining them. The danger for older people is that they are made passive and dependent on social provision and practitioners.

Part Three

Local government and community

eight

Getting a fix on community identity: the catalyst of the local government review[*]

Rick Ball and Jon Stobart

The idea of bounded 'community identity': attaining the unattainable?

For some, the baseline definition of 'community' embues it with a distinct geographical dimension. It is viewed not only as a 'social network of interacting individuals', but also as 'usually concentrated into a defined territory' (Johnston, Gregory and Smith, 1994, p 80). However, the idea of 'community' involves a much wider, more complex and often less geographically focused conception. As Gyford suggests, there are at least two broad domains within notions of 'community' – the affective and the effective (Gyford, 1991a). The former is the conceptual or perceived community of common interest that may well extend beyond the confines of a particular area and perhaps take on global proportions. The latter is the revealed community of interest that can be charted in geographical space; it is the so-called 'action space' of the individual and, in the aggregate, of the group. Clearly, the two perspectives are connected. The affective

---

[*] The work reported in this chapter was funded through a consultancy project completed for Cannock Chase District Council. The views expressed are those of the authors and not of the local authority.

domain, at least to some degree, may follow from an individual's effective action space.

At the heart of the affective/effective distinction and, in particular, the widening gap between them, lies the process of globalisation. The accelerating pace and complexity of life and the bombardment of images and information – what Harvey refers to as "time–space compression" (Harvey, 1989a) – is eroding the fixity of real or perceived boundaries. However, there is a certainty that it is simultaneously serving to sharpen feelings of 'community' via a defensive reaction and so, in effect, precipitating a search for roots (Lash and Urry, 1994). In this way, the mid-1990s Local Government Review (LGR) – where notions of 'community' loomed large in the debate (Midwinter, 1993) – functioned as a catalyst for an enhancement of the significance of the effective domain. Authorities were required to produce local government service delivery proposals for areas that reflected what the Department of the Environment (DoE) referred to as "natural communities" (DoE, 1992; Chisholm, 1994). Thus, while social and spatial forces are working to add complexity to an already complex interconnectivity between places (Massey, 1995), the UK government has been requiring lines to be drawn. There is no alternative to bounded areas for such purposes. However, the outcome has, some would say inevitably, led to confusion and conflict over the conception of local community. Equally, there has inevitably been the reassertion of the argument that the goal of basing a local government system on community loyalties is unrealistic and, essentially, unattainable (Midwinter, 1993).

Accepting the basic unattainability argument, and thus circumventing much conceptual research on the issue of community, this chapter develops a number of interrelated themes around the idea of geographical community. It focuses in particular on a case study of Cannock Chase District and its involvement with the review exercise. The idea of community is set into the context of recent geographical research, in particular, focusing on the catalytic role of the LGR in raising an awareness of definitional issues and the processes and problems created by the virtually enforced construction of geographical notions of community precipitated by the review. In addition to assessing the difficulties and solutions to the boundary delimitation puzzle, it also reflects on outcomes – especially the sharpened awareness of identities – and considers some of the legacies of the whole event as regards ideas of 'community', and the contestation that seems to pervade their formulation.

Community and community identity in geographical domains – providing a context

This discussion is essentially set in the context of an applied geographical perspective on notions of community and the idea of community as spatially relative in some degree and at some scale. Although past flurries of interest by geographers and planners (Burnett, 1994) have been interspersed with quieter times, the question of geographical community retains its interest for anything from theoretical/conceptual work to conventional planning analyses of community.

Planned communities endure as a theme, with attention shifting in line with changing residential geographies. Relph (1991) discusses the deliberate attempt in Greater Toronto to generate a sense of suburban community identity, while both Fishman (1991) and Ward (1993) remind us that the question of the relationships between spatial containment and community identity, especially in new town environments, remains largely unresolved. There has also been work on the development of specific industrial-economic communities and their structures (Iwama 1992; Becker and Bradbury 1994). Much of this work investigates the impact of contemporary change on community structures and development (Simmons, 1995). In contrast, recent work in historical geography by Gilbert (1991), for example, has focused on the idea of community as geographically varying collective identity.

New forms of spatial 'community' are being precipitated by the development and accessibility of the information highway (see Hankey, 1995). For example, Bale (1993) argues that the allegiance to sports clubs – a potent source of affective community – is being stretched via media attention. As such, football club support as an idea of community is increasingly being 'shifted' from a virtually 'clean' and bounded local space to a global unbounded space.

There has been a variety of research directions in the matter of community and local political and governmental structures (Hall,

1977; Cox and Mair, 1988; Burnett, 1994). Of particular interest
here is the growing debate on how to link, through enhanced
involvement, local authorities to communities at the local level
(Morphet, 1993). However, the LGR has raised the issue of
'community identity' to a new level of awareness. The official
requirement for authorities to accord community identity a central
position in their deliberations and proposals on local government
reform, unitary authority status and so on, inevitably gave a fresh
impetus to the subject. In fact, a number of research themes can
be linked expressly to the LGR. For example, Boyne and Law,
reviewing representations made by Welsh authorities, relate some
of the central problems of linking community to local government
boundaries. As they argue, not only may a sense of community be
based around a variety of spatial scales, "there may be different
geographical 'communities' for different services: the 'sense of
community' for nursery education is likely to be expressed at a
smaller spatial scale than the sense of community for transport
planning" (Boyne and Law, 1993, p 544). Moreover, the reality is
that ideas of community identity are flexible, dynamic and ever on
the move.   All communities are at some point 'invented',
sometimes around myths and group stories (Cohen, 1985), but the
number of these inventions is growing, giving people a greater
array of choice over which communities to 'throw themselves into'
(Lash and Urry, 1994, p 316). Under such circumstances, it is easy
to argue that "a single tier of local government cannot give full
expression to the range of community loyalties" (Boyne and Law,
1993, p 544).

This problematic has its counterpart in some theoretical
research. Shields for example, in developing his social theory of
spatiality with the prominence of distinction by division and
community identity, argues that people "transcend and suppress
their own experience in order to identify with broader social
groups ... and ... they also seek to affirm community identities....
[These] are created as the sum of an open set of individual
meanings and experiences" (Shields, 1991, p 263). Although
people may be willing to act in terms of an imaginary community,
the question of boundary production is further complicated by
such compliance.

Although the idea of community as an applied concept – a
locus of service delivery and a reflection of local loyalty – is clearly
important, there are apparent gaps in the research effort. Despite

considerable work on the 'packaging' of ideas of community through either wider (class) or narrower (local business) sectional interests for local political gain (Harvey, 1989a; Cox and Mair, 1988), there has been little or no research on the development of ideas about community identity within 'vested interest' agencies such as local authorities. Certainly, during events such as the LGR, little has been said about the problems and pitfalls encountered, the strategies followed or the development of constructions and representations of local government-based community identity. This is the direction of the present chapter.

Catalyst and reaction – community identity and the Local Government Review

In its guidance notes to the Local Government Commission (LGC), the DoE stressed the importance of the identities and interests of local communities (DoE, 1992). Indeed, the importance of community identity is generally accepted as a key consideration in the determination of local government areas and functions. As the Association of District Councils (ADC) noted, "bonding local authority areas more strongly to the communities they represent and serve ... is what local democracy should be all about" (ADC, 1993). Of course, this is not necessarily seen as clear-cut. For example, the Association of County Councils (ACC) argued that, while local identity remains relevant in modern society, it is not dominant (ACC, 1992). Moreover, they implied, the review could not assume a mosaic of easily identifiable local communities and, with a more complex pattern of modern living, people in the same place will not always want the same things.

Community identity as a concept and an experienced reality is clearly a central matter in the LGR. In the review process, the LGC was required to make recommendations having regard to the need "to reflect the identities and interests of local communities" with local authorities based on "natural communities" (Chisholm, 1994). The range of factors required to be considered was wide (see LGC, 1992; Coombes et al, 1993). Notions of 'community identity' from this perspective involve a consideration of variables such as a locality's history, topography, mobility, industry, transport, demography and sport, leisure and culture (DoE, 1992).

District authorities in Wales emphasised community identity as important for local government; some viewed it as the most important, or indeed the only important criterion (Boyne and Law, 1993, p 543). However, it emerges as a problematical issue due to limitations and ambiguities in finding a definable 'community'. There is a clear tendency for 'senses of community' to be strongest at the village or neighbourhood level, but, as Chisholm argues with regard to the LGR, the underlying problem remained – was it possible to identify "natural communities" which could form the basis for units of local government? (Chisholm, 1994). In other words, the need to demonstrate a 'satisfactory' and defensible notion of community identity in any new local government situation was a basic requirement of the LGR. As such, quite apart from conceptual deliberations about the notion of community (Lash and Urry, 1994), there was the practical need to minimise problems associated with the production of a notion of bounded community.

Processes and problems: constructing a bounded community identity

If we accept that an all-embracing notion of community identity is virtually impossible to delineate in terms of fixed boundaries around definite geographical areas, the question of approximations and constructions comes more sharply into play. During the LGR, local authorities were, in many ways, forced into such constructions either to legitimise their retention or reinforce arguments for changes to the spatial extent of their jurisdiction. They had to accept the limitations and ambiguities of finding a definable 'community' and address practical approaches to the task of boundary drawing. Naturally, such activity was not always undertaken with reluctance: it could give an important fillip to local feelings of identity and belonging regardless of the outcome of the review process. For the local authorities this could mean an important opportunity to engage in a considerable amount of civic 'boosterism' (Ashworth and Voogd, 1995) and for the local residents it often meant explicit recognition, sometimes for the first time, of identity with a locality. Boundaries could thus be 'place-making' at both a promotional and experiential level

(Massey, 1995). There is some moral 'high ground' here. Constructed representations of community identity may serve the needs of the constructors to the detriment of others. In producing the story of community in a particular place, therefore, it is important to problematise the 'construction' process: to look at the strategies and processes of construction, and the implications of the raised awareness of place and community. Such an approach is taken here in looking at the efforts of Cannock Chase District Council to establish the existence and boundaries of local community identity during the LGR process.

The construction process in the Cannock Chase locality

Cannock Chase District lies in southern Staffordshire, immediately to the north of, but arguably distinct from the West Midlands conurbation in spatial terms. The District, created in the reorganisation of local government in 1974, has at its centre the Cannock Chase Area of Outstanding Natural Beauty, around which are grouped a varied set of towns and villages, the largest of which are Cannock to the south and Rugeley to the north of the Chase. Many of these settlements have a strong coal-mining tradition and grew rapidly as mining expanded in the early 20th century. Since then, coal has declined in importance and Littleton Colliery, the last mine in the area, closed in 1993. Today, a range of light manufacturing – many linked to traditional West Midlands metal-working and engineering industries – form the major employment opportunities in an area characterised by relatively high unemployment and low family incomes (1991 Census of Population).

Within this area, the local authority – led by key officers in conjunction with political representatives – sought to construct a notion of community identity which would establish the district as a feasible and legitimate basis for local government. Like many other councils, it went through a process of evaluating ideas of community and exploring alternative bases for community identity. Accordingly, a number of alternative rationales for community were identified: a high plateau community defined in terms of the basic physical geography of the area; an historical social and cultural community centred on its coalmining tradition; a physical community based on the coherence of the area's urban structure; a functional community drawn together by contemporary administrative, shopping and leisure functions, and a perceptual or affective community identified with by the local population (Ball and Stobart, 1993).

In deciding which theme to follow, a number of factors were considered. The chief underlying concern was the end goal of the authority: what was it seeking from the LGR? Was it trying to defend the status quo or legitimise for itself an enlarged role as a unitary authority? Apart from these political considerations, it was the availability of evidence to support the chosen option which was of paramount importance. Having suggested an area of community identity, the authority needed to be confident that it could be justified to the LGC and that it would find support among the local population. Particularly significant in Cannock Chase, it also had to be something which could unite the various constituent groups within the identified area. The history and geographical constitution of the area could potentially lead to divisions within any posited community identity, especially as the Chase forms a large and sparsely populated area in the very heart of the district, dividing rather than uniting loyalties and pulling apart any community identity. This danger is, perhaps, epitomised by the long standing sense of rivalry between Cannock and Rugeley.

The chosen strategy: a coalfield heritage-based community

Lengthy planning, research and consultation eventually produced a case for unitary status for Cannock Chase Council, based on the existence of a community identity throughout an area encompassing all of the pre-existing district and an additional 10 wards. Initially, the area looks unpromising as a geographically identifiable community, as it is split in half by the Cannock Chase High Plateau and further subdivided by the River Trent. However, the coalmining history of the area was quickly identified as a powerful central unifying theme for this community and some strong evidence built upon this base. By outlining the development of mining throughout much of the area, its common historical inheritance was established in economic and (by implication) social terms, and the first factor in community identified by the LGC was fulfilled. Furthermore, it was argued that the 19th- and 20th-century development of this industry was responsible for the geographical coalescence of the various settlements of the district. Not only were these places close in terms of their historic socioeconomic and cultural structures, then, they were also increasingly proximate in a physical sense. The community thus had coherence as well as commonalities.

The local authority recognised from the outset that historical similarities are not enough in themselves to sustain present-day feelings of community identity. Cannock Chase Council therefore built on this foundation a complex superstructure of commonalities within contemporary society, experiences and behaviour. This constructed notion of a functional or effective community contained four levels which reflected closely several of the factors identified by the DoE. First, it possessed a distinctive demographic profile (based on census data), being characterised by "less people in work, more long term illness, more people in local authority housing, less people in service industries, more manual workers and fewer managerial and professional workers" than its surrounding areas (Cannock Chase District Council, 1994). Second, it displayed a certain level of coherence of service provision over much of the community area, with many services (from the magistrates' court to adult social services) covering a broadly similar area, often greater than the current Cannock Chase District. Third, many of the everyday social activities and linkages which form the life-blood of community and cement feelings of identity (schooling, shopping, leisure, etc – Ball and Stobart, 1993) were shown to draw together people from throughout the area. This was often achieved by linking a number of small, tightly knit communities of action centred on a particular school or leisure activity. Fourth, the public transport infrastructure of the area was shown to draw together these various local communities. No part of the area was isolated and most exhibited much stronger links with other parts of the community area than with places beyond its constructed bounds. This last point illustrates an important undertone of this process of construction; the need – or perceived need – not just to demonstrate the internal coherence of the community area, but to differentiate it from its neighbouring communities. While the definition of place in terms of some other is becoming less feasible in a global arena, othering or constructing difference between places appears to remain a significant part of local authority attempts to portray community identity. The practical issues of delineation thus go against the tide of globalisation by emphasising more the local differences between places.

Problems and limitations: challenging the constructed community

The bounded community identity constructed for the Cannock Chase area as part of the local government review was not problem free: it generated tensions both between and within authorities.

Coalition, conflict and management in the policy process

Clearly, the notion of 'community' is a highly contested concept, and this contestation, in its political form, was aggravated by the LGR process and by the endeavours and actions of the more proactive local authorities such as Cannock Chase. Three related aspects of this were important. First, the extent of proactivity with which some authorities took on the quest for unitary status, or at least for a raised profile with central government, was highly variable. This reflected itself both in the emphasis on 'community' in submissions to the LGC, and in the size and depth of the final documents. Second, and partly as a result of this, conflict emerged in various forms at the inter-authority level. Third, in parallel with the ensuing conflict, there was a fairly continuous process of coalition formation and adjustment. All three issues link to the complexion of the authorities involved, as reflected in the process via which 'bids' were assembled, power brokered, aspirations stage managed and conflicting interests appeased, if indeed they were. This merits attention within the context of the contestation of 'community', although, unsurprisingly, it is not possible to chart the finer detail of the policy process.

The importance of community identity within the case-making process for unitary status is clearly reflected in its prominence within the inter-authority debate. Coalitions were formed and developed in a flexible, continuous process, partly around agreement or disagreement over community boundaries. The impetus appears to have come from a combination of officer-led strategic thinking closely developed with key political representatives. There was an initial attempt to predict the strategies and viewpoints of other authorities, in particular those that might be implicated by any annexation. The major orientation in Cannock Chase was to promote a collective voice via a coalition approach. The process, at least in southern

Staffordshire, took on the guise of a 'campaign' orchestrated by a cohort of districts, largely against the inevitable status quo position of the County Council. At the same time, districts that were implicated by aspirations for unitary status were circumvented and not drawn into the coalition. Meetings at chief executive level took place between district authorities as a collective voice was being sought. In parallel, at a less informal level, there were inter-authority officer working groups, but only between selected district authorities. That said, the coalition emerged with agreements being forged incrementally, as informal agreement and support for the independence quest was sought and obtained from, ultimately, like-minded districts in central, eastern and northern Staffordshire. In effect, the aspirations of authorities required a management structure to promote them and it is in this guise that coalitions emerged and developed.

In many senses, it is difficult to gauge the precise or real viewpoint of individual authorities, if indeed they could be said to have such a singular voice. The public (overt) face, designed for internal and external political consumption in the realms of feared outcomes and lost powers, often contrasts sharply with the covert face linked to longer term aspirations of just where (officers and key politicians within) authorities felt they should be in the latter 1990s. Nevertheless, the comparative activities of authorities provide further evidence of how the review debate pivoted around conflicting arguments about community identity.

In the case of the proactive Cannock Chase submission, the reactions of adjacent, implicated authorities emerged overtly in two ways: first, in their own (later) submissions; second, in direct representations made either to Cannock Chase Council, or to the LGC in response to the Cannock Chase approach. Reactions were sometimes confrontational with embittered, emotive language from implicated authorities in southern Staffordshire. These referred to the "alleged affinity" of the Cannock Chase community (Staffordshire County Council, 1994, p 35), claiming it to be "artificial" and a "device" pursued by "factions" (Lichfield District Council, 1994), and initially refused to accept the research base claiming it to have "no justification in terms of a common community identity" (South Staffordshire Council, 1994a). The submissions of adjacent authorities in effect sought to counter the Cannock Chase base argument of an identifiable coalfield community. This also involved a manoeuvring via a range of alternative or counter conceptions of 'community'. These include the 'Tamworth and Lichfield community' (Tamworth Borough Council, 1994) developed more on the basis of local acceptability and service efficiency, the 'community of communities' (South Staffordshire District Council, 1994b) where a disparate array of small settlements is drawn into an integrated unit, and the 24 'natural communities' outside Stoke-on-Trent identified and promoted by the County Council as obviating the sensibility of producing a small number of unitary councils (Staffordshire County Council, 1993, p 9). These representations all used various notions of 'community' to react to and debate the viability of proposed unitary authorities and is give a very real and overt reflection of the contestation that surrounds ideas of community.

Within the constructed community – unity in diversity?

As the constructed representation of community drew together a number of potentially conflicting centres, it is unsurprising that the resultant community area possesses, at its heart, a strong feeling of distinctiveness and identity which weakened towards the outer edges. However, the situation is more complex than this simple core-periphery idea allows as several levels of community identity exist, nesting within one another in a hierarchical fashion. Within the Cannock Chase community area, three definite heartlands of community were identified, centred on Cannock, Rugeley and Burntwood. Each formed a distinct focus for a functional community and possessed strong feelings of community identity. In terms of its ability to unite these three heartlands, the community area constructed by Cannock Chase Council had obvious limitations. Not only was the internal integrity of the posited community somewhat doubtful, but the process of othering came under pressure. The latter difficulty was particularly severe in the case of Burntwood. This cluster of settlements displayed a strong sense of local identity, but was split in terms of allegiances to larger community areas: inhabitants of Chase Terrace and Chasetown identified more with Cannock whilst their neighbours in Burntwood itself looked towards Lichfield. This is effectively a divided heartland of community.

Notwithstanding such limitations, the biggest problem in terms of this 'story' of community identity was the lack of information on the affective community: on individuals' feelings of belonging and identity with particular places and areas. Their history may be shared and their socioeconomic characteristics and patterns of behaviour very similar, but do these really make for a strong community identity? If such basic feelings of belonging are absent, then there is the danger that the construction attempted by Cannock Chase Council identifies an unnatural rather than the real functional and felt community required by the LGR. The real strength and authenticity of the identified community requires further investigation.

Appraisal and assessment – testing the constructions

The integrity of the community area constructed by Cannock Chase Council has been tested on a number of bases. The council itself drew together a range of sources which served to reinforce the idea of an area-wide affective community which corresponded, to an extent at least, to the previously established notion of effective community. They demonstrated the potency of the Chase as an icon for local organisations, with more than 200 using the name 'Cannock Chase' or 'Chase' in their titles. They also analysed external perceptions of the area in terms of its coverage in the regional and national media. The crucial finding here was the extent to which places surrounding the heartlands of Cannock and Rugeley were identified as being part of these areas. This is well illustrated by the reporting of the closure of Littleton Colliery, which, despite being in Huntington and lying outside Cannock Chase District, was firmly identified as being 'Cannock'.

Such evidence is, of course, somewhat anecdotal. More important in testing the constructions of community in the area was the section of the MORI survey (carried out as part of the LGR) which dealt explicitly with feelings of belonging and community identity in the Cannock Chase area. Here, MORI found that, like elsewhere in the county, allegiances were strongest at the local level. People identified most strongly with their village, town or neighbourhood and much less so with larger areas such as districts or counties. In many ways, this confirmed the earlier findings of a number of heartlands of community identity drawn together by communities of action. It thus offered support for the story of community told by Cannock Chase Council: local affective communities being cemented together into larger effective community areas. That said, the strength of community identity in the areas which emerge from such a construction process depends not just on the inherent sturdiness of the building blocks – the local communities – but also on the sureness of the foundation of common history upon which these blocks stand and the continued intensity of the shared experiences which cement together these individual units.

Reflections and legacies of the search for community identity

Unsurprisingly, when faced with the almost intractable conceptual problems of defining and delineating communities, most local authorities sought pragmatic solutions. The degree of 'success' in minimising the limitations of such 'enforced' constructions of community identity is of some importance. Despite the explosion of many communities as people interact over larger and larger distances, they have constructed notions of community based on the shared history, common sociodemographic characteristics and spatial and experiential coherence of the area. Moreover, the attempt to minimise the limitations and produce a feasible, consensus-based representation of community identity appears to have worked. The communities of action thus described appear to find some echo in communities of interest expressed by the people, albeit in some cases having been subjected to local media promotion of the 'chosen' strategy as orchestrated by the local authority. Local authorities have been able to legitimise their constructions and the often rather arbitrary boundaries which they have involved, and find widespread public support for their notions of community areas. Whether this denies the globalisation of community and shows that individuals still feel themselves part of recognisable communities of action and interest, or merely indicates that local authorities and residents alike have been – often willingly – drawn into pointless parochial arguments and boundary drawing is, of course, a moot point. Three things are clear, however: first, community identity, often reflecting the constructions of local authorities, is strongly felt at local level; second, these communities are complex both on a conceptual and spatial level; third, debates about local community unleash strong forces of contestation.

The LGR process has reaffirmed that community exists at various spatial scales (Boyne and Law, 1993), and that community identities are particularly strongly felt at the local level. Both in Staffordshire and countrywide, the MORI surveys confirm that the majority of people feel themselves part of communities based on village, neighbourhood or town rather than district or county. One obvious implication of this for the LGR itself, is that any local government which is to be meaningful in terms of community identity must carefully build on these basic community building blocks – much as has happened in the Cannock Chase area – so that the resultant areas of authority contain a series of nesting communities drawn together under one uniting authority (LGC, 1993, p 34). The question that remains is, of course, how to build a strong 'story' of community identity in 'awkward' places, such as those with dual or multiple centres. The answer perhaps lies in detailed community analysis (Hall, 1977), although that is not always feasible with finite resources.

Outcomes and effects - from vindication to a raised profile

As we have seen, constructed 'stories' of community are likely to generate local tensions and conflicts, and any such representation is open to critical appraisal, not least by those places that are implicated. There can be tension between communities of action and identity – the one often not accurately reflecting the other – so that local government and services cannot be effectively delivered to amalgamations of 'felt' communities. More fundamentally, there has been considerable argument over the 'ownership' of these small communities. This is particularly the case for those, like Burntwood, located on the boundary between two pre-existing districts (Cannock Chase and Lichfield) which then fight for possession of the locality. It can also be seen at a wider scale, however, with campaigns and counter-campaigns mounted by the districts and the counties as they fight for the loyalties of local communities and the allegiances of their individual constituents. The fierce loyalties to old counties may not have been maintained into the contemporary scene (Midwinter, 1993), but the county councils fought an increasingly successful rearguard action in which the public appear to have retained sufficient regard for their counties to be reluctant to see them jettisoned quite yet. At this point, we might return to the moral high ground: whose constructions of community identity are being proferred? In many cases, it is a notion of community engineered by local officers. The question is, to what extent are these constructions acceptable as revelations or are they imposed 'non-natural' perspectives of community?

Another question concerns the relative success or failure of the review process for participants. Between the 'draft' and 'final' recommendations of the LGC, and in the light of the various public consultations, the tranche of coalition authorities discussed in section 4.3.1 emerged in a more public way (LGC, 1994a; 1994b). As supported by Cannock Chase, East Staffordshire, Stafford, Staffordshire Moorlands and, at the last moment, Tamworth, six unitary authorities were proposed (including the addition of a north Staffordshire authority based on Stoke-on-Trent and Newcastle-under-Lyme). That left Lichfield and South Staffordshire to opt for the retention of the two-tier system plus the single unitary authority. It seems that there was great reticence amongst authorities to be seen to be losing any part of their jurisdiction by annexation to a proposed new unitary authority controlled from an adjacent town. Perhaps that view reflected their belief in their own strength of community, perhaps it was merely political parochialism?

For Cannock Chase then, there was a mix of vindication and raised profile from the review exercise, all built around a strong, if contested, representation of community. The LGC opted for status quo plus a unitary authority for Stoke-on-Trent on a range of grounds linked to operating and transitional costs, local views and, no doubt, political considerations. That accepted, 'success' could still be claimed by authorities such as Cannock Chase. Vindication came with the LGC's acceptance, despite the protestations of surrounding districts, of the viability of a 'Greater Cannock' community as a base for unitary status – what the LGC referred to as a "viable alternative structure" (LGC, 1994b, p 5) even if it was not ultimately recommended. This confirmed Cannock Chase Council as the viable core of a unitary authority. In raising its profile, they accepted the marker for the future, perhaps something that was intended in the first place by proactive authorities, certainly as a second best outcome?

Legacies of a raised awareness of community identity

Whatever the outcome in individual cases, the LGR was a catalyst for raising an awareness of geographical communities and bringing the debate about them and their geographical extent to a new prominence. The fundamental tensions in the LGR process and in the establishment and maintenance of a community identity over a large area are, by now, apparent. Within this, the key finding, once again, is that it is local communities that are probably most commonly experienced and certainly most strongly felt, and so these must form the basic building blocks of the larger, area communities 'required' by the LGC. Less clear is how the construction process should take place and how strong and resilient the resultant structures will prove to be. At this stage, though, it is possible to make a number of observations on the legacies of the LGR process for the commission, for the local authority structures and behaviours, and for individuals in surviving or newly created local authority areas.

Given the remit of the LGC and its explicitly stated objective of, wherever possible, creating unitary authorities (partly) on the basis of expressions of community identity, it is unsurprising that they should keenly encourage the construction of such communities. They argue that local government based on such areas would improve its image; make more transparent the accountability of local councillors and officers; bring councils closer to the people who elect them; reduce the impact of national politics on local elections, and be simple and easier to understand than the present two-tier system. The extent to which the public are convinced by these arguments appears somewhat limited and, in most places, popular opinion has favoured the status quo. One significant change is the enhanced role of parish councils: the bodies which come closest to representing the scale of community expressed by most people.

For local authorities, the legacies of the review process would appear more variable and ambiguous. Some (Stoke-on-Trent, Derby and Darlington, for example) have won their arguments for the enhanced status of unitary authorities; others (mostly county councils) have lost out and are to be disbanded; the majority (including Cannock and most other Staffordshire authorities) have remained intact. It would be wrong, however, to think of the last group as losers in the process, as their end goal may not have been unitary status, but simply the defence or reinforcement of their current position. In a very real sense, of course, these authorities have benefited greatly from the LGR process. It has been an excellent opportunity for civic boosterism and important in (legitimising spending on) municipal flag waving. It may even have given authorities a greater taste for playing the 'bidding game' (Ball, 1995). Many authorities have taken the opportunity to project a very positive and corporate image of themselves and their performance in local government to their electorate, to neighbouring authorities and, through the LGC, to the wider world. The local government psyche is clearly affected and that may well generate a range of spin-offs. For example, we may find a greater receptiveness to parishisation and to the use of neighbourhood offices as a consequence (Morphet, 1993). Aspirant unitary authorities or not, the LGR process has been of great significance to such places. Whether or not the corporate image is believed, the very act of drawing boundaries around areas and labelling them 'communities' clearly has important place-making implications for the localities and individual's who live there. As Massey has recently reminded us, drawing boundaries around areas is an exercise as much in place-making as it is in the recognition of similarity (Massey, 1995). The media manipulation that accompanied many local authority strategies for local government reform – particularly in those seeking unitary status – where ideas of a preferred notion of community identity were planted in local newspapers, is an excellent example of a mechanical side to such a place-making process.

The public have also been greatly affected by the review process. Most obviously, those living in areas where significant changes have been recommended (in Avon or Humberside, for instance) will be faced with a totally new composition to their local governance. Throughout the country, though, people have experienced an enormous upsurge in interest in the idea and importance of community identity. The LGC has stressed the importance of community and people's views on community as a vital factor in determining the future shape of local government; district and county councils have pressed their claims to represent real communities of interest and sought to galvanise public opinion around their constructions of community, and national and local surveys have tried to uncover people's real feelings and responses to community. This activity not only heightens awareness of the notion and reality of communities, it also serves to cement the individual's feelings of identity with particular places. Just as drawing a boundary is important in creating identity in places, so prompting people to think about community can be significant in reinforcing their feelings of belonging to those places. Whatever short-term outcomes, community is firmly back on the policy map.

nine

Local government and community

Neil Barnett and Jim Chandler

Introduction

Mackenzie observed in 1961 that people tended to get by with "an ethical commitment to an extremely vague notion of local self-government" (Sharpe, 1970, p 153). Writing at the time when a local govern-ment review was underway following the publication of the Report of the Redcliffe-Maud Commission, Sharpe endorsed this comment and argued that the absence of theory established an unsatisfactory basis for reform. Twenty-five years later, during and in the aftermath of another review there is a similar reluctance to enter into debates on the theories and values of local government.

Indicative of this threadbare commitment to theory has been the way in which the concept of 'community' has been treated both by Redcliffe-Maud and more recently by the Local Government Commission chaired, initially, by Sir John Banham. Both enquiries concerned themselves with 'community' as an issue in the creation of appropriate administrative units, but both have given weight to particular views of community which have allowed them to concentrate their attention primarily upon issues of service delivery and efficiency. It is suggested in this chapter that these reconstructions of local government have studied community only in so far as this awkward concept for British liberal thought can be dismissed from serious consideration. In doing so, the review processes reflect a British tradition of justifying local government on instrumental grounds (Chandler 1995), born out of a British liberal philosophy that emphasises individualism.

Community and the local government commissions

Since the mid-19th century the development of British local government has been towards the creation of a smaller network of larger administrative units. The present review maintains this trend. Although some of the largest units have disappeared, such as the Scottish Regional and Welsh County Councils along with the English counties of Avon, Humberside and Cleveland, their powers have been largely allocated to existing district authorities that now have a unitary status while some smaller districts have been merged with others so that there are now fewer local authorities after than before the review. The review has, however, been nowhere near as radical as was assumed at the outset. The Maud proposal, reflected in Heseltine's White Paper, for a single-tier structure of local government has only been fully realised in Scotland and Wales and two-tier local government remains in many parts of England.

Despite dividing the nation into an even smaller number of local authority areas, both Redcliffe-Maud and Banham have spent a considerable time deliberating about the issue of 'community' and how it should aid their deliberations over the boundaries of local administrative units. There has certainly been deference to the idea of 'community' and to the idea that local government may constitute something more than an agency of service delivery but, in both studies, the concept has never been fully grasped or defined, and has been sidelined in favour of more instrumental values and political expedience.

The Redcliffe-Maud Commission

The work of the Redcliffe-Maud Commission and the government's eventual restructuring of local government in 1972 are revealing. The Commission undertook research into 'community', largely as a result of persuasion from its research director, Sharpe. A key survey into this concept asked a sample of people, within their own homes, to identify an area in which they 'felt at home'. Not surprisingly, people tended to identify very small areas, partly on the assumption that having found where they live, those questioned would be familiar with the town or village.

The Commission concluded from this research that the creation of larger authorities would do little damage to community identity because the existing system did not reflect communities on such a small scale (Redcliffe-Maud, 1969, vol I, para 235 62; vol III, pp 151-61). Community-based units were, moreover, far too small to be capable of administering major functions. Thus:

> Responsibility for all local government services must lie with authorities commanding substantial resources, representing large populations and administering areas, in some cases wide-ranging, which combine town and country. (1969, vol I, para 368 95)

The Commission, nevertheless, paid some deference to the usefulness of parish councils as a grassroots consultative body, and the formation of community councils in urban areas was to be encouraged.

> Our conclusion that local councils must be part of the new system is unanimous. We do not see them as having statutory responsibility for any local government service: but we do see them as contributing a vital element to democratic local government. (1969, vol I, para 371 95)

While bypassing much of their research findings on popular notions of community, the Commission, nevertheless, adopted a cavalier approach to the term 'community' also using it to refer to large areas.

> Our own researches confirmed the community of social and economic interest joining towns of various sizes with the countryside in a mutually advantageous relationship which the present pattern of local authorities fails to reflect. (1969, vol I, Para 243 65)

The eventual pattern which was to emerge in 1972 demonstrated a similarly eclectic view of the concept. The government accepted Maud's arguments concerning the inappropriateness of the majority of the existing local government map for the 'modern day' requirements of service delivery. Urban and rural district councils were abolished and amalgamated into district council areas.

The 1972 Local Government Commission (LGC) established to form the new boundaries stuck largely to the requirement to develop non-metropolitan districts of between 75,000 and 100,000 populations with 40,000 as the absolute minimum. Due to the demands of a number of larger towns that were being forced to merge into new districts, some concessions were made to the many local protests concerning the new local government map of Britain. While there was consultation via public notice and directly with interested parties, the boundaries eventually drawn up owed more to convenience and bargaining between local and central elites than to considerations of community identity.

The absence of a concern for community in the genesis of the 1972 Local Government Act is suggested in Wood's conclusions on the motives behind the reform process.

> The existence of 'acceptable' objectives like democracy and efficiency were little more than a convenience. Government interest in these concepts was limited to support for the standard diagnosis of the ills of local government as undemocratic and inefficient. Reform was based on a mixture of theoretical and institutional political objectives. The need for governmental leadership and parliamentary decision ensured that any concern for theory was frequently subordinated to tactical considerations. (Wood, 1976, p 190)

The Banham Commission

The Banham Commission had explicit instructions from the government to recommend structures which best combined cost-effectiveness with community identities and interests. Proposed authorities had to have the capacity to deliver services and be 'based on communities' (Department of the Environment [DoE], 1993a, Para 4). Significantly, the Commission has been required to 'take account of peoples' expressed preferences' while also using statistical information about the pattern of peoples' lives (DoE, 1993a, Para 5). The government proposed that the LGC used a 'Community Index' which would allow proposals to be analysed according to a range of indices including history, topography, personal mobility, sporting, leisure and cultural affiliations, industrial character, transport and demography.

Not surprisingly, the LGC were made aware at an early stage that it would be difficult to 'pin down' the idea of community. It was a multi-dimensional concept involving affective and effective elements so that a thorough investigation of its implications would involve a varied programme of research including the ranking and weighting of various elements. Pilot research carried out by MORI on behalf of the LGC revealed this complexity and that, in particular, "the measurement of affective community was always going to be difficult and contentious." (Game, 1995, p 71). The Index was, therefore, "virtually abandoned at a distressingly early stage of its life" (Game, 1995, p 71).

In their progress report in December 1993, the LGC stated that it:

> ... had regard to the Index but instead of using it as a weighting/ranking system as a proxy for peoples' opinions, has preferred to go directly to local people for a measure of their own preferences. (LGC, 1993, p 1)

The LGC has subsequently relied on opinion polling conducted in two phases for its assessment of community identity. First, before issuing initial recommendations, a sample of the public in each review area was asked what they thought was important in determining local government structure and their level of contact with district and county councils. In addition, they were asked how strongly they felt they belonged to their neighbourhood village, the nearest town and the areas of the district and county councils. Perhaps not surprisingly it was found that in parallel with the Redcliffe-Maud research that:

> Neither County Council areas nor District Council areas are the areas with which people

> generally associate most strongly. Particularly in rural areas, real communities are usually much smaller than either of them: towns and villages provide the focus for community loyalty and identity. (LGC, 1993, p 33)

Following this discovery the Commission thought that:

> The way ahead is to build upon the basic community building blocks in a way that, on the one hand, combines the need for the local authority to be seen as accessible and accountable and on the other hand the need to provide a firm basis for effective management and service provision. (LGC, 1993, p 34)

In some cases the recommended initial answer (eg, in Derbyshire) was a large unitary authority based upon a county council area with an 'enhanced' role for parish councils.

However, the second phase of the LGC's polling has involved specific questions about the desirability of various arrangements of local authority areas. These polls, which largely identified support for the status quo as opposed to the LGC's initial recommendations, have done much to provide some justification for the outcome in which the majority of shire England is to retain a two-tier system.

The LGC is correct to claim that it has undertaken a public consultation exercise "in a way quite unprecedented in any earlier review" (LGC, 1993, p 1). However, no clear perception of 'community' has been applied. Despite an initial effort in the direction of community opinion the LGC pursued a rather limited public consultation exercise and gave apparently scant recognition of many of the elements later included in the 'Community Index'. Many authorities appear to have been retained by default, including a number of district councils created in 1972.

The concept of 'community'

It is perhaps not surprising that neither Redcliffe-Maud nor Banham have put community at the forefront of their deliberations. The British tradition has been to take at best a one-sided approach to the concept. This approach forms the basis of what is essentially an instrumental attitude towards local government.

It would perhaps have been expecting too much for the respective LGCs to fully consider 'community'. As Plant (1974) points out the word is highly evaluative, and its description can be highly problematic. There are competing ideological standpoints which 'claim' community and, as Hill (1994) says, our idea of community is related to our stance on other aspects of life such as equality, liberty and fraternity. For example, 'community' could be seen in purely evaluative terms as a 'good thing', originating in an ideal state exemplified by the Greek polis and representing something which has intrinsic value. 'Community' in this sense is spiritual, often referred to in nostalgic terms as something which existed in a now lost world of, for example, the English rural village based around its communal green and thatched inn. Tonnies' concept of Gemeinschaft encapsulates this model of an organic society which lives and grows, having its basis in blood relationships and kinship and a unity of being which developed into unity within a locality and attachment to neighbourhood. For Tonnies, Gemeinschaft was natural, and could be described in terms of its existence. The 'modern world' and industrialisation are seen to have brought fragmentation and, in turn, a loss of personal contact and of community spirit. Community in this sense then is contrasted with Gesellschaft, the impersonality of large-scale organisation.

In contrast, classical liberal philosophy places emphasis upon rationalism. Societies are artificial creations representing the aggregation of individual self-interests. Locke's view was that societies exist to protect innate natural rights. Such an understanding leads to a contractual view of community which sees communities based upon individually agreed patterns of social and economic interaction. From this perspective communities will be constantly changing. Custom is replaced by freedom to associate and community could refer to a small locality, a more geographically widespread set of interactions such as shopping and travel-to-work areas or an association based upon a common interest. These elements are, in turn, represented in Tonnies' concept of Gesellschaft, a society based upon the city and brought about by the division of labour following industrialisation.

The tension between the 'spiritual' and 'contractual' interpretations of community must be reflected in deliberations over local government structure. The 'ideal' structure, as Tonnies argued, would encompass both elements (Stafford, 1994). However, this magical combination has proved elusive. As noted earlier, the usually small areas identified as having community spirit have been held to be inappropriate for the contractual purpose of delivering effective and efficient services. Sharpe identified this dilemma as making it "very difficult to evolve a consistent theoretical justification for Local Government that claims to bear some resemblance to actual practice" (Sharpe, 1970, p 159).

Bennett (1989) identifies conceptual and real communities, real communities being those which actually reflect the reality of interactions between people in modern society. Pointing to European examples where basic units of local government have been deemed to be too small for the delivery of services, Bennett sums up this position neatly by stating that "administrative obsolescence is an inevitable consequence of the rapid rate of economic and technological development" (1989, p 303) and that "economic evolution has washed across territorial administrative structure like a wave across a beach" (1989, p 39). Parry, Moyser and Day sum up the position, observing that:

> ... those who would see community as the ground on which a more participatory Britain can be built need first to convince their fellow citizens of its relevance to modern life.... (1992, p 344)

Community and British liberal values

It is not sufficient, however, to note that there has been a dilemma. The important implication for local government structure in Britain is that, in line with the growth of the administrative state, the emphasis has been placed upon the contractual view, in line with a Benthamite utilitarian philosophical tradition. An emphasis upon individualism and economic relationships has led to the acceptance of an instrumental view of local government maintaining that the institution serves a purpose rather than being of intrinsic value.

> The position of local government is ... governed
> by constitutional convention as well as by the
> simple fact that it derives its powers from
> Parliament.   It would, however, be wrong to
> assume that such convention amounts to or
> derives from any natural right for local
> government to exist. It is a convention based on
> and subject to, the contribution which local
> government can bring to good government.
> (Widdicombe, 1986, p 46)

The structure of local government can and should, therefore, change according to the prevailing patterns of economic interaction and the technological changes which affect service delivery. In addition, local government structure can be changed at any time in accordance with the prevailing view of the task at hand.   The British local government system is, therefore, a 'designer system' based upon a practical Chadwickian approach with administrative purpose rather than community at its core (Chandler, 1989a).

The growth in local government expenditure in the post-war years is, therefore, largely associated with the usefulness of local government as an administrative agent for the delivery of an expanded welfare state (see, for example, Rhodes, 1981). The call for reform leading to the establishment of the Redcliffe-Maud Commission was largely founded on the belief that many councils were too small for effective and efficient delivery of such services. Further, the large number of small authorities were held to make the planning and coordination of service delivery difficult and, in particular, it was felt that certain services such as the delivery of education services or strategic land use and transportation planning, required extensively populated geographical areas. These views were largely upheld by the LGC, and partly by the government, although, as has already been noted, for party political reasons the Conservatives in 1972 could not contemplate the abolition of the 'shire' counties and their replacement with the large unitary authorities recommended by the LGC.

The local government reform processes of the 1960s and 1970s took place in an 'end of ideology' culture in which neither of the major parties differed on the need for government intervention in a mixed economy welfare state that had to be founded on large, well-resourced but centrally supervised agencies capable of gaining competitive advantage through the marshalling of economies of scale. The arguments put in favour of economies of scale and of the need for coordination and strategic planning was very much in line with the corporatism prevalent in the economy at this time. The mood is reflected in the recommendations of the Bains Committee (1972) on the internal management of the new authorities, which stressed the advantages of corporate planning systems and the application of more 'rational' management systems.

In contrast to the early 1970s reform, the Banham Commission was established within a political culture that appears to have shed consensus and the values of the mixed economy welfare state in favour of government withdrawal from economic controls to facilitate economic growth through market competition. To draw local government into this framework, the Thatcher administrations developed and applied the concept of the 'enabling' authority and were little concerned with local government's role in strategic planning and delivery of welfare services. In its policy guidance to the Banham Commission the government actively promoted the virtue of contracting out service delivery, and of weakening local government's role in the 'strategic' services of land use and transportation planning. In addition, technological changes, and particularly the growth in the application of information technology had made possible a more flexible response to service delivery, with decentralisation and flexibility the key elements. The language of Bains had been exchanged for the language of Peters and Waterman.

These changes, in theory, developed a scenario in which the formation of many smaller unitary authorities became possible. The application of public choice theory by United States conservatives has been important in rolling back the bandwagon of the 1960s and 1970s that was promoting reconstruction of local government along British lines. Tiebout's (1956) seminal paper on the capacity of ratepayers mobility to restrain bureaucratic growth and inefficiency within an area covered by many small authorities has been highly influential. Later writers such as Ostrom, Bish and Ostrom (1988) have argued on public choice grounds that a pattern of small, irregularly sized, overlapping functionally based authorities can secure the optimum efficiency in service delivery alongside a sense of community demonstrated by popular participation in local decision making.

None of these values were, however, taken on board by the ostensibly new-right British governments.   As in 1972, the outcome of the review process reflects a belief that a pattern of large unitary authorities would be the preferable arrangement. This conclusion may not, as in 1972, be as strongly favoured through adherence to ideas on the economies of scale but it clearly still retains earlier concerns about the convenience to the centre of having a smaller number of easily monitored and regulated local authorities.   Following the battles with local government in the early 1980s the Major governments are not likely to welcome a network of local authorities that are much more complex to resource and control.   In conformity with Gamble's (1994) depiction of the paradox in Thatcherism, whilst the requirement on local authorities to adopt an enabling role through, for example, compulsory competitive tendering, forces respect for the 'free economy', the Conservatives demand for ever tighter controls over local government, reinforces 'the strong state'.

The common ground

In one important respect the restructuring of the 1990s does, however, resemble the early 1970s in that it owes much to political expediency with the government being unwilling to contemplate change in the, for them, more party politically sensitive rural shire areas.   The fact that there were not seen to be such problems in Wales and Scotland serves to underline this point.

It would, of course, be foolish to expect reviews of the structures and administrative boundaries of an elected tier of government to be free of considerations of party political advantage.   However, the debate concerning structure in each review process has been couched in terms of producing a local government which is 'suited to the times'.   The emphasis has been upon attempting to map changed patterns of economic and social interaction and creating boundaries which are congruent with the prevalent technical requirements for service delivery.   The Redcliffe-Maud Commission was clear that local government boundaries needed to reflect the new patterns of interaction brought about particularly by changes in personal mobility and transportation evidenced in travel-to-work and shopping patterns, and that the growth in importance of urban centres had to be recognised.

The task was, therefore, essentially a technical one, including the mapping of what Bennett (1989, p 34) has called 'activity spaces'. For Bennett the ideal would be to have such spaces matched by administrative boundaries, to make them 'truly bounded' and problems are caused either by under or over bounding. Local government structure, then, becomes an issue of spatial economic development. Bours (1989) sees the question being one of 'administrative geography' and of the need to recognise 'spatial policy science' as being useful in seeking congruity between spatial and administrative organisation. To aid the search for such congruity, Bennett (1989) draws upon three stages of spatial economic development:

- Urbanisation, which brings problems of coordination and integration.

- Sub-urbanisation, which brings similar problems but over a wider geographical area.

- Counter-urbanisation, representing a post-industrial society in which technology allows geographic dispersal. In this later stage, local administration may be secured through small units, or, indeed may bypass local units altogether and be fully decentralised to points closer to the consumer.

While Redcliffe-Maud was concerned both with urbanisation and sub-urbanisation, Banham has been concerned with trying to match the new post-industrial environment to suitable administrative units. The answer here, however, is less straightforward and the LGC has in various reports argued both for the benefits of smallness and flexibility and of scale for strategic service delivery. Bennett (1989, p 78) argues that the appropriate response is 'flexible decentralisation' together with 'flexible aggregation', the joining together of small units as and when necessary for specific tasks.

In contrast, British local government has been organised for administrative convenience, with a relatively unified pattern of the population size of each local authority across the tiers. This contrasts with the wide variety of local authority populations found, for example, in the United States or France. A unified clear-cut local authority map makes control and monitoring by central government departments easier. A large number of small authorities would make this task complex, while authorities which were too large may pose a threat to the centre. The design of the system is thus suitable for central administrative elites (Chandler, 1989a). This approach has, in turn, mitigated against the consideration of the full complexity of the nature of 'community' and the recognition that several tiers of local government may be necessary to accommodate varying interpretations. Chandler (1989a) has pointed out that people's perceptions of relevant community may vary according to the administrative function/service that they are considering. A small Gemeinschaft community may be fine for some areas and some functions while others may need a larger area both geographically and in terms of population, and a different interpretation of community. Asking people where they 'feel at home' or what they think about certain reform options can only scratch the surface of this complexity.

A liberal alternative

Centralisation and the resultant eclipse of the values of community is, however, a peculiarly British disease. Within other liberal polities, and in particular the United States, an alternative liberal ideology can secure continued respect for the integrity and value of the community alongside a liberal emphasis on the value of individual liberty.

This position is most clearly developed in the ideas of de Tocqueville, who like the Federalists a generation earlier, perceived that the greatest threat to individual liberty lay not so much in the restraints of single individuals against one another but in the repression that would result from an unfettered central government controlled by an individual or small oligarchy. Individuals, argued de Tocqueville, need some form of joint governance to act together to develop commonly held goods and services, but these common goods should be established and governed solely by the group that benefit from these services. Thus, for the provision of, for example, minor roads, local policing or social services, only the members of a community directly contributing to and benefiting from these services should control those services. Where the community was of sufficiently small size its government should be through direct participative democracy so that each contributor to its policies could best be able to maximise their individual interest in its operation.

De Tocqueville found such a political arrangement in the townships of New England where all citizens of a community can assemble to approve legislation and the appointment of officers for the town.

> The native of New England is attached to his township because it is independent and free: his cooperation in its affairs ensures his attachment to its interests.... He takes a part in every occurrence in the place; he practices the art of government in the small sphere within his reach, he accustoms himself to those forms without which liberty can only be advanced by revolutions.... (de Tocqueville, 1963, vol 1, p 68)

Issues that affected more than a single township had to be governed by the representative government of the state or at an even higher level of national defence and foreign and commercial relationships, the federal government. The values underlying such a decentralised system of government aided by constitutional safeguards ensured that the higher levels of government did not encroach on matters that affected predominantly a particular community. Through such an arrangement the community can provide its own services while safeguarding the freedom of the individual by ensuring each person in the community can jointly determine the policies that affect them and, through ensuring that matters affecting the community are only dealt with by its members, minimising interference from those outside the community.

The ideas expressed by de Tocqueville reflect a concern for the idea of community that is widely reflected in the values of several earlier and later continental European and United States theorists. Rousseau's vision of a democratic community government based on the notion of consensus expressed as the General Will is made a more practical reality in de Tocqueville's analysis of the United States. In recent years this view is also echoed in Dahl's (1967) depiction of the United States polity as a series of Chinese boxes with smaller community governments determining the decisions confined within their walls being enclosed by larger boxes representing wider communities. The concept of subsidiarity as perceived by the European Commission, as opposed to the expedience of national interest espoused by the then Prime Minister John Major, similarly reflects the view that individual liberty can be best reconciled with the need for efficient communal action by passing power down to the lower strata of government that is capable of effectively determining and implementing particular policies.

British centralism

Despite the influential tradition in the United States of reconciling the freedom of the individual with the need for communal action through the process of the separation of the powers and pluralism, British political theory remained, in line with its political elites, increasingly inclined towards a centralist position (Chandler, 1989a). This tendency did not derive from any lack of familiarity with pluralist thought. Mill was familiar with the views of de Tocqueville and from his writings it is possible to build a defence of local government based upon individual freedom and the tendency for humans to form communal associations. In his essay 'On liberty' Mill recognised that individual freedom, "implies a corresponding liberty in any number of individuals to regulate such things as regards them jointly..." (1975a, p 125). Mill's most basic defence of local government in his essay concerning 'Representative government', argues,

> ... that those who have any ideas in common, which they do not share with the general body of their countrymen may manage the joint enterprise by themselves. (1975b, p 368)

Individual liberty, therefore, is here consistent with the perceived need for common activity. The classic 'liberal dilemma', however, is to determine what the limits on individual liberty are once the necessity for common action has been determined. Mill, like de Tocqueville, appears to believe that this problem is best resolved by ensuring that individual liberty would be maximised through governments covering the smallest practicable community so as to ensure that although everyone can participate in decisions this power is given to as few individuals or groups as is possible. This would enable each person to participate in joint activities to the maximum extent.

While Mill built an intellectual framework for justifying community governments based on several tiers each appropriate to the needs of differing groups for differing functions, he cast the logic of his ideas to one side and concluded in his essay on 'Representative government' that:

> The authority which is most conversant with principles should be supreme over principles, while that which is most competent in details should have the details left to it. The principle business of the central authority should be to give instruction, of the local authority to apply it. (1975b, p 377)

Although willing to allow communities some discretion over local matters, Mill did not sufficiently trust the wisdom of the community to allow localities a measure of sovereignty on parochial matters. This reluctance to follow the logic of his earlier argument reflected values that were strongly engrained in the battles being waged by the emergent British Liberals in the first half of the 19th century and had been intellectually expressed by Mill's utilitarian mentor Jeremy Bentham. The ideal state for Bentham was based on a representative parliament at the national level which would best express the policies necessary to secure 'the greatest happiness for the greatest number'. Differing local views would represent geographically particularist interests seeking to benefit a small section of society rather than the whole. Thus, where differences arose localities must be subordinate to the sovereignty of parliament, and hence local decision making, for Benthan, was to be through a system of devolved administration rather than government.

The generation and support for this position had important political roots. The barrier to economic progress for early 19th-century radicals in Britain was the landowning class who dominated parliament. Their position was secured by their hold on local political life and, through this, the capacity to gain entry to parliament. As Justices of the Peace, landowners controlled the parish governments through the supervisory role assigned to the civil procedures of the Courts of Quarter Sessions and more generally through the deference landowners could exact from the tenant farmers and landless labourers. Such influence ensured that in rural areas and small towns local government followed the values of landowning interests. In many larger towns and cities new manufacturing could also be politically subordinated either to landowners' control over the local government system or to the power of self-selecting guilds of local craftsmen and artisans who had, through traditional rights, secured control of many chartered boroughs.

British liberals considered that they had to remove these interests from control of local politics if local community action was ever going to advance the progress of industrial development. Such action could only be accomplished by centralising legislation from a liberal parliament and was secured, in part, after the 1832 electoral Reform Act that placed liberal values securely in Westminster. The 1834 Poor Law Reform Act began a process of translating powers held by the parishes to the inspection and manipulation of central government, thus undermining the influence of landed interests operating through the Quarter Sessions. Within the larger industrialising cities the 1835 Municipal Corporations Act was designed to ensure liberal interests took control of these centres for economic growth and could, therefore, gain greater autonomy. Until the 1920s the larger cities, through private acts secured with the agreement of parliament, were, consequently, able to generate considerable independence from the centre. However, the emergence of the Labour Party in municipal politics led to Parliament, by the 1920s, withdrawing its consent to all but the most minor local acts (Keith-Lucas and Richards, 1978, pp 39-40).

A spirited Tory defence of the traditional system of parish government did nothing to alleviate liberal suspicions of the dangers to progress inherent in the idea of community. The lawyer and campaigner on behalf of the parish, Toulmin Smith, defended the traditional structures on the basis of a romanticised notion of community based on the values of deference and order. A later, more sophisticated, defence of a community established on a hierarchy of deference towards respected traditional leaders was popularised by Gneist late in the 19th Century and became the central issue to be challenged by Redlich and Hirst (1903, pp 380-418) in their powerful but strongly liberal defence of the restructured system of local government in Britain.

The political concern of early British liberals to restructure local government so as to remove landed Tory or unreformed Whig domination of local politics, therefore, brought a serious suspicion of the motives and competence of local politicians into a British constitution being reformed under primarily liberal principles. Outside the large cities local politics was seen as being based on conservative narrow-minded interests that were inimical to progress. Community was, consequently, seen as a reactionary inward-looking force permitting powerful local notables to dominate more progressive individuals as opposed to serving as a means for securing individual freedom and liberty.

The attitudes developed during the 19th century towards community remain as part of the largely unquestioned assumptions of elite British political culture today. Both recent local government reform commissions have, as a consequence, been incapable of grappling with the full complexity of 'community' and have given it so little weight that it has been easy both for them and the government to dismiss this awkward concept. The utilitarian approach has led to less emphasis being placed upon the spiritual elements of community and has, therefore, enhanced the instrumental element leaving local government with a weak foundation (Chandler, 1995). In contrast to established values towards local government in the United States or western Europe this has made it easier in Britain for central government to erode local autonomy.

Local government in Britain is not recognised as having a right to exist. Vincent and Plant (1984) refer to 'mechanical' and 'moral' forms of organisation: mechanical associations emphasise the importance of the distribution of economic resources and are typified by bureaucracy, rules, rights and entitlements; moral organisation on the other hand requires membership, altruism and spirit. The British administrative tradition is to have a 'mechanistic' approach. However, any review which is serious about the value of local government to democratic governance could and should refer to a wider range of arguments and philosophical standpoints. An alternative view of community is one such means by which the status of local government could be justifiably enhanced.

Conclusion

The acceptance of an alternative justification for local government to the one established by the British administrative tradition would have led both reviews along different paths and required them to give more attention to different questions. Rather than seeking an elusive match between various economic and social indicators and the technological requirements of service delivery, we could instead have followed Dahl (1967, p 959) and thought about:

> ... appropriate units of democracy as an ascending series, a set of Chinese boxes each larger and more inclusive than the other, each in some sense democratic though not always in the same sense, and each not inherently less nor inherently more legitimate than the other. (Parry, Moyser and Day, 1992)

Such a standpoint would lead us to spend more time debating which services are best allocated to which level of government. Why should our starting point not be that of trying to facilitate participation as much as possible, for example? Work by Parry, Moyser and Day (1992) revealed little evidence to support the view that a strong sense of local identity and community spirit leads to greater participation. However, similarly, research has shown that the connection between local authority size and efficiency in service delivery is also tenuous. If successive reviews had taken as their starting point the belief that individual freedom is best enhanced by devolving power to the smallest group possible to recognise mutual interests, the British local government map would look considerably different to the one which now exists.

Part Four

Community, participation and empowerment

ten

Community networking: developing strength through diversity

Alison Gilchrist and Marilyn Taylor

"Only connect", wrote E.M. Forster. He was referring to power and passion as the driving forces of life and the malaise experienced by many people in the contemporary society described in Howard's End. This concern is echoed in current attempts to revive notions of 'community' and mutual responsibility. Communitarians on both left and right conjure up an ideal community, based on traditional values of cooperation and family duty. Society, however, has developed a more kaleidoscopic feel, characterised by diversity and difference, fragmentation, discontinuity and individualism.

It is arguable that for the most marginalised groups in our society, it is social disintegration and powerlessness rather than social cohesion that characterise their everyday interactions. For many years, community work has sought to reverse this experience by developing organisational and political capacity in such areas. The emphasis has been on breaking down isolation and building 'community capacity' as a vehicle for both giving communities a voice and developing self-help activities. In this era of measurable outcomes, the number and sustainability of self-help and voluntary organisations is increasingly recognised as a performance measure in community development and regeneration initiatives (Community Development Foundation [CDF], 1995). But this paper argues that fostering and developing informal links and associations is just as vital – indeed, that they are the mesh in which organisational capacity must be embedded if it is to be both sustainable and responsive to the diversity and tensions that characterise most 'real-life' communities.

What are the skills needed to develop such networks? And what are their strengths and weaknesses? This chapter reflects on the process of mobilising a city-wide network against racism in Bristol and the lessons that it has for networking as a way of enhancing the power of marginalised communities to take action. It explores how a 'community of resistance' might be developed whereby links are formed and strengthened between individuals in ways which enable, encourage and empower them to work together to achieve shared aspirations or resist a common threat. A network is defined as a pattern of actual and potential connections between people, based partly on their formal organisational roles and partly on informal relationships arising from friendship, shared interests, joint affiliation and simple acquaintance. Networks are seen as larger and more complex types of organisation than a simple cluster of individuals. Nevertheless they are less formally structured than a voluntary association or constituted organisation. Networking refers to those activities by which links between people are established, cultivated and activated for specific purposes. It is an active process of making and maintaining contacts, which can range from the deliberate targeting of a key individual, through the art of 'being in the right place at the right time', to the serendipitous encounters and conversations which throw up unexpected, but useful connections (for a more detailed discussion, see Gilchrist, 1995).

The organisation of the Festival Against Racism

The idea of the Festival Against Racism (FAR) was developed by the Bristol Anti-Racist Alliance (ARA). ARA wished to find a way of overcoming the fragmentation of anti-racist work across the city in order to promote anti-racism as mainstream 'common sense', rather than as a marginal or specialist activity. The aim of the Festival was to embed anti-racism into the lives of ordinary citizens and the policies and practices of Bristol's civic institutions. Four central motifs were chosen which encapsulated the basic principles of anti-racist work espoused by the Alliance, namely: *Equality*, *Justice*, *Diversity* and *Solidarity*. The Festival was designed, first, to provide opportunities for people throughout Bristol to become involved in some kind of anti-racist activity in their local communities or workplaces, for example. Second, it was seen as a way of crystallising visible signs of anti-racist commitment from the solution of the local civil society. Third, it offered an opportunity for people to develop working relationships with other organisations, without getting into formal contractual arrangements or ideological disagreements.

The Festival offered a framework within which any organisation or group who subscribed to these basic values and principles could participate. The intention was to offer a kind of "freedom within boundaries" (Hoggett, 1991), which would enable people to take part on their own terms in a collective and multi-faceted assertion that 'racism is wrong'. The Festival was a means of making anti-racist activities normal, respectable, accessible and fun.

After an initial period of informal consultation and a cautiously enthusiastic public meeting, a leaflet was produced and widely circulated. This set out the key aims of the Festival, inviting participation and sponsorship. The main responsibility for coordinating the Festival fell to two volunteers, who were supported in this role by a notional steering group, a small fund-raising committee and informal contact with a few close allies. Fortnightly meetings took place, which were widely publicised and open to anyone interested in contributing to the Festival. These offered the opportunity for democratic decision making and accountability, but in practice they were poorly attended and most of the key policy and organisational decisions were taken by the central organisers, usually after informal discussions between themselves and others who were close to the core group.

The absence of any formal management structure, along with pressures of time and the lack of administrative facilities meant that the organising strategy which emerged for the Festival made substantial and explicit use of informal connections and opportunities. From the outset, the main resource for the Festival consisted of an extensive and rich web of contacts, spanning the labour movement, 'left' and progressive movements, the local music scene and much of the city's community and youth work sectors. These had been garnered by the organisers over years of professional and political involvement in various organisations and projects and allowed the Festival to draw on facilities, materials and energy beyond the immediate resources of the organising cluster. The organisers' track record and reputations meant that many people were prepared to trust the concept of the Festival and, despite some reservations about its 'white' origins, to associate themselves with the idea publicly. Knowledge of local networks also allowed the organisers to hook into more formal coalitions and umbrella bodies to reach potential sponsors and participants with whom they had no previous direct contact.

Over several weeks of intensive networking, media publicity, lobbying and follow-up administration, the core group was able to draw up a programme of over a hundred events and activities, lasting some six weeks. Participating organisations were drawn from key areas of Bristol's civil society – political groups, community and youth organisations, trade unions, religious bodies, schools, some statutory services and even a few commercial firms.

The programme itself not only gave information about the different events, it provided a directory of anti-racist organisations and opportunities for many local organisations and businesses to endorse the spirit of the Festival through adverts publicising their own commitment to anti-racism. The programme represents one of the most significant outputs of the Festival, the tangible evidence of a local, if somewhat ephemeral anti-racist movement.

The significance of networking as a method of organising

The use of networks represented a practical response to the specific circumstances of ARA's task, in particular the problem of limited resources dispersed over a wider range of agencies, but it also had a more fundamental philosophical rationale. The Festival aimed to create and strengthen connections between people around the specific issue of anti-racism. It used the four motifs of Equality, Justice, Diversity and Solidarity to mobilise people and resources around a basic consensus that racial discrimination would not be tolerated in the lives of Bristol citizens. The aim was to develop an active and visible solidarity between those who experienced racism directly (predominantly the members of minority ethnic groupings) and those who were angered or ashamed by racist behaviour and attitudes. The intention was to construct (Cohen, 1985) a 'community of resistance' around racism, which would endure beyond the period of the Festival itself. The basic philosophy behind this approach was that anti-racism should not be seen as the responsibility of Black people, nor the preserve of experts or 'race relations' professionals, but a basic unifying value underpinning the whole 'civic community'.

As such, the medium of the Festival was to be a crucial part of the message: that racial equality and cultural diversity should be woven into the fabric of everyday life and become the normal expectation for all citizens. In this respect the process of contacting people and making links between organisations became as important as the Festival itself. An open, enabling structure was needed emphasising possibilities of participation and collaboration, which people could determine for themselves in the light of their own circumstances and ideological inclinations.

The 'do-it-yourself' nature of the Festival was designed to promote a sense of individual and collective responsibility. It was up to 'ordinary' people to develop their own ways of tackling racism within the normal course of their lives. It created an opportunity for people to express their opposition to racism in whatever ways they found appropriate and accessible. The fragmentation and 'territorial' disputes which had become a feature of 'race relations' over recent years were avoided by discouraging any sense of 'political correctness' around anti-racism, and ensuring instead an atmosphere of constructive debate and cooperation.

The format of a six-week long programme of activities allowed high levels of participation and enormous diversity. Furthermore, it was able to accommodate difference and disagreements, because nothing more was required beyond a willingness to associate with the aims and values clearly stated in all the publicity material. Taking part involved simply organising an event or activity around the theme of anti-racism, however unambitious, and making sure the information was available to be included in the programme.

People were invited to contribute in all manner of means. Most organisations received the official leaflet or read about the Festival in the local press or community mailings. In addition, hundreds of individuals were approached informally to encourage them to contribute an activity or to volunteer for a particular task. The use of personal connections had the additional advantage of allowing people in relatively powerful positions to give a personal indication of support, without prematurely risking the status and credibility of the organisation they represented. It also allowed the resources of other agencies to be diverted to assist the organisation of the Festival. This might occur explicitly through a sponsorship or secondment, but it also happened through donations in kind and voluntary gifts of time, expertise and influence. The whole initiative carried a high element of uncertainty – the politics were controversial and the practicalities of such an ambitious project had been only briefly sketched out. The use of informal networks allowed that initial risk to be distributed across a wider range of stakeholders than just the core organisers.

Nonetheless, the ways in which contacts were made through existing links and relationships to persuade people to become involved, inevitably gave rise to a network that was focused on the specific identities of the core group members. Many of the links that were created and used in the organisation of the Festival relied on the personal biographies, circumstances and characteristics of the organisers, rather than their formal, organisational roles. These idiosyncratic ingredients gave the Festival a distinct 'flavour' and ideological bias. The demands of organisation similarly meant that resources tended to flow towards the administrative centre. This trend could have become highly controlling, by creating a powerful centralised hub, with spokes radiating out instructions to the participants on the periphery. Whilst this model evolved to some extent, it was counterbalanced by the existence of formal and informal mechanisms by which participants could influence core decision making.

Furthermore, deliberate efforts were made to set up horizontal links between participating organisations, to support joint initiatives and foster greater awareness between participants of the range of people and projects committed to anti-racism. The development of horizontal, vertical and cross-cutting links between different sectors and levels of Bristol's civil society was seen as contributing to the longer term development of a local movement against racism. It was hoped that the experience of working together would contribute to the building of longer term alliances. In turn this would lead to the eventual development of a 'community of resistance'; an awareness and sense of belonging to a network of allies, who share a common cause.

Creating links with higher status organisations was crucial to this longer term objective. A deliberate strategy adopted in the initial stages of planning the Festival was to seek the sponsorship of key voluntary sector bodies, such as the Race Equality Forum, the local trades union council, and major Black and minority ethnic organisations. This had two important objectives. First, it would demonstrate that the Festival had support from people in significant leadership positions and open up channels of communication to wider constituencies. This endorsement gave the Festival its initial status and credibility, and opened up access to much needed resources. Second, it enabled the Festival to build a model of social partnership and alliance, which has been crucial in planning subsequent actions, including the most recent Festival in 1996. By connecting the Festival networks into key local power structures, and emphasising the more durable and overarching bonds born of common citizenship within a particular locality, the long-term aim was to create a 'civic community' with the thicker and multi-layered ties that are required for 'strong' rather than 'thin' democracy (Barber, 1984). While the web of interlocking networks was fragile, consisting of many 'weak ties' (Granovetter, 1973) the hope was that it could be sustained from a sufficient number of strong links in the civic community to give it status, energy, credibility and a degree of resilience.

Networking and community development

Community development offers a strategy for professional intervention in social and political processes. The Festival organisers drew on core values of community development – self-determination, participation, empowerment and inclusion. The philosophical rationale behind the Festival echoed that of community development in its concern to enable people from marginalised or oppressed sections of society to influence decisions which affect their lives and to develop their own solutions to common problems.

How does the practice of networking relate to community development? It is possible to see networks as opening up 'circuits of power' (Clegg, 1989). By mobilising the "web of networks submerged in everyday life" (Melucci, 1988, p 248), networking can be seen as reconnecting circuits which have been in disrepair. Without such circuits, activities and events are difficult to mobilise (much as appliances have to be plugged into an electrical circuit if they are to work), but with them, things can start to happen. However, an isolated circuit is not enough on its own, and another step is needed if reactivated circuits are not to become just one more circuit to jostle alongside others in an increasingly fragmented world and with limited shelf-life (see Clegg, 1989, p 274). Networking also, crucially, needs to throw the switches which connect disused circuits into what Clegg defines as the more 'privileged pathways', both formal and informal, which supply the power and link in with the more sustainable reserves of power.

The metaphor of circuits of power is useful in the case of community development for a number of reasons. First, it reminds us of the centrality to community development of issues of power and empowerment. Second, it sees power as something which flows, rather than as a finite entity which is held by one party and will be diminished if it is given away. It highlights the importance of creating channels through which power can flow. Third, it offers a way of tackling different kinds of power. Contemporary theorists argue that power works not just in the overt exercise of power over another agent, but also through creating the agendas and rules of engagement within which we see the world and the way things are, through the unquestioning internalisation of values and ideologies (Lukes, 1974; Foucault, 1977; Clegg, 1989). Of particular relevance in this respect is Clegg's 'circuit of social integration' which is conceptualised in terms of rules that fix relationships of meanings and membership (Clegg, 1989).

The Festival can be seen as an illustration of a more general community work approach, whereby specific projects (events, trips, groups) are organised as important activities in their own right but which also act as vehicles for the development of individual and collective capacity. The creation of overlapping networks within the community, which are also 'plugged in' to sources of power, resources and information, is a key strategy for community development and one which has been neglected in recent years (Thomas, 1995). It can be argued that the Festival allowed an alternative set of views of 'the way things are' to surface by making visible, to use Melucci's terms (1988), existing links and shared beliefs through many different voices and media, giving people the opportunity to celebrate their differences within a common stand against racial discrimination. The pluralist nature of the network is able to accommodate different approaches without risking factionalism or splintering, for example, in the Festival's case, the related but different discourses of anti-racism and multi-culturalism (see Cain and Yuval-Davis, 1990).

However, networking is not without its problems. So far, we have portrayed networks largely as a positive and efficient form of organisation, offering opportunities to develop trust over a wide set of people, with loose links that encourage a sense of commonality, while encompassing diversity. But networks can also be exclusive and oppressive, blocking rather freeing up power. They can be secretive and unaccountable rather than being informed by their surrounding communities and they can be extremely unstable (Taylor and Hoggett, 1994). Three particular issues therefore need to be addressed if they are to open up new circuits of power rather than reinforcing existing ones: access and inclusion; accountability; and sustainability.

Access and inclusion

It would be easy to read into the informal, opportunistic nature of a network an assumption that little active development and maintenance has to be done. If networks are to be a tool for community cohesion rather than exclusion, then little can be left to chance. Otherwise networks would simply reproduce (indeed reinforce) prevailing inequalities and social fractures. The Festival attempted to address these issues through a four-fold strategy:

- information and communication: active extension of the network, broadcasting the message far and wide;

- providing formal opportunities for people to become involved in the planning of the Festival through regular open meetings;

- offering incentives to make the Festival accessible to all through grants for disabled access and other positive action measures;

- dispersing responsibility for the delivery of the Festival activities.

In urban regeneration, MacFarlane (1993) and Skelcher, McCabe and Lowndes (1996) suggest that community empowerment does not depend only on membership of strategic planning groups. Continuing involvement and informal contact with other participants is a crucial factor. For many, responsibility for the planning and delivery of specific projects is a more significant route to empowerment – more direct, more clearly bounded, and simply more fun. Active participation and dispersal of responsibility was inherent in the nature of the Festival itself. The responsibility of the organisers was to develop and promote the framework within which a range of actions could take place – and to ensure that information was spread as widely as possible in order to maximise the number of people who could take part. The delivery of the programme depended crucially on the willingness of a large number of people to put on events. The Festival simply would not have happened without them. In these circumstances it is perhaps of less significance that few people took the opportunity to be involved in the formal planning of the Festival and that the bulk of this fell onto the shoulders of the core group. This could be compared with the Festival held in 1996 – a music festival held over a day (with high profile performers), where the opportunity to take part was largely confined to attending on that one day, meaning that most people were passive rather than active participants. The potential of a network to spread power and organisational capacity can therefore be said to depend partly on the nature of the activities in which members can be involved and the extent to which key organisers are linked into other constituencies.

Accountability

Whatever its purpose, if the planning and administration of the network falls on few people, accountability becomes a crucial issue. Can networks be made accountable without unduly formalising them? Day and Klein (1987) argue that accountability implies both a shared set of expectations and a common currency of justification. The underlying values of the Festival – Equality, Justice, Diversity and Solidarity – provided the political and ethical frameworks, while the main aims were featured in all communications and publicity material.

Accountability also requires transparency. The ongoing face-to-face nature of much of the continuing contact work that was needed to keep the show on the road would have afforded many informal opportunities for participants to check out what was going on. Indeed Day and Klein (1987) also argue the growth of more formal systems of accountability is essentially a response to the disappearance of more informal, face-to-face opportunities to keep in touch with what is going on in contemporary society. But the happenstance of informal contacts can still be exclusive. More formal accounts are needed, like the sporadic 'update' bulletins sent to participating organisations, alongside regular verbal reports to the major sponsoring agencies.

Providing a loose framework and 'giving an account', while necessary, are still not sufficient. Two other ingredients were used by FAR to increase accountability: first, early consultations which allowed the organisers to 'take into account' the views of others; second, an evaluation carried out after the event to allow feedback from participants which was then written up into a report for funders and others. As we have already seen, the opportunity was there for people to come to meetings, to hear or question what was going on and contribute ideas. But few people took this up, preferring to invest their limited time and energy on getting on with organising their own Festival events. This is an important reminder of the limitations of formal meetings as a mechanism for accountability and an example of one of the major tensions inherent in networking as a form of organisation. Clearly one of the advantages of a network is its informality and dependence on too many formal mechanisms will surely change it into something else.

Leat (1988) has distinguished between responsive accountability, explanatory accountability and accountability with sanctions. While much of the accountability of the organisers was responsive, depending on their professional and democratic principles of giving an account. The sponsors clearly had a right to expect explanatory accountability, which they got through both regular reports and the final evaluation. It could also be argued that the dispersal of responsibility for organising Festival events ensured a degree of accountability with sanctions. If participants were not happy with the way the Festival was being organised, they could simply 'opt out' or 'exit' (Hirschmann, 1970). Clearly this option would be a more powerful weapon in some hands than others, and its effectiveness would also depend on how many were prepared to exercise this sanction. With this in mind, the organisers made considerable efforts to persuade, reassure and even 'chivvy' to ensure the active involvement of certain key organisations.

Sustainability

Networking offers a valuable means of organising at certain points and for some purposes. Networks can be seen as flexible and adaptable forms of organisation and empowerment, which are suitable for circumstances requiring broad participation, speed and innovation (see Powell, 1990). But loading too much onto these circuits may cause the fuse to blow. They are not an appropriate vehicle for sustained formal activity or service delivery. The responsibilities of internal democracy, management of resources and external accountabilities require more formal structures, especially where conflicts of interest or policy disagreements are likely to arise.

Without formal roles, decision-making mechanisms and procedures, networks are more vulnerable than other organisational forms to cyclical involvement, to shifting allegiances, loss of interest and changing circumstances. Inactivity, and the resultant loss of contact, will lead the circuits of power that have been created to deteriorate as connections become corroded, or people move into new relationships, ventures and interests. If networks are to survive, they need some form of sustaining activity to keep them afloat between peaks of interest (Milofsky and Hunter, 1994). But sustaining activity requires more resources and increasing formalisation and may lead to its aims being taken over or distorted by an elite (see Tarrow, 1994 for a discussion of the impact of formalisation on social movements). If this happens, it is likely to be more difficult either to mobilise the wider network or for its wider membership to benefit.

Milofsky and Hunter (1994), in developing theories of voluntary and community action, suggest there is a middle ground. They have developed the concept of 'background communities' to describe how networks feed into more formal activities and organisations. They describe these background communities as loose informal alliances that throw up formally organised coalitions when informal associational processes cannot get a task done. Through the numerous 'junction points' and 'organisational intelligence' that these networks offer, they store individual and organisational capacity that can be drawn on when needed for specific purposes. Every foray into a more formally organised activity brings more experience into the background community, even if specific activities represent very disparate and even conflicting interests. Background communities also act as a 'Greek chorus', offering feedback on more formal activities and organisations and, in that sense, have a role in holding more formal organisations to account.

In this formulation, the task of the community worker becomes focused not on the survival of particular organisations per se, but on the development of capacity within the whole community. This requires:

- building overlapping networks, based on thick and varied links between people and offering a variety of access points;

- encouraging the organisation of 'events' which make networks visible, reinforce links and give people a sense of common identity;

- switching neighbourhood-based networks into more influential and better resourced circuits – throwing the switches that allow power to flow into marginalised communities;

- ensuring that expertise gained through specific actions flows back into the community at large and is translated into the capacity to respond to further needs and opportunities;

- ensuring that information flows in and out of networks and that more formal activities exercise responsive accountability to 'background communities' and take their views and experience into account.

Conclusion

The arguments presented here draw on a model of power which sees it as residing in the relationships between people and their organisations. Networking not only has the potential to change the dynamic equilibrium within these relationships, but also opens up access to new circuits of power, which can benefit (empower) all concerned. The Festival was a deliberate attempt to develop a network which could both challenge power relationships in Bristol and change the beliefs and attitudes around which power and opportunities are structured. The network strategy for organising the Festival was an efficient and effective mechanism for mobilising and strengthening a 'community of resistance' to racism in Bristol.

The success of the Festival must ultimately be judged in three ways. First, has a circuit of power been activated in a way that gives groupings across the network the contacts and confidence they need to pursue their diverse interests within a broad alliance? Second, has the alternative 'way of seeing things' that the Festival sought to promote been sustained and reflected in changed practice? Third, have the goals of the Festival become part of a civic community in Bristol which is active in combating the racism in its midst and celebrating its own diversity?

Participation in the Festival was experienced as empowering by those who organised events. Many others took part in the activities or helped distribute publicity materials. The positive momentum generated by the Festival has left behind a legacy of increased confidence amongst individuals, a heightened sense of belonging, greater trust and knowledge amongst potential allies, and a more public commitment from many organisations that they are prepared to take up and challenge issues of racism. People felt linked into a larger initiative which drew in power from other sources and which reduced the anxiety and isolation felt by many in their attempts at anti-racist work.

No evaluation has been carried out of the extent to which networks built during the 1994 Festival were sustained. No Festival took place in 1995, but a different kind of festival was mounted, as we have seen, in 1996. How far this drew on and strengthened similar networks might be one measure of the success of the 1994 initiative.

But the success of the networking activity that went into the 1994 Festival Against Racism has to be judged not only in the perpetuation of the Festival in subsequent years. A more comprehensive measure would be to assess how far the 1994 Festival established a 'background community' on a wider front, storing capacity, spinning off formal activities and achievements and acting as a reference group for such initiatives.

As with many community development projects, it is difficult to evaluate the outcomes of the Festival which are directly attributable to the processes by which it was organised. On the basis of discussions with key participants and subsequent events, it would appear that there has been an improvement in the capacity of local activists and professionals to respond to racist incidents and to work together around longer term projects. To some extent this reflects better relationships between key individuals;

greater knowledge of people's values and organisational roles, but also increased trust. The connections between the individuals (and their organisations) have been consolidated, not on the basis of consensus, but with a recognition of mutual solidarity and respect.

Networking is a crucial and undervalued method of community development, especially in circumstances requiring rapid mobilisation of scarce resources towards an innovatory project. Its effectiveness is two-fold. As an organising tool, networking through informal contacts allows relatively easy access to sources of power, expertise and practical support, which might not be as readily or quickly available through formal approaches. Similarly the use of network-type organisations enables information and influence to spread across a range of individuals, by making use of the communication systems of other bodies. Most importantly, however, the networking approach to community development, actively recognises the importance of informal and formal ties between individuals. It is these, rather than any particular project or organisation, which are the real basis for the construction and maintenance of the bonds of 'community', 'solidarity' and collective empowerment.

eleven

Do the people want power? The social responsibilities of empowering communities[*]

Chris Hart, Kathryn Jones and Manmohan Bains

Introduction

This chapter reports on research in progress. We investigate the degree to which the assumptions underpinning current approaches to the policy of empowerment (and its associated concepts and manifestations, eg, charters) have been operationalised and what it would take to have a society of empowered citizens. Our work on charters, citizenship and local initiatives aimed at empowering 'communities' has been focused in fieldwork which is being conducted in Chartersville, West Midlands. Designated as a City Challenge area, Chartersville might be characterised as an extremely deprived inner-city area. A major goal of Chartersville City Challenge is to elicit involvement and active participation from local residents in decision making about the area. We took this opportunity to examine the degree to which the assumptions of the consumer citizen can be applied in a particularly focused locality with identifiable groups of residents. Given the large amounts of resourcing provided by the City Challenge into enhancing local empowerment we translated assumptions about

---

[*] This chapter reports on part of an ongoing research project. Because of the sensitive nature of the research, the name of the focus of the research has been changed.

the consumer citizen into the following questions: to what degree do local people want power? What else would they need in terms of say, information, to exercise any power? When provided with channels to decision makers, what level of organisational decision making do people need to access to achieve *actual* empowerment?

We will go on to present our analysis, but it may help the reader if we first of all give some indication of where we will be going. In consideration of our questions and from our empirical studies we soon realised that empowerment was a political tool with multiplicity of ironies, and which might have a number of unintended consequences. Looking at empowerment as an *ironic phenomenon* allowed us to do two complementary things. First, we were able through the field research to assess the degree to which people take what power is made available to them from official agencies. Even though that power was very limited being focused in practice on the operational sphere rather than at the strategic level where real empowerment is possible. Out of this we were able to make visible some of the ironic structures and consequences that might happen generally if people did not take what little power was on offer. It also allowed us to look at the role of the professional service provider; how they manage involvement and balance the practice with the rhetoric while themselves being given titular empowerment in the form of devolved accountability. Second, it allowed us to investigate the necessary and sufficient needs for empowerment; what the logical conclusions might be *if* people were given the opportunity to have influence at the strategic level of decision making. We only touch on this second dimension, but because of its importance we will be writing an account of this at a later stage in the research.

The chapter begins with an overview of the empowerment movement, identifying some of the key notions and vocabulary. This is followed by an analysis of the degree to which residents of Chartersville are involved participants in decisions affecting their area. The final section of the chapter discusses the findings from Chartersville in the wider context of what might logically happen if people do not accept the kind of power on offer.

John Major's empowerment paradigm

The way in which the policy of empowerment has actualised itself is largely dependent upon a particular view of 'urban citizenship' and the relationship of the state to the citizen; in short, a particular definition of citizen and power. John Major's empowerment movement is rooted in the tradition of *watchdog liberalism* (Lowery, 1992, pp 70-4). According to this view citizenship is based on individual property rights. The right to own, use, dispose of and accumulate property are the rights of each responsible individual. These rights enable the individual to engage in two types of social activity. They can engage in the exchange of goods and services, and they can exercise choice and decision making when selecting goods and services to meet their wants and needs. A key assumption here is that it is the individual that can best determine what their needs and wants are, and how best these can be fulfilled. This further assumes that a range of alternatives exist from which an individual can choose.

This contractual basis of citizenship has been extended from the private sector to the provision of public services and in some cases voluntary services. In the consumption of direct payment goods and services the model of the individual is that of *consumer citizen*. Their power is assumed to reside in their being able to make choices over what goods to purchase. Whatever their position in the consumer hierarchy the individual will, it is assumed, have some measure of power. With the reorientation and restructuring of the public sector the citizen and services are expected to take on the attitude and features of consumerism. Choice among alternatives is seen as the means to individual power (Tiebout, 1956). The public as tax payer and voter is expected to take responsibility for choosing which services they need and for exercising voice to make complaints about services they find unsatisfactory.

A key structural feature of the public choice view is the devolved and fragmented organisation of service providers. Small-scale easily defined units of operation are preferred over large, centralised bureaucracies. There are two aspects to this. The local branch of a devolved agency can be more easily monitored, evaluated and controlled centrally by government ministers. Second, local residents can exercise influence over the local agency. They are expected to exercise voice, and exit if local service providers fail to satisfy their individual needs. Therefore, staff at the local level are accountable both internally and externally. They are on the one hand accountable for quantifiable performance to government regulators, commissioners or service purchasers. On the other hand they are accountable to the expectations of actual customers and their representatives (eg, pressure groups).

Threats to the professional are therefore two-fold. Re-organisation in terms of devolved management is eroding traditional career hierarchies and progression markers. Front-line staff, usually at supervisory level, are now expected to take responsibility for functions and roles once dispersed to specialists around an organisation. Included in these job responsibilities are: continuous collection and compilation of statistics on perform-ance; implementation of health and safety in their sphere of work; bidding for budget allocations and financial management of funding; and staff performance reviews. At the same time they are required to establish structures for the involvement of people from outside the organisation. These people are not necessarily users or consumers of the service. In the voluntary sector they often include local councillors, general practitioners and those that make a career from volunteering to be members of various committees.

Power and the ways in which it is developed, located, facilitated, monitored, evaluated, regulated, moved and circulated is therefore central to empowerment. This is because changes to the organisation of the public sector are based on a definite approach to the relationship of the individual to the state in terms of the structuring of power between the two. Having outlined something of this relationship we will now look at the meaning of empowerment and disempowerment.

Empowerment and disempowerment

From the view of a service provider accountability is a dual structure. Government either directly or through agencies monitors the quality, standards and value for money of services provided. Simultaneously, consumers have access to complaints mechanisms, information and regulatory and consumer bodies (eg, OFFWAT, *Which* etc). However, the degree to which individual service providers experience consumer power is variable. Some providers experience a high degree of consumer involvement (eg, schools) and thereby have coalition-based decision making. Other providers grant little power to users: instead of power, users are made accountable for the provision of information by which the provider can evaluate them (eg, Inland Revenue). Therefore, along with the promise of increased rights, information and remedies to poor service goes control and regulation of the consumer (Lister, 1990, p 453). It is this duality that is difficult to describe. This is because models of the consumer citizen and re-structuring of the public sector give the impression of a simple continuum of increasing consumer power. Figure 1 shows this continuum.

As we have already indicated not all agencies have followed this linear movement in the reorientation of their service provision. Few agencies have in reality gone all the way. Nevertheless, the principle of 'movement' towards consumer involvement is embedded in the political rhetoric of empowerment.

At the heart of the notion of empowerment is the movement towards the consumer citizen model for social policy formulation. As this has been discussed in detail elsewhere (Lowery, 1992; Staples, 1990, p 21) a single definition will suffice to remind readers of its meaning. Staples provides a snappy definition: "'empowerment' ... the process by which power is gained, developed, seized, facilitated, or given ..." (1990, p 29). He also states the change aspect empowerment necessitates: "an individual or group moves from a condition of relative powerlessness to relative power through the empowerment process". The move from relative powerlessness to relative power is a movement from *dis*-empowering structures and behaviours by service providers to actions and structures that encourage empowerment of people as consumers.

Assumptions about the consumer citizen are not necessarily the foundation for the concept of empowerment. Alternative approaches to watchdog liberalism could be used as the basis for empowering service users and others. Regrettably, discussion of these is outside the scope of this chapter. This is because the reality of the situation is that watchdog liberalism is the dominant political paradigm (Cooper, 1993). Major's charter movement is based on the watchdog liberalist assumption that people should be responsible for themselves and therefore be active in public service decision making. We now turn to a case study that examines the realities of empowerment. We intend to show through this something of the effects of promising empowerment and not being able to deliver anything more than opinion seeking.

Figure 1: Continuum of consumer power

Bureaucratic service	Supply led	Information provision	Seeking opinions	Discussion of agency proposals	Agency – consumer exploration of issues	Join decision making	Decisions devolved to consumers
Based on paternalistic professionalism	Professional diagnosis of needs	Aims of agency	Surveys	eg Community care plans			

Source: Modified from Skelcher (1993) pp 14

Community empowerment in City Challenge: a case study

> The tremendous enthusiasm it has bred is not just within local authorities but among the communities themselves, where local people have for the first time been given the power to shape the future of their areas. (DoE press release July 1992; taken from Mabbot, 1993)

Chartersville is one of the most socially, economically and culturally deprived inner urban areas in the West Midlands. Characteristically the area displays many of the social ills of inner-city life. A population of 12,000 live in an area distinguished by high levels of unemployment; a significant proportion of unskilled residents, lone parents and low income households; a poorly maintained housing stock; poverty and ill-health and inadequate community, childcare and shopping facilities. The population includes 40% from the ethnic minorities – mainly Afro/Caribbean and Asian.

Chartersville was awarded City Challenge status in 1992. Prior to this the area had undergone several phases of regeneration instigated by both local and national government. There had been slum clearance in the 1930s and 1940s, redevelopment in the 1960s and the Inner City Partnership and Urban Renewal Areas in the 1970s and 1980s. The question seems to be what will make this initiative different?

> True social and economic regeneration in poor urban areas will not occur simply by public or private sector-led initiatives: the community from all its different facets has to be involved in the process for the initiative to succeed in developing ownership and thereby having lasting effect. (DoE, 1992c, p 17)

City Challenge differed from previous initiatives in that local authorities were required to make a competitive bid for funding and that there was a stress placed on partnership between the public and private sector and the participation and involvement of local residents. Involving the community at the developmental, planning and implementation stages of City Challenge, giving them a say in how their area was to be redeveloped so that they can become stakeholders in the redevelopment, is a major premise of the City Challenge ethos.

Community involvement in Chartersville City Challenge

MacFarlane (1993) reported on the steps necessary to ensure adequate involvement and empowerment of the community in any City Challenge context. In this case Chartersville City Challenge has met many of the criteria which he established for good practice. City Challenge has undertaken to involve the residents of Chartersville in the life of the area and the project by implementing an infrastructure for consultation and redress. The organisation has created a mechanism for including the community in the decision-making process in terms of a community forum. Community residents also make up a quarter of the City Challenge board of directors (4 out of 16). Both the community directors and the forum executive are elected by the community in an annual election.

To some extent the corporation has also tried to ensure that the entire area has adequate representation in terms of the geographic area, areas of interest and those members of the community which might suffer specific discrimination. For example, the community forum serves the whole area, a child care forum serves the needs of parents (special interest) and a Bangladeshi youth forum meets the need of the Bangladeshi youth of the area (specific discrimination).

However, MacFarlane also identified a number of criteria which would reduce the effectiveness of community involvement, which also apply in this case. The consultation period in the preparation of the bid was insufficient – a mere 12 weeks to make long-term policy decisions. The consultation process was also considered by some to be inadequate and ineffective. A variety of methods were used to involve the community at the planning stages of the project – meetings, opinion polls, surveys, working groups. However, the influence that local residents had over the setting of key projects was still minimal. For example, the refurbishment of the shopping centre was considered by most residents to be of prime importance, yet other projects have been given greater priority. The demographic make-up and geographic placing of the area means that the community is fragmented and does not always act as a conducive whole – the corporation had to establish an infrastructure for consulting with the entire community. In some key areas the community tends to be sidelined, exercises to really involve the community such as 'planning for real' failed because the people doing the facilitating didn't have "a good understanding themselves of what would and would not work" (interview with chief executive, City Challenge, March 1994).

Many of the problems described above were beyond the control of the City Challenge organisation, due to the way in which the funding process was run. Indeed, the organisation is now offering key aid in terms of facilities and training in order to increase the effectiveness of the various community forums, providing a resource centre and skills training for members of the community to help residents realise their full potential.

However, there remains one key problem – the interest of the residents in this empowerment process. The underlying assumption of the City Challenge project (both nationally and locally) is that local communities will be willing participants in the regeneration scheme. Indeed, many residents of Chartersville were pleased to see that they were at last being involved in decision making about their area. Yet, in reality the involvement of the community has been negligible. City challenge community workers seem to be doing all they can to involve the community in the project, but it does not appear to be working.

The difficulty faced by the development workers was that the bid had assumed that there was a 'community' in place to become involved in the project. In fact Chartersville was composed of two separate and isolated districts which had been grouped together for the purpose of the bid. Indeed, there was a common perception among community workers there if they had been able to go *into* Chartersville before the money had been allocated, and build a forum for consultation, then community participation might be altogether different. As one community leader stated, City Challenge was an "imposed agenda being done for us ... if they are serious about partnership they would have put in the community workers to give residents a chance from the word go" (Colenutt, 1994, pp 36).

The residents in Chartersville seem unsure whether or not they are being *listened to*, although 45% felt that their views were taken into account by City Challenge, 41% couldn't be sure at all. At an open day designed to inform and educate the residents of the area about the various aspects of the project, only a small minority of the people who attended were those that the project needs to involve and interest if the redevelopment is to work. The interim assessment of the impact of City Challenge points to a lack of local interest – 9% of those interviewed had taken part in meetings which decided on the future of NSA, and only 5% indicated that they had taken part in the community forums set up by City Challenge, interestingly, more (12%) had attended residents or housing association meetings (Tricker, 1996). A key question therefore, is why are the residents seemingly unwilling to become involved in their area? Perhaps if we turn to the question of who holds the power, the answer might be found.

Stakeholder Power Matrix

> The problems have created problems.... I think it's not the question of physical environment, but it's the power that people have and it's the lack of choices that were available to them, the powerlessness that then meant they resented the environment. (interview with chief executive, City Challenge, March 1994, discussing previous attempts at regeneration in the area)

The City Challenge initiative was perceived to be different from the traditional top-down approach to regeneration, in that local residents were to be given real say in the shaping of their environment and future, that is they were to be empowered to make local decisions. To adequately assess how Chartersville residents have been empowered to take ownership of the redevelopment scheme it is first necessary to identify ways in which this empowerment can be measured.

There is much discussion in the literature on varying notions of power and empowerment process. Particular attention has focused on the difference between strategic and operational power. The key distinction between them is the ability to set targets, allocate priorities and determine policy (strategic) and the ability to decide how this will be carried out (operational). Strategic-level decisions are policy-level decisions on a long-term basis. Operational-level decisions are service-level decisions on a day-to-day basis. There is a general confusion regarding where the ability to allocate resources fits into the notion of power. Many, including Skelcher (1993) would determine that this falls into strategic decision making. Yet, there is a distinction to be made between power over financial policy and power over resource provision.

For the purpose of this analysis Winstanleys' (1995) stakeholder power matrix has been employed. It was originally developed in order to measure the changing nature of power as a consequence of the widespread local government restructuring of the 1980s and 1990s. She defined stakeholders as "any group or individual who can affect or is affected by the achievement of an organisation's purpose" (Winstanley, 1995). Winstanley tries to clarify the fuzzy boundaries between the modes of power that stakeholders can exert by distinguishing between high-level influence over resource allocation and service-level influence over resource allocation. While some stakeholders are able to influence financial policy, others are only able to utilise what is made available to them. This matrix is shown in Figure 2 below.

Figure 2: The stakeholder power matrix

	High		
		Arm's-length power	Comprehensive power
Criteria power		A	B
		C	D
	Low	Disempowered	Operational power
		Low	**High**
		Operational power	

There are four potential levels of stakeholder power using this matrix:

A   Arm's-length   –   strategic power

B   Comprehensive   –   strategic and operational power

C   Disempowerment   –   no real power

D   operational power   –   operational power

Strategic power is the power the stakeholder has in determining the aims and objectives of an organisation, in the setting of performance criteria and in evaluating that performance. Operational power is the power the stakeholder has in determining what services to provide, the allocation of limited resources and in how services should be provided.

Stakeholder power matrix for Chartersville City Challenge

In this case, however, the matrix is being used to determine which stakeholders hold the controlling influence and exert power over the decision-making process within the City Challenge programme in Chartersville. There are a number of stakeholders who are affected by and hold influence in the regeneration scheme. This is illustrated in Figure 3 below.

Figure 3: The stakeholder power matrix for Chartersville City Challenge

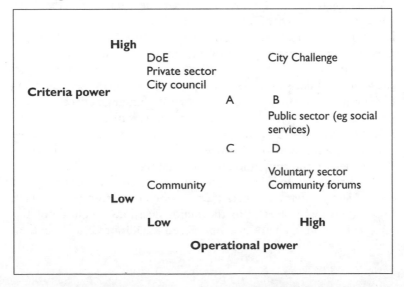

Within quadrant D the community forums (which cover not only single issue groups, such as childcare, safety and housing, but also the forum established for the whole area) exert varying degrees of influence in the City Challenge programme. While they are able to demand services and projects which they feel they need, they have no direct influence over financial policy. In other words they exert power but only at operational level. Each forum has a community worker attached to it who acts as a liaison officer or a facilitator carrying out projects identified by the community for the community. For example, the forum set up to meet the needs of young children, determines the aims and objectives of the child care information officer. However, the forum has no real control over what funding the officer receives, or whether or not the project continues. And whilst the community workers are answerable to the community they are accountable to City Challenge. All community workers must carry out their tasks within the wider framework of objectives identified by City Challenge. The main community forum is responsible for administering a budget to plan and build projects for the community. However, as a percentage of the entire budget it appears to be negligible.

The City Challenge company exerts enormous influence over the project (quadrant B), since it is responsible for the whole regeneration process it involves itself in both strategic and operational decisions. However, the company is still accountable to the Department of the Environment, which provides the public funding each financial year, and it set the agenda for the City Challenge project nation-wide. Hence the DoE holding arms-length power (quadrant A). The fact that the Challenge process is meant to be a partnership between the public and private sector means that the private sector is also able to exert pressure on strategic-level decisions. As the scheme is principally designed for economic regeneration of the area, private funding is necessary for projects such as site redevelopment and refurbishment. The private sector works within a framework set by City Challenge, and therefore is able to influence strategic-level decisions, because it provides a significant amount of capital for the project.

Although the local residents have a say in various aspects of the project, in many respects they can be considered to still have little or no real influence in the major decisions taken about the area. Therefore they are disempowered (quadrant C). While they enjoy a say on 'community redevelopment', for example, in health and housing, through consultation at the planning stages of various projects, strategic-level economic and social regeneration decisions can be made without the backing of the residents. The various forums have no right to veto any of the projects they dislike or are against.

The City Council (quadrant A) set the strategic objectives for the regeneration of Chartersville, however, once the funding was secured, it handed over the management of the project to the City Challenge company, and now has no direct influence over operational decisions. The public sector services however, do (quadrant B). Under the City Challenge umbrella they are able to make decisions about what types of services should be provided and on the allocation of resources. Although their control over the project is not as significant as City Challenge's, it still has some form of comprehensive power. Finally, the voluntary organisations which are also partners in the regeneration process, have an influence over operational decisions (quadrant D). Many are working with City Challenge for the duration of the project and therefore their wider strategic decisions are made by the company.

In some respects the notion of stakeholder power is a more complex process than the one described above. Each stakeholder is dependent on the other to a varying degree of need. For example, City Challenge is reliant on the city council to approve planning applications; the public sector is reliant on the voluntary sector to take up some of the slack in service provision, and the private sector is dependent on City Challenge in terms of project setting and delivery. However, what is at issue is the notion of power. The prime stakeholder who will ultimately determine the success or failure of the project is the community. Yet, at the strategic level, they have little or no real say in what happens to the area. Whilst they were consulted at the beginning of the project to determine what they assessed to be the prime targets for regeneration, time and again they are thwarted in their effort to exercise real control. In the final analysis of the level of power-holding, the inter-dependent relationship between agencies and the citizen is still top-down. An indication of the type of accountability faced by the various stakeholders is shown in Table 1.

Table 2: Political and managerial accountability of stakeholders in Chartersville City Challenge

Stakeholder	Representatives on City Challenge board?	Number	Report back to	Political accountability	Managerial accountability
City Challenge	Yes	2 (chief executive and financial director)	Constituent group	DoE	City council community forum
City Council	Yes	5 (nominated by city council)	As above	DoE	National government
Public sector	Yes	3 (nominated)	As above		
Private sector	Yes	3 (nominated by Chamber of Commerce)	As above	Shareholders	Executive committee
Voluntary sector	No			Executive committee	Executive committee
Community forum and wider community	Yes	3 (community directors elected by local residents)	As above	Local residents	Local residents

Potential community response

To gain an understanding of the potential responses of the residents of Chartersville to this apparent disempowerment at a strategic level, the Exit, Voice, Loyalty and Neglect model, developed by Lyons and Lowery (Lowery, 1992, p 76) was applied.

Figure 4: Dimensions of response to dissatisfaction, response types and illustrative behaviour

```
                        Active
          Exit          ·      Voice
  eg  leaving the area   ·      eg  attending meetings,
                         ·          belonging to
                         ·          organisations/groups,
                         ·          contacting officials,
                         ·          signing petitions,
                         :          talking to neighbours

  Destructive · · · · · · · · · : · · · · · · · · Constructive

  eg  not caring, believing  ·   eg  trusting officials to do
      involvement won't help/ ·       the right thing,
      work                   ·        believing that issues will
                             ·        be sorted out,
                             ·        defending community
                             :
          Neglect            ·   Loyalty
                        Passive
```

Within the model, there are three interdependent variables which will influence the responsive actions of the citizens (Lowery, 1992, p 80). Prior satisfaction – how previous attempts to involve the local residents were perceived; investment – the level of time, effort and energy residents have put into the area; and finally, availability of alternatives – principally an influence on the exit scenario – if residents decide to leave is there somewhere else for them to go?

We will look at this model in relation to the stakeholder's power matrix. Those residents of Chartersville who are members of the community forum are obviously taking an active and constructive role in the regeneration of the area. They are using their voice. This type of involvement is essentially what the government at local and national level want citizens to achieve. Looking at the wider community two other scenarios come into play, that of loyalty and neglect. Both are dangerous in terms of the passivity of local residents, however, they are perhaps the most obvious reactions to the regeneration and probably typify the area as a whole. While many are happy to see the redevelopment of Chartersville, most locals are constrained by the time or do not have the inclination to get involved. To a certain extent this response is understandable. Previous programmes gave residents little or no say in how redevelopment should occur. The difficulty comes however, with the ultimately destructive scenario of neglect and exit. Many will not be able to exit the area, simply because of the lack of alternatives available to them. Consequently, they will adopt the next best approach, if time and again they fail to get their voices heard. Cynicism seems to be setting in amongst the people of Chartersville and generally they seem to no longer care about the City Challenge project.

Discussion

There are many things that could be discussed and argued over concerning the policy of empowerment – reorganisation and re-structuring of public services; need for professionals in many spheres to learn new skills associated with business operations; the shift towards an entrepreneurial culture as well as the impact on client needs, are among some of the issues. We want to look at two areas: the amplification of disempowerment because of empowerment structures; and the consolidation of professional power because of disenchantment and disempowerment of communities. We will talk about each of these in relationship to the case study.

The disempowerment process

Although certain sectors of the community are exercising their right as consumer citizen to use their voice, the question remains, what effect, if any, will this have? Figure 5 below, provides a representation of the process of encouraging community participation and evoking community empowerment at the operational level, while at the same time involving private and public sector agencies in strategic-level planning. It is this cycle of disempowerment that can at present best explain the seeming apathy to get involved. In this scenario, empowerment actually increases the power of the power holders because they are failing to relinquish power in any meaningful way. They may appear to offer involvement to the consumer, but the decisions locals are being asked to influence have already been taken at a strategic level, so their input is effectively ignored. For example, the residents of Chartersville consider the refurbishment of the shopping centre to be of prime importance, however, other projects have been given higher priority by the corporation. Locals have only been allowed to get involved with service-level decisions, they have no access to the strategic (long-term economic) or structural (governmental) levels of decision making. The fact that the agency cannot even deliver the level of participation it promised, coupled with the visible signs of inequality in the power-holding stakes, appears to be leading to the resentment and criticism of the agency by local residents. In turn they are appearing to become less active and more passive in their involvement in the project, which is effectively amplifying this disempowerment process because the organisation has to make more and more decisions without the input of local citizens.

Skelcher (1993) describes this paradox whereby service providers appearing to employ methods of empowerment are actually disempowering their consumers. Organisations are effectively creating a myth of empowerment by ignoring consumer demands; making closed decisions; not providing alternative choices; breaking promises; withholding information; not providing adequate support. Perhaps most significantly they are paying lip service to the notion of empowerment by engaging consumers in lesser decisions and not involving them in those considered by the community to be the significant ones. This typifies the current situation developing in Chartersville.

Professional reconsolidation

In Chartersville the demand to involve local residents was the responsibility of City Challenge personnel, professional managers and community workers. The policy of empowering local residents was and continues to be a stated policy of City Challenge. This policy was based on the assumption that local people would not only want to be involved in the decision-making processes of City Challenge but should be involved. However, as we have seen from the case study, very few people were attracted by any of the initiatives aimed at facilitating involvement. Lack of interest has not changed the policy. It continues to be a major corporate value expoused by City Challenge. Therefore, a situation is currently emerging in which decisions that were to involve local people are increasingly being framed by professional staff *prior* to the consultation process. It is on this development that we have begun to focus some attention in the research: the re-consolidation of professional power.

In terms of the initial structure of access to involvement there were two main spheres. Local people were allowed access to only one of these spheres. The areas for involvement were initially broad including health, education and housing. But local residents were not to be allowed to influence any decisions concerning economic and industrial redevelopment of their area. Looking at this in formal terms the former sphere translates into service-level power while the latter is mainly areas of strategic and structural power. Service-level power is the most visible aspect of a service local people are aware of, for example, opening hours, access, attitude of employees (customer care) and the like. At the strategic level, power resides with City Challenge personnel and central government. Local residents have no real say in decisions concerning policies, resource allocation or the prioritising of programmes. In effect this is disenfranchising the community, who are becoming less active in those spheres where their voice might still count. For example, in the election of local residents to the City Challenge board.

Figure 5: The cycle of disempowerment

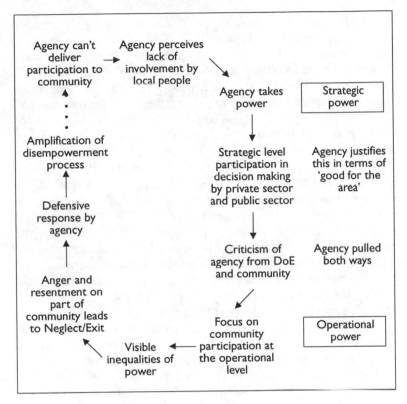

This is why we are seeing a reconsolidation of professional rather than bureaucratic power. Individuals are making decisions on behalf of the organisation in order that decision making is seen to be being done. There seem to be two reasons for this. One is the administrative necessity, the need to get the job done in the limited time available. The other is the need to be managerially accountable to the DoE. This is not an isolated development or professionals attempting to recapture power. It is occurring within the cycle of disempowerment. An inverse relationship is developing, the less power people feel they have, the more power is being taken by professionals to compensate and fill potential vacuums in the decision-making process and structures.

Conclusion: the centralisation of power

To understand why communities are not being effectively empowered, we need to look further afield. Cooper suggests that there is in fact a hidden agenda at the national level. "Major and his government wished to distance themselves from taking responsibility for the state of public services by presenting themselves instead as the party concerned to improve quality" (Cooper, 1993, p 152). This apparent concern over quality has manifested itself in two ways. First the public service providers have to meet government set standards and criteria within the finite resources made available to them. Second they must also involve local citizens in the decision-making process over which services to provide. Effectively the public sector is being pulled in two directions.

However, local service providers cannot deliver the participation that local residents demand, because they do not have the power to do so, their real accountability is elsewhere. Yet this process has been hidden from the consumer citizen, they hold responsible front-line staff and those at the local level, because they are being made promises at the national level. Conversely, by demanding the empowerment of the citizen by the public sector, the government has also moved the responsibility for the success or failure of projects onto the individual. If those individuals within the community fail to get involved, there is no recourse to the government. In shifting this responsibility, the government is effectively denying their part in the whole process. Individuals are being given the chance to take control and ownership of their local areas, if they do not, the government can justify its attack on local councils because it is through them that the empowerment movement is supposed to be implemented. By being held accountable to both their funders and their users, and without any redress of their own, local service providers will undoubtedly fail in the eyes of one or both, and "provide the government, with a legitimate reason ... for intervention in the public sector" (Cooper, 1993, p 152).

twelve

Community participation and urban regeneration in Britain

Rob Atkinson and Stephen Cope

Introduction

The issue of community participation in urban regeneration has received considerable attention in both Britain and the United States since the end of the 1980s (Hambleton and Taylor, 1993; Robinson and Shaw, 1991). This attention lies in stark contrast to developments in the 1980s when governments, inspired by neo-liberal theories (Green, 1987; King, 1987), stressed the role of markets and the private sector as the most effective method of economic and urban regeneration. This chapter investigates the idea of community participation in the development of urban regeneration strategies (Atkinson and Cope, 1994; Atkinson and Moon, 1994a; Hambleton and Thomas, 1995). First, it examines the nature of community participation by exploring the ideas of 'community', 'participation' and 'empowerment'. Second, it outlines the dominant approach to urban regeneration in the 1980s, and examines government initiatives seeking to involve local communities in the processes of urban regeneration. Third, it assesses the role of community participation in urban regeneration strategies. In particular, it looks at how communities can be and are empowered to participate in formulating and implementing urban regeneration strategies.

Reinventing community participation

The idea of community, though always a salient concept, has returned to the mainstream of urban policy analysis. Kymlicka observed that "in the 1980s and 1990s, community has resurfaced" (1993, p 366), with "community ties ... recast into humanity's natural domicile" (Bauman, 1995, p 150). For example, the local government review process provided "the opportunity of relating the structure of local government more closely to communities with which people identify" (Department of the Environment, 1991, p 6). There is increasing interest in communitarianism, with its emphasis on "rebuilding community institutions ... [because] ... society has cannibalized communities" (Etzioni, 1993, p 134). Governments "seem to use 'community' as if it were an aerosol can, to be sprayed on to any social programme, giving it a more progressive and sympathetic cachet" (Cochrane, 1986, p 51). From community policing to community care and from community architecture to the community charge, the idea of community rests on "an emotional appeal" to an imagined past and idyllic future (Worsley, 1987, p 238). For Chamberlain, community politics represents "a new age of romanticism" (1986, p 12). It seems that people "never ... are against the community" (Williams, 1992, p 8).

The meaning of community is contested. Though the idea of community is underpinned by the notion that "people have something in common" (Hill, 1994, pp 34-5), that 'something' is in fact many 'somethings'. Hillery counted 94 different definitions of 'community', nearly all of which suggest that it "consists of persons in social interaction within a geographic area and having one or more additional common ties" (1955, p 111). There are multiple meanings of community. For example, Plant wrote that community "has been linked to locality, to identity of functional interests, to a sense of belonging, to shared cultural and ethnic ideas and values, to a way of life opposed to the organisation and bureaucracy of modern mass society" (1974, p 13). There are social and spatial dimensions in defining 'community'. Burns, Hambleton and Hoggett wrote:

> *Communities of interest* reflect the common material concerns or characteristics of their members and/or the issues of common interest around which they group.... *Communities of*

> *place* can be thought of as a particular kind of
> imagined community. (1994, p 227)

However, place "does not deterministically shape residents' way of
life", though "commonality might be grounded in a territorial
area" (Hill 1994, pp 34-5). Increasing globalisation is
transforming and even threatening traditional 'localised'
communities, and creating opportunities for the emergence of
'non-localised' communities (Goetz and Clarke, 1993; Kirby,
1993; Sassen, 1991), such as 'virtual' communities fostered by the
Internet. Following Gray:

> The idea of community is a potent symbol of the
> culture losses of the eighties.... To accept the
> globalisation of the economy is, in effect, to make
> the survival of communities everywhere
> conditional on changes in a world market which
> care nothing for the stability of the societies it
> exists to serve. (1995, p 26)

The meaning of community is relative. Cohen argued people
"define themselves by reference to a 'significant other' ... [and] ...
construct community symbolically, making it a resource and
repository of meaning, and a referent of their identity" (1985, pp
117-18). People belong to many communities with varying
degrees of attachment at the same time. They "have multiple
identities and linkages" (Burns, Hambleton and Hoggett, 1994, p
228). There is thus fluid and overlapping membership of
communities. Etzioni believed "communities are best viewed as if
they were Chinese nesting boxes, in which less encompassing
communities ... are nested within more encompassing ones"
(1993, p 32). Communities are both inclusive and exclusive. To
belong to a community is dependent on others not belonging.
Membership of a community implies marginalisation of those on
the periphery inside and exclusion of others outside the
community. Burns, Hambleton and Hoggett observed:

> On the one hand, community is a unifying
> concept, the expression of common interest,
> solidarity, integration and consensus.... On the
> other, community is not a singular concept but in
> reality represents a mere umbrella under which

> shelter a multitude of varying, competing and
> often conflicting interests. (1994, p 224)

This challenges the way in which the notion of community is uncritically used by both governments and many community activists, that tend to assume that simply by adding 'community' it somehow legitimates a policy. However, the notion of community intersects with a multiplicity of issues (such as class, race and gender), creating a range of conflicting and competing interests that embrace both fragmentation and difference (Phillips, 1993). Even in relatively homogeneous single-class spatial communities, there are significant divisions of interest based around gender and age (Campbell, 1993). Furthermore, just as conflicts exist within communities, conflicts exist between communities competing for limited resources within the same urban area. Communities are thus constructed within this context of competition and conflict. Phillips argued:

> Neither community nor solidarity will come to us
> ready made; both have to be constructed through
> the active involvement of people trying to sort
> out their differences themselves. (1993, p 20)

However, despite fragmented divisions within and between communities, the view that the public should increasingly participate in the making of government decisions has gained increasing importance since the 1960s (Boaden et al, 1982). Public participation is all about people 'taking part' in government (Gyford, 1991, pp 52-79; Hill, 1994, pp 32-68; Richardson, 1983, pp 8-28). Arnstein stated:

> ... citizen participation is a categorical term for
> citizen power. It is the redistribution of power
> that enables the have-not citizens, presently
> excluded from the political and economic
> processes, to be deliberately included in the
> future. (1969, p 216)

She constructed an eight-rung ladder of citizen participation – see Figure 6 below (1969, p 217). This ladder is useful because it recognises that "there are significant gradations of citizen participation" (Arnstein, 1969, p 217). At the bottom of the ladder, therapy and manipulation represent forms of non-participation because their aim "is not to enable people to participate in planning or conducting programs, but to enable powerholders to 'educate' or 'cure' the participants" (1969, p 217). In the middle, placation, consultation and informing are tokenistic forms of citizen participation, as "citizens may indeed hear and be heard ... [but] ... lack the power to insure that their views will be *heeded* by the powerful" (1969, p 217). At the top, citizen control, delegated power and partnership are "levels of citizen power with increasing degrees of decision-making clout" (1969, p 217). Arnstein acknowledged that these rungs do not represent purely distinctive and mutually exclusive forms of citizen participation. Furthermore, she recognised that the powerless and the powerful are heterogeneous blocs with "a host of divergent points of view, significant cleavages, competing vested interests, and splintered subgroups" (1969, p 217).

Figure 6: Arnstein's ladder of citizen participation

DEGREES OF CITIZEN POWER
8. Citizen control
7. Delegated power
6. Partnership
DEGREES OF TOKENISM
5. Placation
4. Consultation
3. Informing
NON-PARTICIPATION
2. Therapy
1. Manipulation

Burns, Hambleton and Hoggett further criticised Arnstein's ladder of citizen participation (1994, pp 153-79). They argued that a citizen may enjoy different degrees of participation in different spheres of influence (eg, housing estate, housing department, local authority) and in different areas of decision making (eg, making, financing and administering policy), thus making a single ladder a highly generalised measure of citizen participation. Furthermore, they noted that "the rungs of the ladder should not be considered to be equidistant" (1994, p 161). Burns, Hambleton and Hoggett then constructed a new 12-rung ladder of citizen empowerment – see Figure 7 below (1994, p 162; see also Burns, 1991). Their ladder of citizen empowerment, though more elaborate than Arnstein's ladder of citizen participation, still "simplifies a much more complex reality" (Burns, Hambleton and Hoggett, 1994, pp 161-4). There are several critical issues requiring examination before applying this ladder of citizen empowerment to analysing community participation in urban regeneration strategies.

Figure 7: Burns, Hambleton and Hoggett's ladder of citizen empowerment

CITIZEN CONTROL
12. Independent control
11. Entrusted control
CITIZEN PARTICIPATION
10. Delegated control
9. Partnership
8. Limited decentralised decision making
7. Effective advisory boards
6. Genuine consultation
5. High-quality information
CITIZEN NON-PARTICIPATION
4. Customer care
3. Poor information
2. Cynical consultation
1. Civic hype

First, it is important to identify who constitutes the community. A government agency will have "different relationships" with "different publics" (Stewart, 1983, p 120). There are many different communities representing consumers, producers, citizens, residents, voters, taxpayers, pressure groups, ethnic groups, religious groups and so on. Some interests or places may not form communities; some communities may not want or may not be able to participate. The role of a state agency seeking community participation, and of other bodies impinging on relations between a state agency and its 'publics', is critical in shaping communities. For example, many local authorities have undertaken a community development role to provide a voice for less powerful groups in their areas (Association of Metropolitan Authorities [AMA], 1989; AMA, 1993; Blackman, 1995, pp 142-65; Smith and Chanan, 1986). The European Union plays an increasingly important role in urban regeneration, and recently courted the Coalfields Communities Campaign seeking funding to regenerate run-down areas (Fothergill, 1995).

Second, it is necessary to examine how much weight is attached to the views of communities, especially compared to those of elected politicians, appointed bureaucrats and expert professionals within state agencies. Furthermore, given the existence of many 'publics', a state agency plays a pivotal role in mediating between the competing and conflicting demands of communities and in allocating resources between different communities. Burns, Hambleton and Hoggett noted "the reactionary parochialism which can exist in some communities" (1994, p 164), and argued local authorities should not decentralise decision making if it hands over power to an intolerant and obnoxious community.

Third, community participation involves forms of community power (Dowding et al, 1995; Polsby, 1980). Consequently, understanding community participation requires an understanding of power relations between a state agency and its 'publics'. The literature on community participation is largely disappointing in its coverage of power, largely preferring to hide behind anodyne concepts like 'empowerment'. Many have discussed empowerment without examining what power is (Pirie, 1991; Skelcher, 1993). As a result empowerment may mean little more than symbolic incorporation and cynical entrapment. In contrast

Clarke and Stewart argued (see also Stewart and Taylor, 1995, pp 11-19):

> Empowerment is about increasing the power of the public in relation to the institutions and organisations whose activities affect their way of life. By power we mean the extent of influence and control exercised over such activities. Power is differentially distributed in society and empowerment must be concerned therefore with strengthening the position of those who lack the power to influence or control. (1992, p 2)

Understanding community power is essential in understanding community participation. Following Dowding:

> The distinction between 'power over' and 'power to' may be described as 'outcome power' and 'social power': the first because it is the power to bring about outcomes; the second for it necessarily involves a social relation between at least two people. (1991, p 48)

Being powerful involves possessing and mobilising resources, effecting and securing intended outcomes of decision making, shaping and manipulating interests of other actors, controlling and filtering agendas of decision making and creating and maintaining structures of decision making. Consequently different empowerment strategies arise from different conceptions of power.

Notwithstanding the above, the ladder of citizen empowerment developed by Burns, Hambleton and Hoggett provides a useful framework within which community participation can be assessed in urban regeneration strategies.

Urban regeneration in the 1980s

In 1979 the Thatcher government embarked upon a neo-liberal experiment designed to reduce the role of the state and 'bring the market back in'. As a result urban areas, although relatively low-down the government's list of priorities, were subject to several initiatives encouraging the private sector to take a lead role in urban regeneration, albeit one subsidised and facilitated by the state (Atkinson and Moon, 1994b; Deakin and Edwards, 1993; Imrie and Thomas, 1993a; Thornley, 1991).

Given the changes taking place within the wider economy, most notably the decline of the manufacturing sector and rise of service industries, forms of growth and demand for new investment in urban areas were largely based around offices, retailing outlets and up-market housing. As a result the property development industry came to play a major role in urban regeneration – leading to the notion of property-led urban regeneration (Imrie and Thomas, 1993b; Turok, 1992). This development partly caught the government by surprise. However, given its emphasis upon the primacy of the market, it encouraged this development via grants, tax relief, relaxation of planning regulations, and so on. A key element of this emerging strategy was the marginalisation of local government and local people in the redevelopment of areas suffering from urban decline (Cabinet Office, 1988). The private sector, following the market dictate of securing the highest returns, largely focused its attentions upon flagship developments in or adjacent to city centres and/or existing concentrations of office complexes. The assumption underlying these developments was that by allowing wealth creators to transform the landscape of urban areas and create new jobs the benefits would eventually 'trickle down' to deprived communities.

During the mid-1980s this strategy transformed the built environment of some of Britain's most derelict urban areas (notably London's Docklands). However, the combined effects of the worldwide stock-market crash in 1987 and the subsequent onset of recession, severely undermined the position of the property-development industry. At the same time the government was increasingly criticised for its lack of a coherent urban strategy, its continued exclusion of local government and the failure of local communities to benefit from urban regeneration initiatives (Audit Commission, 1989; National Audit Office, 1990). In response the government began to make overtures to local government seeking to bring it into urban regeneration initiatives (Cabinet Office, 1990; Hunt, 1990), albeit on terms largely dictated by central government. Furthermore, there was growing emphasis on the community's role in urban regeneration and the need to ensure that disadvantaged groups derived some benefit from developments in their areas.

Bringing the community back into urban regeneration

The government responded by launching City Challenge in late 1990 and early 1991 (Atkinson and Moon, 1994b; De Groot, 1992; Kamis, 1992; Oatley, 1995). As conceived by the then Secretary of State for the Environment, Michael Heseltine, City Challenge was to be based upon a competitive bidding process. Guidelines issued to authorities taking part in the bidding process emphasised that "City Challenge is about local initiative" (Department of the Environment, 1992b, p 1), and that any economic transformation should benefit local residents. The Department of the Environment advised:

> The mix of objectives will depend on the area selected. However they should tackle the problems which are perceived by the residents of the area and by potential investors as being crucial to its regeneration. (1992b, p 5)

Two rounds of City Challenge occurred before the government embarked upon a major review of urban policy in 1993, the outcome of which was the Single Regeneration Budget (SRB). Like City Challenge, SRB stresses the role of local communities in the development of urban regeneration strategies and the consequent benefits for them (Mawson et al, 1995; Stewart, 1994). SRB also uses competitive bidding, but monies available via this mechanism are relatively small compared to total expenditure. Bids will be expected to meet one or more of the following objectives (Department of the Environment, 1993b, p 5):

- enhance the employment prospects, education and skills of local people, particularly the young and those at a disadvantage, and promote equality of opportunity;

- encourage sustainable economic growth and wealth creation by improving the competitiveness of the local economy, including business support;

- improve housing through physical improvements greater choice and better management and maintenance;

- promote initiatives of benefit to ethnic minorities;

- tackle crime and improve community safety;

- protect and improve the environment and infrastructure and promote good design;

- enhance the quality of life of local people, including their health and cultural and sports activities.

The key notion developed in both City Challenge and SRB is that of local partnership between local government, the private sector, voluntary bodies, local communities and, where applicable, other government agencies such as training and enterprise councils and English Partnerships. Although successful bids "will be expected to maximise the leverage of private sector investment and intensify the impact of public sector resources by achieving greater coherence of spend" (Department of the Environment, 1993b, p 5). However, the idea of partnership remains unclear in official discourse (Hastings, 1996), with Fordham observing that "there is little consensus amongst policy-makers or practitioners about what terms like 'community consultation', 'empowerment', or 'capacity building' mean" (1995, p 31). The government has been unwilling to spell out exactly what partnership entails, other than expressing vague hopes that greater coordination and synergy will focus minds and maximise resources. Furthermore, these new initiatives have emerged out of a long period of conflict between central and local government and may represent a more subtle form of central control over 'the urban regeneration game' in which central government sets the 'rules of the game' that localities have to accept if they wish to at least have the possibility of access to scarce funds (Atkinson and Moon, 1994a; Oatley, 1995).

These initiatives have developed as part of a wider New Right agenda emphasising the superiority of competitive market-based forms of organisation over state intervention (Hoggett, 1996; Walsh, 1995). More specifically, there has been a growing emphasis on competition between urban areas to attract private and public sector investment. A key part of this competitive process is 'place-marketing' or 'boosterism' (Paddison, 1993), whereby local partnerships attempt to improve the human, social and cultural capital of their localities by attracting investment. Harvey defined this process of using public funds to underwrite private sector profits as urban entrepreneurialism, when he argued:

> The new entrepreneurialism typically rests ... on a
> public–private partnership focusing on investment

> and economic development with the speculative
> construction of place rather than amelioration of
> conditions within a particular territory as its
> immediate (though by no means exclusive)
> political and economic goal. (1989b, p 8)

One of the government's key criteria for successful bids is the extent to which they are able to 'lever-in' additional resources and, given the lack of resources available to deprived communities, this criterion invariably means that the private sector will have a privileged place in any urban regeneration partnership. Furthermore, both City Challenge and SRB embrace the paradox that while successful bids involve cooperation and collaboration locally, they entail competition between cities nationally and, consequently, there are always winners and losers. With reduced government funding of other urban regeneration-related programmes (Nevin and Shiner, 1995, p 6), City Challenge and SRB success means that funding reductions elsewhere may be partially offset, while failure may exacerbate the position of deprived communities. In this context, the addition of the community to the partnership may bestow an added degree of legitimacy upon urban policy initiatives, in exchange for which selected communities receive additional resources while the total monies available for urban regeneration decline (Nevin and Shiner, 1994; 1995).

Although City Challenge and SRB are relatively recent initiatives, problems are beginning to emerge in securing community participation. One problem has been the speed at which bids had to be prepared; sufficient time was not allowed for anything other than the most superficial forms of consultation and in some cases not even that. Even where well-organised community organisations already existed, the agenda appears to have been largely set by those in local government and the private sector. As a result the partnerships created have been unequal, with local communities very much the junior partner responding to initiatives from elsewhere rather than actively participating in setting the agenda (Davoudi and Healey, 1995; MacFarlane and Mabbott, 1993; Mawson et al, 1995, pp 95-7). Not only is more time needed to allow greater participation but more resources are needed to enable communities to organise themselves and put forward suitably detailed proposals. There needs to be an emphasis on sustainable regeneration and building community capacities not just for a single project over a few years but over the longer term if politicians and professionals are not to dominate the process. An essential part of this process will be the construction of community-based organisations to run local regeneration schemes and to link into more extensive regeneration strategies covering the wider urban area and region. It is only in such fora that negotiations over the allocation of resources and the coordination of strategic action can take place.

Community participation is time consuming, and as many people as possible need to develop organisational skills and acquire knowledge. There is a very real danger that participation will become too dependent upon a (potentially unrepresentative) few and, if they become exhausted, activity will collapse. Such problems are compounded in the most deprived communities suffering from a sense of powerlessness and abandonment, and consequently a major investment of time and resources is needed to support existing community organisations and encourage the growth of new ones. Community participation, other than mere superficial consultation, requires the commitment of significant resources, most notably from central and local government.

Genuine participation thus requires a fundamental re-think of attitudes by politicians and officials in central and local government. They need to recognise the legitimate right of local people to participate as an equal partner in setting the regeneration agenda. Such a re-think requires both structural change (that is, organisational restructuring and decentralisation to bring government physically closer to communities) and cultural change (that is, the replacement of long established bureaucratic and professional forms with genuinely participative forms of action) (Gaster, 1996). Furthermore, the private sector, as a partner, must accept the legitimacy of community views and accommodate those views. Even if it means less profitable forms of development, private sector provision of high-quality training schemes, in cooperation with the public and voluntary sectors, and the targeting of jobs on local people must be central to urban regeneration schemes. These developments will need to be accompanied by (often radical) organisational restructuring to facilitate community access to and control of resources (Burns, Hambleton and Hoggett, 1994).

Even if such restructuring was enacted, significant problems would remain. There is no guarantee that the most deprived areas will be targeted; bids may focus on areas with significant development potential to attract private sector investment, thus maximising leverage and economic development.   Such an approach would run the risk of reproducing the problems of the property-led schemes, with community simply being added on to give greater legitimacy.   Also most schemes will focus upon relatively small areas, raising the crucial issue of territorial justice – why should one area be given preference over others? Schemes may focus on only one aspect of the problem (eg, poor housing), and ignore other interconnected problems (eg, unemployment), with the result that short-term improvements will be undermined (Power and Tunstall, 1995).

In addition, the existence of programmes (such as City Challenge and SRB) may lead to the formation of groups claiming to represent the community, as scarce funds act as an impetus to group formation. But the danger remains that such groups may become too closely identified with particular programmes and their success and longevity become largely dependent upon those programmes. It is also likely that, given community participation is one of the criteria for a successful bid, where groups do not exist local authorities will seek to stimulate their formation. Consequently such groups will become the creatures of local government. Even where community groups already exist there is the potential that they will simply become incorporated into the partnership and lose their links with the local community. It is therefore important that strong representative ties between community groups and the wider community exist if such groups are to adequately represent the interests of the community within a partnership.

Furthermore, communities that receive government monies through urban regeneration programmes exist within a wider locality and, consequently, such programmes directed towards particular spatial locations should be part of a wider strategy. What is required is a clearly elaborated integrated strategy for the whole area and its constituent local communities, and an explicit commitment to target benefits to the most disadvantaged (both individuals and areas). In the early days of SRB, each of the newly created Integrated Regional Offices (now known as Government Offices for the Regions) was to provide a regional strategy, but this idea was soon abandoned. Local partnerships are highly likely to become arenas for conflicts between partners with inter- and intra-community conflicts over the distribution of resources and benefits. To deny the likelihood of such conflicts is naive.

These difficulties are not limited to City Challenge and SRB projects. Research on community participation in local government revealed similar problems (Burns, Hambleton and Hoggett, 1994), as did more specific research on urban regeneration schemes in Scotland (Barr, 1995; Hastings, 1996; Hastings and McArthur, 1995; McArthur, 1993). For example, in a study of housing regeneration in Ferguslie Park, Kintrea concluded:

> ... not just the official and politicians in Ferguslie needed more experience in the techniques of participation, but that the whole process of identifying and progressing the Partnership was antipathetic to effective community involvement. (1996, p 304)

Kintrea also noted that rather than work cooperatively with existing community groups, the Ferguslie Park Partnership imposed its own management structures to which they were expected to adapt. Later the Partnership actually replaced a long-standing community organisation with forms of representation more amenable to its aims (see Chapter 6). Generally the greatest danger associated with such partnerships is that community participation is seen by local communities as a form of symbolism and incorporation, running the risk of exacerbating a sense of marginalisation and powerlessness, increasing feelings of hopelessness and accentuating conflict thereby creating ever more 'dangerous places' (Campbell, 1993).

Community participation and urban policy analysis

If notions of community participation and community em-powerment are taken seriously, then local people must be an integral part of the urban policy process, while recognising that communities are not homogenous entities waiting to participate. However, central and local government representatives, perhaps hard-pressed, tend to consult community groups where they exist and, where they do not, simply develop policies and seek community involvement later. This approach is mistaken, as it would be more sensible to involve groups where they exist, examine their representativeness and, if low, provide resources for the development of a wider and more representative range of local groups. Where no groups exist, it is important to invest resources so that local communities can develop their own identity and define the problems they face so they can be tackled. Such an approach may be time consuming and troublesome, particularly for local government, but in the long run it is most likely to sustain locally relevant and viable urban regeneration strategies.

It is therefore vital that the local community be involved at all stages of the urban policy process – problem definition, agenda-setting, goal-setting, policy appraisal, policy implementation, policy review, policy succession and policy termination (Atkinson and Cope, 1994, p 8). As a result community-focused urban policy analysis needs to address the following questions (Atkinson and Cope, 1994, pp 15-17; Atkinson and Moon, 1994b, pp 17-19):

- What is the problem-focus of urban policy?

- How is the problem to be explained?

- What is the aim of the policy?

- How is the aim to be achieved?

- How is the policy to be resourced?

- How will the policy be managed?

- Does the policy have political support?

- Is there an adequate legislative base?

- What are the measures for monitoring?

- Who benefits?

- Are issues of social equity being tackled?

If urban policy is to incorporate community participation, the community must be involved in framing and responding to all 11 questions. While City Challenge and SRB (plus other initiatives in Scotland) have partly attempted to address these issues, there is no evidence to suggest that the community has been integrated into the overall urban policy process (Davoudi and Healey, 1995; Hastings and McArthur, 1995).

The last two questions are central concerns in securing genuine community participation, requiring adequate measures of 'who benefits' and social equity to be developed that are relatively straightforward, easy to monitor and readily understood by non-specialists. For example, job creation must be closely monitored from the beginning of any project, and all partners (including the private sector) must recognise their commitment to achieve agreed targets. Even before the project is underway, recruitment campaigns, advice centres and training schemes should be in place, preferably involving local offices of central government, local government and community groups. Furthermore, rather than simply focusing on the total numbers of jobs created there must be a disaggregation that distinguishes between full-time permanent, part-time permanent, full-time temporary and part-time temporary jobs. Also job distribution on the basis of gender, race and age should be monitored. The wage rates attached to jobs created should be monitored, otherwise projects run the risk of replacing inadequate state benefits with unstable low-income jobs and thereby simply replacing one form of poverty with another. Realistic attempts must also be made to estimate not only the number of jobs directly created but also those indirectly created without relying too heavily on abstract econometric models and supposed multiplier effects. Moreover, the distribution of jobs between areas and groups of people must be closely monitored.

While the above may be seemingly prohibitively expensive and time consuming, thereby slowing up development, failure to integrate local people's perceptions and needs, particularly from excluded communities, into urban regeneration projects will undermine their legitimacy in the eyes of local people and may lead to expensive policy failures. Local communities should be involved at all stages of the urban policy process from policy design to policy review. Response from some quarters will be that the technical issues involved are so complex as to prohibit the involvement of lay people. However, these problems largely result from the nature of organisations and their intra-organisational power relations and 'outside worlds' – that is, the way in which organisations divorce themselves from the 'people', legitimised by their possession of technical and specialist knowledge (Hirst, 1976). Hirst argued there is no reason why such knowledge cannot be made more widely available through education and public information (1976, p 117). Furthermore, he argued that technical knowledge is mainly a function of access, with knowledge kept 'secret' and thus shielded from public access. Greater access would open-up organisations to greater scrutiny and would improve service delivery which "depends on there being a set of pressures for service improvement which reside *outside the state*" (Burns, Hambleton and Hoggett, 1994, p 153). Research in the United States has indicated citizens' assessment of policy impacts are often far more sophisticated than politicians, professionals and bureaucrats envisaged, providing a valid form of performance measurement that can be fed back into the policy process and acting as a counterweight to the more technical forms of performance measurement (Brudney and England, 1982). Furthermore, the use of citizens' juries, representing the 'general public', "offer the opportunity to bring into the public domain experience and judgement too often excluded from it" (Stewart, Kendall and Coote, 1994, p 5). Resources need to be made available to communities to facilitate their acquisition of knowledge and organisational skills, accompanied by the decentralisation of power, information and decision making. This crucial aspect of community participation explicitly challenges the power of politicians, professionals and bureaucrats in the public sector and of the private sector. Issues of community benefit and social equity must be of equal, if not of more, importance than profitability, thus requiring a critical ongoing culture of community participation.

Community participation cannot act as a panacea. Locally, urban regeneration strategies may be constrained by wider structural forces combining to severely limit their effectiveness. Nationally, central government may be powerless to influence global economic forces. However, these structural limits should not lead to either fatalism or a blind adherence to the 'invisible hand' of the market, because forms of governance do matter and effective policies require the development of corresponding local and regional structures – similar to those surrounding SRB (Davoudi and Healey, 1995; Morgan, 1995). Mainstream programmes will need to be 'bent' to support urban policy initiatives and thus operate in a synergic manner.

Generally community participation poses major challenges for government bodies organised along bureaucratic lines, embracing the vast majority of government agencies, which despite recent managerial and organisational reforms, are still palpably bureaucratic. Genuine democratic participation disrupts bureaucratic routines and the search for a consensus makes long-term bureaucratic planning impossible (Offe, 1975). Offe contended:

> ... too much responsiveness towards its clientele would almost necessarily push administrations beyond the limits of what they can do and are required to do within the framework of a capitalist organization of the economy. At least, such responsiveness would not only *reflect* conflicts most directly, but also *create* conflicts in case its pretended reliance upon democratic decision making is not parallelled by its ability to act according to the emerging decisions of its clientele. (1975, p 140)

Conclusion

As argued, there are distinct limits on community participation in urban regeneration strategies, partly originating in wider structural forces, which have increasingly led local partnerships to market themselves nationally and internationally (Harvey, 1989b). Success can lead to inward investment (eg, Manchester), while failure can lead to further decline (eg, Liverpool). However, even in 'successful' cities there is no guarantee that the most deprived communities will benefit, thus enhancing the case for community participation despite the danger that such participation will simply act as a legitimating device and provide the state with new and more effective means of conflict management and social control.

Notwithstanding the above, there is a need for greater community participation in urban regeneration strategies, while recognising the problems of operationalising the concept of and of securing community participation in urban regeneration partnerships. Though City Challenge and SRB offer a partnership approach, they fall short of citizen control as outlined in the ladder of citizen empowerment developed by Burns, Hambleton and Hoggett (see Figure 7). Indeed, City Challenge and SRB bids were generally made with only minimal (if any) consultation with affected communities. As a result the agenda was largely set before communities became involved.   Even after local communities became involved, significant questions remain about the extent of their involvement and their capacity to maintain involvement over time.   Moreover, serious questions remain over the extent to which public and private sector members of partnerships have embarked upon structural and cultural change within their own organisations to accommodate community participation and develop innovative urban regeneration strategies, preferring to rely upon 1980s-style property-led forms of regeneration which have failed to tackle to underlying urban problems (such as unemployment) as perceived by many communities.

City Challenge and SRB can therefore be placed, at best, in the middle of the ladder of citizen empowerment, though even this position may be far too high-up on the ladder.   The partnership approach emerging in SRB projects "may be more appealing to government than increased direct 'participation' because it is probably easier to manage the 'stakeholders' and the way they interact" (Barlow, 1995, p 57).   This view corresponds closely to other studies of public participation in government.   For example, Boaden et al observed:

> ... though there have been great moves towards public involvement in local service provision in recent years, little has been achieved by way of a fundamental shift in power....   In the end, élite perspectives have won out, and participation has served the purposes of building up a consensus for the proposals of those in power, thereby legitimating them. (1982, p 179)

Communities represent only one set of 'stakeholders', and are generally much less powerful than other 'stakeholders' (eg, local authorities, central government, private developers) that command far greater resources and thus dominate the urban policy process. This imbalance of power resources needs to be redressed if calls for community participation in urban regeneration are to be more than symbolic, and before urban regeneration strategies climb up the ladder of citizen empowerment.   Increasing community participation will enhance their effectiveness and legitimacy and, as a result, strategies 'bringing the community back in' do not necessarily represent a 'zero-sum' game but may represent a 'positive-sum' game where all may benefit.

The case for greater community participation in regenerating urban areas requires communities to be involved at all stages of the urban policy process, from problem definition to policy appraisal. This case may be countered by those (usually vested interests) sceptical of the intellectual prowess of communities. But this scepticism needs to be challenged. Following Fishkin, an important distinction needs to be made between "what the public thinks, given how little it knows" and "what the public *would* think, if it had a more adequate chance to think about the questions at issue" (1991, p 1). However, community participation in urban regeneration will not act as a panacea for all problems. Indeed, it may create new problems as various 'stakeholders' compete (and cooperate) with each other to achieve their ends. Moreover, we need to recognise that communities are social constructs, which are both inclusive and exclusive. There will inevitably be conflicts over who constitutes and represents the community and what comprises its needs. Such conflicts are the essence of politics, and should be acknowledged and accepted into the urban regeneration process.

Bibliography

Abrams, P. and McCulloch, A. (1976) *Communes, sociology and society*, Cambridge: Cambridge University Press.

Abrams, P., Abrams, S., Humphreys, R. and Snaith, R. (1989) *Neighbourhood care and social policy*, London: HMSO.

Abu-Lughod, J. (1994) 'Diversity, democracy and self-determination in an urban neighbourhood: the East Village of Manhattan', *Social Research*, Spring, pp 181-203.

Allan, G. and Crow, G. (1991) 'Privatisation, home-centredness and leisure', *Leisure Studies*, vol 10, pp 19-32.

Anderson, B. (1991) *Imagined communities: reflections on the origin and spread of nationalism*, London: Verso.

Anthias, F. and Yuval-Davis, N. (1992) *Racialized boundaries: race, nationa, gender, colour and class and the anti-racist struggle*, London: Routledge.

Arber, S. and Ginn, J. (1991a) 'The invisibility of age: gender and class in later life', *Sociological Review*, vol 39, no 2, pp 261-91.

Arber, S. and Ginn, J. (1991b) *Gender and later life*, London: Sage.

Arnstein, S.R. (1969) 'A ladder of citizen participation', *Journal of the American Institute of Planners*, vol 35, pp 216-24.

Ashworth, G. and Voogd, H. (1995) 'Place marketing', in S. Ward and J. Gold (eds) *Place promotion*, Chichester: Wiley.

Association of County Councils (1992) 'Changing the shape of local government: the continuing controversy', Briefing Paper no 12.

Association of District Councils (1993) Local government review, Community identity, Summary.

Association of Metropolitan Authorities (1989) *Community development: the local authority role*, London: AMA.

Association of Metropolitan Authorities (1993) *Local authorities and community development: a strategic opportunity for the 1990s*, London: AMA.

Atkinson, R. and Cope, S. (1994) 'Urban policy evaluation: science or art?', Paper presented at ESRC 'Urban policy evaluation' seminar, University of Wales College of Cardiff, September.

Atkinson, R. and Moon, G. (1994a) *Urban policy in Britain: the city, the state and the market*, Basingstoke: Macmillan.

Atkinson, R. and Moon, G. (1994b) 'The City Challenge Initiative: an overview and preliminary assessment', *Regional Studies*, vol 28, pp 94-97.

Audit Commission (1989) *Urban regeneration and economic development*, London: HMSO.

Avineri, S. and de-Shalit, A. (1992) *Communitarianism and individualism*, Oxford: Oxford University Press.

Avon County Planning Department (nd) *Social stress in Avon 1991.*

Bakhtin, M.M. (1981) *The dialogic imagination: four essays by M.M. Bakhtin*, Austin: University of Texas Press.

Bakhtin, M.M. (1986) *Speech genres and other essays*, Austin: University of Texas Press.

Bale, J. (1993) *Sport, space and the city*, London: Routledge.

Ball, R.M. (1995) *Local authorities and regional policy in the UK: attitudes, representations and the local economy*, London: Paul Chapman Publishing.

Ball, R.M. and Stobart, J. (1993) 'Community identity and the local government review: an exploration of the Cannock Chase area – Phase II report', Consultancy Report submitted to Cannock Chase District Council and the Local Government Commission.

Ball, R.M. and Stobart, J. (1994) 'Community identity and the local government review – the Cannock Chase community area and the Staffordshire MORI survey date: an evaluation?', Division of Geography, Staffordshire University.

Banks, M. (1996) *Ethnicity: anthropological* constructions, London: Routledge.

Barber, B. (1984) *Strong democracy: participatory politics for a new age*, Berkeley: University of California Press.

Barford, J. (1993) 'The key to empowerment: inform 92', *Audiovisual Librarian*, vol 19, no 1, pp 45-50.

Barke, M. and Turnbull, G. (1992) *Meadowell: the biography of an 'estate with problems'*, Aldershot: Avebury.

Barlow, J. (1995) *Public participation in urban development: the European experience*, London: Policy Studies Institute.

Barnes, C. (1991) *Disabled people in Britain*, London: Hurst and Co, British Council of Organisations of Disabled People.

Barr, A. (1995) 'Empowering communities – beyond fashionable rhetoric?   Some reflections on Scottish experience', *Community Development Journal*, vol 30, pp 121-32.

Bauman, Z. (1993) *Postmodern ethics*, Oxford: Blackwell.

Bauman, Z. (1995) 'Searching for a centre that holds', in M. Featherstone, S. Lash and R. Robertson (eds) *Global modernities*, London: Sage.

Baumgartner, M. (1988) *The moral order of a suburb*, New York: Oxford University Press.

Becker, B. and Bradbury, S.L. (1994) 'Feedback on tourism and community development: the downside of a booming tourist economy', *Community Development Journal*, vol 29, no 3, p 268-76.

Bell, C. and Newby, H. (eds) (1974) *The sociology of community: a selection of readings*, London: Frank Cass.

Bennett, R. (ed) (1989) *Territory and administration in Europe*, London: Pinter.

Benwell Community Development Project (1981) *West Newcastle in growth and decline*, Benwell CDP.

Bhabha, H.K. (1990) 'Dissemination: time, narrative, and the margins of the modern nation', in H.K. Bhabha, *Nation and narration*, London: Routledge.

Blackman, T. (1995) *Urban policy in practice*, London: Routledge.

Blackman, T. and Stephens, C. (1993) 'The internal market in local government: an evaluation of the impact of customer care', *Public Money and Management*, October-December, pp 37-43.

Boaden, N. Goldsmith, M. Hampton, W. and Stringer, P. (eds) (1982) *Public participation in local services*, Harlow: Longman.

Bourke, J. (1994) *Working-class cultures in Britain 1890-1960*, London: Routledge.

Bours, A. (1989) 'Management by territory and the study of administrative geography', in R. Bennett (ed) *Territory and administration in Europe*, London: Pinter, pp 72-90.

Boyne, G. and Law, J. (1993) 'Bidding for unitary status: an evaluation of the contest in Wales', *Local Government Studies*, vol 19, no 4, pp 537-57.

Bristol Broadsides (1980) *Corrugated ironworks. Poems and stories by the Hut Writers*, Bristol: Bristol Broadsides.

Bristol Broadsides (1986) *A Southmead festival of words*, Bristol: Bristol Broadsides.

Bristol City Council (1994) *Poverty in Bristol*, Bristol.

Brown, S. (1995) 'Crime and safety in whose "community"? Age, everyday life and problems for youth policy', *Youth & Policy*, vol 48, pp 27-48.

Brownill, S. (1993) 'The Docklands experience: locality and community in London', in R. Imrie and H. Thomas (eds) *British urban policy and the urban development corporations*, Liverpool: Paul Chapman.

Bruce Doern, G. (1993) 'The UK citizen's charter: origins and implementation in three agencies', *Policy and Politics*, vol 21, no 1, pp 17-29.

Brudney, J.L. and England, R.E. (1982) 'Urban policy making and subjective service evaluations: are they compatible?', *Public Administration Review*, vol 42, pp 127-35.

Buchanan, G. (1986) 'Local economic development by community business', *Local Economy*, no 2, Summer, pp 17-28.

Bulmer, M. (1986) *Neighbours: the work of Philip Abrams*, Cambridge: Cambridge University Press.

Burnett, A. (1994) 'The use of community in local politics', Paper presented at the Institute of British Geographers Annual Conference, Nottingham.

Burns, D. (1991) 'Ladders of participation', *Going Local*, vol 18, pp 14-15.

Burns, D., Hambleton, R. and Hoggett, P. (1994) *The politics of decentralisation: revitalising local democracy*, Basingstoke: Macmillan.

Butler, A., Oldman, C. and Greve, J. (1983) *Sheltered housing for the elderly*, London: Allen & Unwin.

Byrne, D. (1989) *Beyond the inner city*, Milton Keynes: Open University Press.

Cabinet Office (1988) *Action for cities*, London: HMSO.

Cabinet Office (1990) *People in cities*, London: HMSO.

Cain, H. and Yuval-Davis, N. (1990) 'The equal opportunities community and the anti-racist struggle', *Critical Social Policy*, vol 29, pp 5-26.

Campbell, B. (1993) *Goliath – Britain's dangerous places*, London: Methuen.

Campbell, B. (1995) 'Neighbourhood from hell', in *The Guardian Weekend*, 1 July.

Cannock Chase District Council (1994) *The case for unitary status*, Cannock.

Carter, P. (1993) *'I just feel happier that day': health promotion and pleasure in older people*, Newcastle upon Tyne: Social Welfare Research Unit, University of Northumbria at Newcastle.

Carter, P. and Everitt, A. (forthcoming) 'Conceptualising practice with older people: friendship and conversation', *Ageing and Society*.

Castells, M. (1991) *The informational city: information technology, economic restructuring and urban-regional process*, Oxford: Basil Blackwell.

Central Statistical Office (1993) *Regional trends*, vol 28, London: HMSO.

Chamberlain, M. (1986) 'Community romance', *New Statesman*, 9 May, vol 111, pp 12-13.

Chandler, J.A. (1989a) 'The territorial dimension of local government – a lost issue?', Paper presented to the Political Studies Association Conference, University of Warwick.

Chandler, J.A. (1989b) 'The liberal justification for local government: values and administrative expediency', *Political Studies*, vol 37, pp 604-11.

Chandler, J.A. (1995) 'Democracy and the defence of local government in Britain', in J.A. Chandler and S. Leach (eds) *Strategic government: the democratic deficit in local government*, London: Association of County Councils, pp 6-19.

Chisholm, M. (1994) 'The community index in the Local Government Review', Paper presented at the IBG, Annual Conference, Nottingham.

Churchill, H. and Everitt, A. (1996) *Home from home: conversations with older people in sheltered housing*, Newcastle upon Tyne: Social Welfare Research Unit, University of Northumbria at Newcastle.

Clapman, D. and Munro, M. (1988) *A comparison of sheltered and amenity housing for older people*, Edinburgh: Scottish Office.

Clarke, J. (1981) 'Capital and culture: the post war working class revisited', in R. Dale et al, *Politics, patriarchy and practice*, vol 2, Brighton: Falmer Press.

Clarke, M. and Stewart, J. (1992) *Citizens and local democracy: empowerment: a theme for the 1990s*, Luton: Local Government Management Board.

Clegg, S. (1989) *Frameworks of power*, London: Sage.

Cochran, C.E. (1989) 'The thin theory of community: the communitarians and their critics', *Political Studies*, vol XXXII, pp 422-35.

Cochrane, A. (1986) 'Community politics and democracy', in D. Held and C. Pollitt (eds) *New forms of democracy*, London: Sage.

Cochrane, A. (1991) 'The changing state of local government: restructuring for the 1990s', *Public Administration*, vol 69, pp 281-302.

Cohen, A.P. (1985) *The symbolic construction of community*, Chichester and London: Ellis Horwood and Tavistock Publications.

Cohen, A.P. (ed) (1986) *Symbolising boundaries. Identity and diversity in British cultures*, Manchester: Manchester University Press.

Cole, M. et al (1990-91) 'The citizen as "individual" and nationalist or "social" and internationalist? What is the role of education?', *Critical Social Policy*, vol 10, no 3, Winter, pp 68-87.

Colenutt, B. (1994) *Community empowerment in urban regeneration*, London: Docklands Consultative Committee.

Collins, C. (1991a) 'Partnerships: what's it all about?', *CiN* (Newsletter of the Community Information Network), no 1, pp 2-5.

Collins, C. (1991b) *Community participation in the Ferguslie Park 'partnership': a report to the Ferguslie League of Action Groups*, Paisley: FLAG.

Collins, C. (1992) *What's this all about then? Tenant participation in the Ferguslie Park 'partnership'*, Report written for the Tenants' Information Service.

Collins, C. (1996a) 'To concede or to contest', in C. Barker and P. Kennedy (eds) *To make another world: studies in protest and collective action*, Aldershot: Avebury, pp 69-91.

Collins, C. (1996b) 'The pragmatics of emancipation: a critical review of the work of Michael Huspek', *Journal of Pragmatics*, vol 25, pp 791-817.

Collins, C. and Lister, J. (1996a) 'Hands up or heads up: community work, democracy and the language of partnership', in M. Shaw and I. Cooke, *Radical community work: perspectives from practice in Scotland*, Edinburgh: Moray House.

Collins, C. and Lister, J. (1996b) 'From social strategy to partnership: Ferguslie Park and its significance for community work practice', *Concept*, vol 6, no 2, pp 3-7.

Collins, R. (1994) *Four sociological traditions*, Oxford: Oxford University Press.

Community Development Foundation (1995) *Guidelines to the community involvement aspect of the SRB Challenge Fund*, London: CDF.

Community Development Project Inter-Project Editorial Team (1977) *Gilding the ghetto: the state and the poverty experiments*, London: CDP Inter-Project Editorial Team.

Confederation of British Industry (1988) *Initiatives beyond charity: report of the CBI Task Force on business and urban regeneration*, London, CBI

Coombes, M., Openshaw, S., Wong, C. and Raybould, S. (1993) 'Community boundary definition: a GIS design specification', *Regional Studies*, vol 27, no 3, pp 280-86.

Cooke, P. (1989) (ed) *Localities: the changing face of urban Britain*, London: Unwin Hyman.

Cooper, D. (1993) 'Citizen's charter and radical democracy: empowerment exclusion within citizenship', *Social and Legal Studies*, vol 2, no 2, pp 149-71.

Corlett, W. (1989) *Community without unity. A politics of Derridian extravagance*, Durham, USA: Duke University Press.

Cox, K. and Mair, A. (1988) 'Locality and community in the politics of local economic development', *Annals of the Association of American Geographers*, vol 78, pp 307-25.

Croft, S. (1989) 'User-involvement, citizenship and social policy', *Critical Social Policy*, vol 26, Autumn, pp 5-17.

Crow, G. (1989) 'The post-war development of the modern domestic ideal', in G. Allan and G. Crow (eds) *Home and family*, Basingstoke: Macmillan, pp 14-32.

Crow, G. and Allan, G. (1994) *Community life: an introduction to local social relations*, Hemel Hempstead: Harvester Wheatsheaf.

Crow, G. and Allan, G. (1995a) 'Beyond 'insiders' and 'outsiders' in the sociology of community', Paper presented to the Annual

Conference of the British Sociological Association, University of Leicester, April.

Crow, G. and Allan, G. (1995b) 'Community types, community typologies and community time', *Time and Society*, vol 4, no 2, pp 147-66.

Cruddas Park Adult Education Group (1990) *Sod the dishes*, Cruddas Park Community Trust.

Cruddas Park Community Council, Minutes.

Cunning Young and Partners (1988) *Ferguslie 2000: a new Paisley pattern*, Report to Scottish Development Agency.

Dahl, R.A. (1967) 'The city in the future of democracy', *American Political Science Review*, LXI.

Davies, J.G. (1972) *The evangelistic bureaucrat*, London: Tavistock.

Davis, M. (1990) *City of quartz*, London: Verso.

Davoudi, S. and Healey, P. (1995) 'City Challenge – a sustainable mechanism or temporary gesture?', in R. Hambleton and H. Thomas (eds) *Urban policy evaluation*, Liverpool: Paul Chapman.

Day, P. and Klein, R. (1987) *Accountabilities: five public services*, London: Tavistock.

Day, G. and Murdoch, J. (1993) 'Locality and community: coming to terms with place', *Sociological Review*, vol 41, no 1, pp 82-111.

Deakin, N. and Edwards, J. (1993) *The enterprise culture and the inner city*, London: Routledge.

De Groot, L. (1992) 'City Challenge: competing in the urban regeneration game', *Local Economy*, vol 7, pp 196-209.

Dempsey, K. (1990) *Smalltown*, Melbourne: Oxford University Press.

Dempsey, K. (1992) *A man's town*, Melbourne: Oxford University Press.

Dennis, N., Henriques, F. and Slaughter, C. (1969) *Coal is our life: an analysis of a Yorkshire mining community*, London: Tavistock.

Department of the Environment (1991) *The structure of local government in England: a consultation paper*, London: DoE.

Department of the Environment (1992a) *Policy guidance to the Local Government Commission for England*, London: HMSO.

Department of the Environment (1992b) *City Challenge bidding guidance 1993-94*, London: DoE.

Department of the Environment (1992c) *Working partnerships – implementation agencies: an advisory note*, February, London: DoE

Department of the Environment (1993a) *Policy guidance to the Local Government Commission for England*, London: HMSO.

Department of the Environment (1993b) *Bidding guidance: a guide to funding from the Single Regeneration Budget*, London: DoE.

De Tocqueville, A. (1963) *Democracy in America*, P. Bradley (ed) New York: Alfred Knopf.

Devine, F. (1992) *Affluent workers revisited*, Edinburgh: Edinburgh University Press.

Dhooge, Y. (1982) 'Livelihood II: local involvement', in S. Wallman and associates, *Living in South London*, Gower, pp 103-23.

Dickens, P. (1988) *One nation?*, London: Pluto.

Dodson, J. and Kendall, D. (nd) Newcastle upon Tyne multi agency crime prevention initiative, *Residential survey*, Northumbria Police.

Dominelli, L. (1990) *Women and community action*, Venture Press.

Donnison, D. (1988) 'Secrets of success', *New Society*, 29 January, pp 11-13.

Dowding, K.M. (1991) *Rational choice and political power*, Aldershot: Edward Elgar.

Dowding, K.M., Dunleavy, P., King, D. and Margetts, H. (1995) 'Rational choice and community power structures', *Political Studies*, vol 43, pp 265-77.

Durkheim, E. (1982) *The rules of sociological method*, London: Macmillan.

Durkheim, E. (1893) *The division of labour in society*, Free Press (1964).

Elias, N. (1974) 'Foreword – towards a theory of communities', in C. Bell and H. Newby (eds) *The sociology of community: a selection of readings*, London: Frank Cass.

Elias, N. and Scotson, J.L. (1965) *The established and the outsiders: a sociological enquiry in community problems*, London: Frank Cass and Co.

Elias, N. and Scotson, J.L. (1994) *The established and the outsiders*, London: Sage, 2nd edn.

Estes, C., Swan, J. and Gerrard, L. (1982) 'Dominant and competing paradigms in gerontology: towards a political economy of ageing', *Ageing and Society*, vol 2, no 2, pp 151-64.

Etzioni, A. (1993) *The spirit of community*, New York: Touchstone.

Etzioni, A. (1995a) *The spirit of community: rights, responsibilities and the communitarian agenda*, London: Fontana.

Etzioni, A. (ed) (1995b) *The new communitarian thinking: persons, virtues, institutions and communities*, Virginia: University Press of Virginia.

Evans, K., Fraser, P. and Walklate, S. (1995) 'Whom can you trust? – the politics of 'grassing' on an inner city housing estate', Paper presented to the BSA Conference, Leicester.

Evans, K., Fraser, P. and Walklate, S. (1995) 'Grassing: whom do you trust in the inner city', *Sociological Review*, August 1996.

Fairclough, N. (1989) *Language and power*, London: Longman.

Faith in the City (1985) *Report of the Archbishop of Canterbury's Commission on urban priority areas*, London: Church House Publishing.

Ferguslie Park Strategy Group (1988) *Setting the pattern, Ferguslie Park: a review of the area initiative, 1984/88*, Strathclyde Regional Council: Paisley.

Fishkin, J.S. (1991) *Democracy and deliberation: new directions for democratic reform*, New Haven: Yale University Press.

Fishman, R. (1991) 'The garden city tradition in the post-suburban age', *Built Environment*, vol 17, no 3/4, pp 232-41.

Fletcher, P. (1991) *The future of sheltered housing: who cares?*, London: National Federation of Housing Associations Policy Report.

Fordham, G. (1995) *Made to last – creating sustainable neighbourhood and estate regeneration*, York: Joseph Rowntree Foundation.

Forrest, R. and Gordon, D. (1993) *People and places: a 1991 census atlas of England*, University of Bristol: SAUS Publications.

Fothergill, S. (1995) *The struggle over European funding*, London: Local Government Information Unit.

Foucault, M. (1977) *Discipline and punishment*, Harmondsworth: Penguin.

Fowles, A.J. (1993) 'Changing notions of accountability: a social policy view', *Accounting, Auditing and Accountability Journal*, vol 6, no 3, pp 97-108.

Frankenberg, R. (1957) *Village on the border: a social study of religion, politics and football in a North Wales community*, London: Cohen & West.

Frazer, E. and Lacey, N. (1993) *The politics of community: a feminist critique of the liberal-communitarian debate*, Hemel Hempstead: Harvester Wheatsheaf.

Freire, P. (1972) *The pedagogy of the oppressed*, Harmondsworth: Bristol.

Fyfe, N. (1993) 'Making space for the citizen? The (in)significance of the UK citizen's charter', *Urban Geography*, vol 14, no 3, pp 224-7.

Gamble, A. (1994) *The free economy and the strong state: the politics of Thatcherism*, 2nd edn, London: Macmillan.

Game, C. (1995) 'Assessing community identity and public opinion', in S. Leach (ed) *The Local Government Review: key issues and choices*, Birmingham: Institute of Local Government Studies, pp 64-81.

Gardiner, M. (1992) *The dialogics of critique: M.M. Bakhtin and the theory of ideology*, London: Routledge.

Gaster, L. (1996) 'Centralisation, empowerment and citizenship', *Local Government Policy Making*, vol 22, pp 57-64.

Gaster, L. et al (1995) *Interim evaluation of the Ferguslie Park partnership*, Edinburgh: Scottish Office Central Research Unit.

Gibson, A. (1992) *Older people and leisure in the West End of Newcastle*, Newcastle upon Tyne: Social Welfare Research Unit, University of Northumbria at Newcastle.

Giddens, A. (1991) *Modernity and self-identity*, Oxford: Basil Blackwell.

Gilbert, D. (1991) 'Community and municipalism: collective identity in late-Victorian and Edwardian mining towns', *Journal of Historical Geography*, vol 17, no 3, pp 257-70.

Gilchrist, A. (1995) *Community development and networking*, London: CDF.

Gittins, D. (1985) *The family in question*, London: Macmillan.

Glucksmann, M. (1990) *Women assemble*, London: Routledge.

Goetz, E.G. and Clarke, S.E. (1993) *The new localism*, Newbury Park: Sage.

Goldthorpe, J., Lockwood, D., Bechhofer, F. and Platt, J. (1969) *The affluent worker in the class structure*, Cambridge: Cambridge University Press.

Granovetter, M. (1973) 'The strength of weak ties', *American Journal of Sociology*, vol 78, pp 1360-80.

Gray, J. (1995) 'Hollowing out the core', in *The Guardian*, 8 March.

Green, D.G. (1987) *The new right*, Brighton: Wheatsheaf.

Green, J. (1995) 'Crime, poverty and unemployment: the case of West Newcastle', Paper prepared for the BSA Annual Conference, Leicester.

Green, J.M. (1995a) *Postmodernist community action?*, 'Rivers of blood' conference, University of Durham, April.

Green, J.M. (1995b) *A project from hell: an evaluation of the Search Project*, Newcastle upon Tyne: Social Welfare Research Unit, University of Northumbria at Newcastle.

Gyford, J. (1991) 'Does place matter? Locality and local democracy, the Local Government Management Board', *The Belgrave Papers*, no 3.

Gyford, J. (1991) *Citizens, consumers and councils*, Basingstoke: Macmillan.

Hall, D. (1977) 'Applied social area analysis: defining and evaluating areas for urban neighbourhood councils', *Geoforum*, vol 8, pp 277-310.

Hall, J.K. (1995) '(Re)creating our worlds with words: a sociohistorical perspective of face to face intervention', *Applied Linguistics*, vol 16, no 2, pp 206-32.

Hall, S. (1990) 'Cultural identity and diaspora', in J. Rutherford, (ed) *Identity, community, culture, difference*, London: Lawrence & Wishart.

Halliday, M.A.K. (1978) *Language as social semiotic: the social interpretation of language and meaning*, Cambridge: Cambridge University Press.

Hambleton, R. and Taylor, M. (eds) (1993) *People in cities: a transatlantic policy exchange*, Bristol: SAUS Publications.

Hambleton, R. and Thomas, H. (eds) (1995) *Urban policy evaluation*, Liverpool: Paul Chapman.

Hankey, P. (1995) 'Hanging out in cyberspace', in *The Guardian*, 21 April, p 24.

Harvey, D. (1989a) *The urban experience*, Oxford: Blackwell.

Harvey, D. (1989b) 'From managerialism to enterpreneurialism: the transformation in urban governance in late capitalism', *Geografiska Annaler*, vol 71B, pp 3-17.

Hartmanm, H. (1987) 'The family as the locus of gender, class and political struggle: the example of housework', in S. Harding, *Feminism and methodology*, Milton Keynes: Open University Press.

Hastings, A. (1996) 'Unravelling the process of "partnership" in urban regeneration policy', *Urban Studies*, vol 33, pp 253-68.

Hastings, A. and McArthur, A. (1995) 'A comparative assessment of government approaches to partnerships with the local community', in R. Hambleton and H. Thomas (eds) *Urban policy evaluation*, Liverpool: Paul Chapman.

Hedges, A. and Kelly, J. (1992) 'Identification with local areas', Report to DoE.

Hempel, S. (1991) 'A faint chorus of approval', *Nursing Times*, vol 87, no 34, pp 16-17.

Hill, D.M. (1994) *Citizens and cities: urban policy in the 1990s*, Hemel Hempstead : Harvester Wheatsheaf.

Hillery, G.A. (1955) 'Definitions of community: areas of agreement', *Rural Sociology*, vol 20, pp 111-23.

Hirschmann, A. (1970) *Exit, voice and loyalty: responses to decline in firms, organisations and states*, Harvard: Harvard University Press.

Hirst, P. (1976) *Social evolution and sociological categories*, London: Allen & Unwin.

Hoggart, R. (1958) *The uses of literacy*, Harmondsworth: Penguin.

Hoggett, P. (1991) 'A new management in the public sector?', *Policy and Politics*, vol 19, pp 243-56.

Hoggett, P. (1993) 'What is community mental health?', *Journal of Interprofessional Care*, vol 7, no 3, pp 201-9.

Hoggett, P. (1994) 'The politics of the modernisation of the UK welfare state', in R. Burrows and B. Loader (eds) *Towards a post-fordist welfare state?*, London: Routledge.

Hoggett, P. (1996) 'New modes of control in the public service', *Public Administration*, vol 74, pp 9-32.

Homans, G. (1951) *The human group*, London: Routledge and Kegan Paul.

Hope, T. and Shaw, M. (eds) (1988) *Communities and crime reduction*, London: HMSO.

Hope, T. (1995) 'Community crime prevention', in M. Tonry and D.P. Farrington, 'Building a safer society – strategic approaches to crime prevention', *Crime and Justice*, vol 19, Chicago: University of Chicago.

Hughes, G. (1996) 'Communitarianism and law and order', *Critical Social Policy*, vol 16, no 4, pp 17-41.

Hunt, D. (1990) Speech given at British Urban Regeneration Association, 13 February.

Hymes, D. (1974) *Foundations in sociolinguistics: an ethnographic approach*, Philadelphia: University of Pennsylvania Press.

Imrie, R. and Thomas, H. (eds) (1993a) *British urban policy and the urban development corporations*, London: Paul Chapman Publishing.

Imrie, R. and Thomas, H. (1993b) 'The limits of property-led regeneration', *Environment and Planning C: Government & Policy*, vol 11, pp 87-102.

Iwama, H. (1992) 'The internal structure of a mining-manufacturing community and its formation processes: a comparison of Ube and Hitachi', *Geographical Review of Japan*, series A, vol 65, no 8, pp 635-52.

Jacobs, B. (1992) *Fractured cities*, London: Routledge.

Jeffers, S., Hoggett, P. and Harrison, L. (1996) 'Race, ethnicity and community in three localities', *New Community*, vol 22, no 1, pp 111-26.

Johnson, R. (nd) 'Two ways of remembering: exploring memory as identity', Unpublished paper.

Johnston, R.J., Gregory, D. and Smith, D.M. (eds) (1994) *The dictionary of human geography*, 3rd edn, Oxford: Blackwell.

Joseph Rowntree Foundation (1995) *Inquiry into income and wealth*, York: Joseph Rowntree Foundation.

Kamis, C. (1992) 'Wolverhampton', *Local Work*, vol 34, pp 6-7.

Keith-Lucas, B. and Richards, P.G. (1978) *A history of local government in the 20th century*, London: Allen and Unwin.

Kelly, G. (1995) 'Falling off the edge? After City Challenge: organising effective succession strategies', *Newcastle City Challenge Seminar Series*, 28 July.

Kemp, A. (1993) *The hollow drum*, Edinburgh: Mainstream.

King, D.S. (1987) *The new right*, Basingstoke: Macmillan.

Kintrea, K. (1996) 'Whose partnership? Community interests in the regeneration of a Scottish housing scheme', *Housing Studies*, vol 11, pp 287-306.

Kirby, A. (1993) *Power/resistance: local politics and the chaotic state*, Bloomington: Indiana University Press.

Klein, M. (1986) *The selected Melanie Klein*, J. Mitchell (ed), London: Penguin.

Kymlicka, W. (1993) 'Community', in R.E. Goodin and P. Pettit (eds) *A companion to contemporary political philosophy*, Oxford: Blackwell.

Lash, S. and Urry, J. (1994) *Economies of signs and space*, London: Sage.

Lawless, P. (1989) *Britain's inner cities*, London: Paul Chapman.

Leat, D. (1988) *Voluntary organisations and accountability*, London: NCVO.

Lewis, N. (1993) 'The citizen's charter and next steps: a new way of governing?', *The Political Quarterly*, vol 64, no 3, pp 316-26.

Lichfield District Council (1994) *The Lichfield and Tamworth Authority: proposed Cannock Chase unitary authority – response by Lichfield District Council*, Lichfield.

Lifelines (1994) The Southmead Community Play, remembered, devised and created by people of Southmead, script by Neil Beddow.

Lister, R. (1990) 'Women, economic dependency and citizenship', *Journal of Social Policy*, vol 19, no 4, pp 445-67.

Local Government Commission for England (1992) *Guidance on the approach to the reviews*.

Local Government Commission for England (1993) *Reviewing local government in the English shires: a progress report*, London: HMSO.

Local Government Commission for England (1994a) *The future local government of Staffordshire: draft recommendations*, July, London: HMSO.

Local Government Commission for England (1994b) *Final recommendations on the future local government of Staffordshire: a report to the Secretary of State for the Environment*, September, London: HMSO.

Lockwood, D. (1975) 'Sources of variation in working-class images of society', in M. Bulmer (ed) *Working-class images of society*, London: Routledge and Kegan Paul, pp 16-31.

Logan, J. and Molotch, H. (1987) *Urban fortunes*, Berkeley: University of California Press.

Lovell, R. (1992) 'Citizen's charter: the cultural challenge', *Public Administration*, vol 70, pp 395-404.

Lowery, D. (1992) 'Citizenship in the empowered locality: an elaboration, a critique and a partial test', *Urban Affairs Quarterly*, vol 28, no 1, pp 69-103.

Lukes, S. (1974) *Power: a radical view*, London: Macmillan.

Mabbot, J. (1993) 'The role of community involvement', *Policy Studies*, vol 14, no 2, pp 27-35.

MacFarlane, R. (1993) *Community involvement in City Challenge: a good practice report*, London: NCVO publications.

MacFarlane, R. and Mabbott, J. (1993) *City Challenge: involving local communities*, London: National Council for Voluntary Organisations.

Macintyre, S. (1980a) *Little Moscows*, Croom Helm.

Macintyre, S. (1980b) *A proletarian science*, Cambridge: Cambridge University Press.

Mackenzie, W.J.M (1961) *Theories of local government, Greater London papers no 2*, London: London School of Economics.

McCulloch, A. (1990) *Rationale and proposal for the evaluation of the Cruddas Park and Loadman Street Project*, Newcastle Polytechnic.

McArthur, A. (1993) 'Community partnership – a formula for neighbourhood regeneration in the 1990s?', *Community Development Journal*, vol 28, pp 305-15.

McCulloch, A. (1994) *Cruddas Park/Loadman Street Project: final report and evaluation*, University of Northumbria.

McGregor, A. et al (1992) *Community participation in areas of urban regeneration. A report to Scottish Homes*, Edinburgh: Scottish Homes.

McIntyre, J. (1991) 'FLAG information', Unpublished report on meeting of 24 August.

Maffesoli, M. (1989) 'The sociology of everyday life (epistemological elements)', *Current Sociology*, vol 37, pp 1-16.

Maffesoli, M. (1991) 'The ethics of aesthetics', *Theory, Culture and Society*, vol 8, pp 7-20.

Maffesoli, M. (1996) *The time of the tribes. The decline of individualism in mass society*, London: Sage.

Massey, D. (1988) 'A new class of geography', *Marxism Today*, May, pp 12-17.

Massey, D. (1995) 'The conceptualisation of place', in D. Massey and P. Jess (eds) *A place in the world?*, Oxford: Oxford University Press/Open University.

Mawson, J. et al (1995) *The Single Regeneration Budget: the stocktake*, Birmingham: Centre for Urban and Regional Studies, University of Birmingham.

Melucci, A. (1988) 'Social movements and the democratisation of everyday life', in J. Keane and J. Meir (eds) *Nomads of the present*, London: Hutchinson.

Midwinter, A. (1993) 'Shaping Scotland's new local authorities: arguments, options, issues', *Local Government Studies*, vol 19, no 3, pp 351-67.

Mill, J.S. (1975) 'On liberty', in R. Wollheim (ed) *John Stuart Mill: three essays*, Oxford: Oxford University Press.

Mill, J.S. (1975) 'Representative government', in R. Wollheim (ed) *John Stuart Mill: three essays*, Oxford: Oxford University Press.

Milofsky, C. (1987) 'Neighbourhood-based organisations: a market analogy', in W.W. Powell (ed) *The non-profit sector: a research handbook*, New Haven: Yale University Press.

Milofsky, C. and Hunter, A. (1994) 'Where non-profits come from: a theory of organisational emergence', Paper presented to Association for Research on Non-profit Organisations and Voluntary Action, San Francisco, October.

Mitchell, J. (1990) *The myth of dependency*, Edinburgh Scottish Centre for Economic and Social Research, *Forward Series*, no 3.

Mogey, J. (1956) *Family and neighbourhood*, London: Oxford University Press.

Morgan, K. (1995) 'Reviving the valleys? Urban renewal and governance structures in Wales', in R. Hambleton and H. Thomas (eds) *Urban policy evaluation*, Liverpool: Paul Chapman.

Morphet, J. (1993) 'Getting closer to the people', *Town and Country Planning*, May, pp 113-15.

National Audit Office (1990) *Regenerating the inner cities*, London: HMSO.

Nevin, B. and Shiner, P. (1994) 'Behind the chimera of urban funding', *Local Work*, vol 52.

Nevin, B. and Shiner, P. (1995) 'The Single Regeneration Budget: urban funding and the future for distressed communities', *Local Work*, vol 58.

Newcastle City Council Chief Executive's Department (1990) *Minority ethnic communities: report of the research manager, chief executive's department*, Newcastle City Council, Racial Equality Sub-committee, 21 November.

Newcastle Journal, 16 October, 1992.

Newcastle Westend Partnership with the Research Section, Newcastle City Council (1994) *Newcastle upon Tyne City Challenge profiles*, Newcastle upon Tyne: Newcastle Westend Partnership.

Oatley, N. (1995) 'Competitive urban policy and the regeneration game', *Town Planning Review*, vol 66, pp 1-14.

Offe, C. (1975) 'The theory of the capitalist state and the problem of policy formation', in L.N. Lindberg, R. Alford, C. Crouch and C. Offe (eds) *Stress and contradiction in modern capitalism*, Lexington, DC: Heath.

Oliver, M. (1992) 'Changing the social relations of research production?', *Disability, Handicap and Society, Special Issue: Researching Disability*, vol 7, no 2, pp 101-14; and other articles in this issue.

Ostrom, V., Bish, R. and Ostrom, E. (1988) *Local government in the United States*, San Francisco: Institute for Contemporary Studies.

Paddison, R. (1993) 'City marketing, image reconstruction and urban regeneration', *Urban Studies*, vol 30, pp 339-50.

Pahl, R. (1984) *Divisions of labour*, Oxford: Basil Blackwell.

Pahl, R. and Wallace, C. (1988) 'Neither angels in marble nor rebels in red: privatisation and working-class consciousness', in D. Rose (ed) *Social stratification and economic change*, London: Hutchinson, pp 127-49.

Parry, G., Moyser, G. and Day, N. (1992) *Political participation and democracy in Britain*, Cambridge: Cambridge University Press.

Parry, I. and Thompson, L. (1993) *Effective sheltered housing: a handbook*, London: Institute of Housing.

Phillimore, P., Beattie, A. and Townsend, P. (1994) *Health and inequality: the Northern Region 1981-91*, Newcastle upon Tyne, Department of Social Policy, University of Newcastle upon Tyne.

Phillips, A. (1993) *Democracy and difference*, Cambridge: Polity Press.

Phillipson, C. and Walker, A. (eds) (1986) *Ageing and social policy: a critical assessment*, Aldershot: Gower.

Pinto, R. (1995) 'Revitalising communities: a moment of opportunity for local authorities', *Local Government Policy Making*, vol 21, no 5, pp 30-41.

Pirie, M. (ed) (1991) *Empowerment: the theme for the 1990s*, London: Adam Smith Institute.

Plant, R. (1974) *Community and ideology*, London: Routledge and Kegan Paul.

Polsby, N.W. (1980) *Community power and political theory*, New Haven: Yale University Press.

Powell, W.W. (1990) 'Neither market nor hierarchy: network forms of organisations', in B. Staw (ed) *Research in organisational behaviour*, vol 12, Greenwich, CT: JAI Press.

Power, A. and Tunstall, R. (1995) *Swimming against the tide*, York: Joseph Rowntree Foundation.

Procter, I. (1990) 'The privatisation of working-class life: a dissenting view', *British Journal of Sociology*, vol 41, no 2, pp 157-80.

Ram, M. (1995) 'The politics of research: local consultation in a City Challenge context', *Sociology*, vol 29, no 2, pp 275-92.

Redcliffe-Maud (1969) *Report of the Royal Commission on Local Government in England*, vol I and vol III, Cmnd 4040, London: HMSO.

Redlich, J. and Francis, H.W. (1903) *Local government in England*, vol II, London: Macmillan.

Relph, E. (1991) 'Suburban downtowns of the Greater Toronto area', *Canadian Geographer*, vol 35, no 4, pp 421-25.

Rex, J. and Moore, R. (1967) *Race, community and conflict*, London: Oxford University Press.

Rhodes, R.A.W. (1981) *Control and power in central-local government relations*, Farnborough: Gower.

Richardson, A. (1983) *Participation*, London: Routledge and Kegan Paul.

Roberts, E. (1984) *A woman's place*, Oxford: Basil Blackwell.

Robinson, F. and Shaw, K. (1991) 'Urban regeneration and community involvement', *Local Economy*, vol 6, pp 1-73.

Robson, B. (1988) *Those inner cities*, Oxford: Clarendon Press.

Robson, B. (1989) *Those inner cities: reconciling the economic and social aims of urban policy*, Oxford: Oxford University Press.

Ross, E. (1983) 'Survival networks: women's neighbourhood sharing in London before World War I', *History Workshop*, no 15, Spring, pp 4-27.

Rosser, C. and Harris, C. (1965) *The family and social change: a study of family and kinship in a South Wales town*, London: Routledge and Kegan Paul.

Safe Neighbourhoods Unit (1991) *The Southmead survey*, for Bristol City Council and Bristol Safer Cities Project.

Sandel, M.J. (1982) *Liberalism and the limits of justice*, Cambridge: Cambridge University Press.

Sassen, S. (1991) *The global city: New York, London, Tokyo*, Princeton: Princeton University Press.

Saunders, P. (1990) *A nation of home owners*, London: Unwin Hyman.

Savage, M., Barlow, J., Duncan, S. and Saunders, P. (1987) 'Locality research: the Sussex programme on economic restructuring, social change and the locality', *The Quarterly Journal of Social Affairs*, vol 3, no 1, pp 27-51.

Scottish Business in the Community (1990) *Urban renewal: the partnership approach*, Edinburgh: ScotBIC.

Scottish Homes (1990) *Renfrew/Inverclyde District Plan, 1990*, Paisley: Scottish Homes.

Scottish Office (1988) *New life for urban Scotland*, Edinburgh: HMSO.

Scottish Office (1989) *A pattern for new life: strategy for the regeneration of Ferguslie Park*, Edinburgh: HMSO.

Scottish Office (1990a) *Urban Scotland into the 90s: proceedings of the conference held in the Forum Hotel, Glasgow, from 14-16 May*, Edinburgh: HMSO.

Scottish Office (1990b) *New life two years on*, Edinburgh: HMSO.

Scottish Office (1991) *Ferguslie Park partnership: three year progress report*, Edinburgh: HMSO.

Scottish Office (1993) *Progress in partnership*, Edinburgh: HMSO.

Scottish Office (1995) *Programme for partnership*, Edinburgh: HMSO.

Seabrook, J. (1984) *The idea of neighbourhood*, London: Pluto.

Seebohm Report (1968) *Report of the Committee on local authority & allied personal services*, London: HMSO.

Sharpe, L.J. (1970) 'Theories and values of local government', *Political Studies*, vol 18, pp 153-74.

Shields, R. (1991) *Places on the margin: alternative geographics of modernity*, London: Routledge.

Simmons, M. (1995) 'Long pit road to recovery', in *The Guardian*, 2 August.

Skeffington Report (1969) *People and planning*, London: HMSO.

Skelcher, C. (1993) 'Involvement and empowerment in local services', *Public Money and Management*, vol 13, pp 13-20.

Skelcher, C., McCabe, A. and Lowndes, V. with Nanton, P. (1996) *Community networks in urban regeneration: 'it all depends who you know...!'*, Bristol: SAUS Publications.

Skogan, W.G. (1988) 'Community organisations and crime', in M. Tonry and N. Morris (eds) *Crime and justice: a review of research*, Chicago: University of Chicago Press.

Smith, J. and Chanan, G. (1986) 'Public service and community development', *Local Government Studies*, vol 12, pp 7-14.

South Staffordshire District Council (1994a) *South Staffordshire's response to the draft recommendations*, Codsall.

South Staffordshire District Council (1994b) *The case for South Staffordshire*, Codsall.

Spencer, J., Tuxford, J. and Dennis, N. (1964) *Stress and release in an urban estate*, London: Tavistock.

Stacey, M. (1969) 'The myth of community studies', *British Journal of Sociology*, vol 20, no 2, pp 134-47.

Stacey, M., Batstone, E., Bell, C. and Murcott, A. (1975) *Power, persistance and change*, London: Routledge and Kegan Paul.

Stafford, W. (1994) 'Ferdinand Tonnies: a candidate for the canon?', *Politics*, vol 14, no 1, June, pp 15-20.

Staffordshire County Council (1993) *Local Government Review: making the right decision*, Stafford.

Staffordshire County Council (1994) *Local Government Review: submission part II – authorities for Staffordshire*, Stafford.

Stallybrass, P. and White, A. (1986) *The politics and poetics of transgression*, London: Methuen.

Staples, L.H. (1990) 'Powerful ideas about empowerment', *Administration in Social Work*, vol 14, no 2, pp 29-42.

Stewart, J. (1983) *Local government: the conditions of local choice*, London: Allen & Unwin.

Stewart, J., Kendall, E. and Coote, A. (1994) *Citizens' juries*, London: Institute for Public Policy Research.

Stewart, M. (1994) 'Value for money in urban public expenditure', *Public Money and Management*, vol 14, pp 55-61.

Stewart, M. and Taylor, M. (1995) *Empowerment and estate regeneration*, Bristol: The Policy Press.

Strathclyde Regional Council (1988) *Generating change – urban regeneration: the Strathclyde experience*, Glasgow: SRC.

Strathclyde Regional Council (1991) 'Analysis of community participation within the formal structures of the partnership', Unpublished council report.

Sugden, N. (1994) *Friends are like diamonds ...* , Newcastle upon Tyne: Social Welfare Research Unit, University of Northumbria at Newcastle.

Tamworth Borough Council (1994) *A unitary solution*, Tamworth.

Tarrow, S. (1994) *Power in movement: social movements, collective action and politics*, Cambridge: Cambridge University Press.

Taylor, M. and Hoggett, P. (1994) 'Trusting in networks? The third sector and welfare change', in I. Vidal (ed) *Delivering welfare: repositioning non-profit and cooperative action in Western European welfare states*, CIES: Barcelona.

Thomas, D.N. (1995) *Community development at work: a case of obscurity in accomplishment*, London: CDF.

Thompson, E.P. (1970) *The making of the English working class*, Pelican.

Thornley, A. (1991) *Urban planning under Thatcherism*, London: Routledge.

Tiebout, C. (1956) 'A pure theory of local expenditures', *Journal of Political Economy*, vol 64, no 3, pp 416-24.

Tizard, J.N. and Holman, K. (1995) 'Communities, governance and local democracy: roles and relationships', *Local Government Policy Making*, vol 21, no 5, pp 3-8.

Tonnies, F. (1887) *Community and association*, London: Routledge and Kegan Paul (1955).

Tonnies, F. (1957) *Community and society*, C.P. Loomis (trans and ed), New York: Harper Row.

Tonry, M. and Farrington, D.P. (1995) 'Building a safer society – strategic approaches to crime prevention', *Crime and Justice*, vol 19, Chicago: University of Chicago Press.

Townsend, P. (1962) *The last refuge*, London: Routledge and Kegan Paul.

Tricker, M. (1996) 'The impacts of the first two-and-a-half years of the City Challenge Programme – an interim assessment', Aston: Aston Business School.

Tritter, J. (1994) 'The citizen's charter: opportunities for users' perspectives?', *The Political Quarterly*, vol 65, no 4, pp 397-414.

Truman, J. and Brent, J. (1995) *Alive and kicking! The life and times of Southmead Youth Centre*, Bristol: Redcliffe Press.

Turok, I. (1992) 'Property-led urban regeneration: panacea or placebo?', *Environment & Planning A: Government & Policy*, vol 24, pp 361-79.

Vincent, A. and Plant, R. (1984) *Philosophy, politics and citizenship – the life and thought of the British idealists*, London: Basil Blackwell.

Volosinov, V.N. (1973) *Marxism and the philosophy of language*, London: Seminar Press.

Volosinov, V.N. (1986a) *Marxism and the philosophy of language*, London: Harvard University Press.

Volosinov, V.N. (1986b) 'Discourse in life and discourse in poetry', in A. Shukman (ed) *Bakhtin school papers*, Oxford: RPT Publications, pp 5-30.

Wahlberg, M. and Geddes, M. (1995) 'Taking the initiative on local democracy', *Local Government Policy Making*, vol 21, no 5, pp 9-26.

Wallace, C. and Pahl, R. (1986) 'Polarisation, unemployment and all forms of work', in S. Allen, A. Waton, K. Purcell and S. Wood (eds) *The experience of unemployment*, Basingstoke: Macmillan, pp 116-33.

Wallman, S. (1984) *Eight London households*, London: Tavistock.

Walsh, K. (1995) *Public services and market mechanisms: competition, contracting and the new public management*, Basingstoke: Macmillan.

Walzer, M. (1991) 'Constitutional rights and the shape of civil society', in R. Calvert (ed) *The constitution of the people: reflections on citizens and civil society*, Lawrence: University Press of Kansas.

Walzer, M. (1995) 'The communitarian critique of liberalism', in A. Etzioni (ed) *The new communitarian thinking: persons, virtues, institutions and communities*, Virginia: University Press of Virginia.

Ward, C. (1993) *New town, home town: the lessons of experience*, Calouste Gulbenkian Foundation.

Warwick, D. and Littlejohn, G. (1992) *Coal, capital and culture*, London: Routledge.

White, M. (1995) '"Neighbours" plan gets £20m aid', in *The Guardian*, 7 June.

Widdicombe, D. (1986) *Report of the Committee into the Conduct of Local Authority Business*, Cmnd 9797, London: HMSO.

William Roe Associates (1994) *An evaluation of community involvement in the Ferguslie Park partnership*, Edinburgh: The Scottish Office Central Research Unit.

Williams, R. (1992) 'Homespun philosophy', in D. Jones and S. Platt (eds) *Borderlands: nations and nationalism, culture and community in the new Europe*, London: Channel 4 and New Statesman & Society.

Williams, W. (1956) *The sociology of an English village: Gosforth*, London: Routledge and Kegan Paul.

Willmott, P. (1986) *Social networks, informal care and public policy*, London: Policy Studies Institute.

Willmott, P. and Young, M. (1960) *Family and class in a London suburb*, London: Routledge and Kegan Paul.

Wilson, R. (1963) *Difficult housing estates*, London: Tavistock.

Winstanley, D. (1995) 'When the pieces don't fit: a stakeholder power matrix to analyse public sector restructuring', *Public Money and Management*, April-June, pp 19-26.

Wood, B. (1976) *The process of local government reform 1966-1974*, London: George Allen & Unwin.

Wood, J., Walker, G., Bannister, E. and Kay, I. (1989) *Feasibility study into the prospects of social and economic regeneration in the Loadman Street and Cruddas Park (West) area of Newcastle*, np.

Workers' Educational Association/Ferguslie Elderly Forum (1992) *The reminiscences of the Ferguslie Elderly Forum*, Paisley: WEA.

Worsley, P. (ed) (1987) *The new introduction to sociology*, Harmondsworth: Penguin.

Young, M. and Willmott, P. (1957) *Family and kinship in East London*, London: Penguin.

Zizek, S. (1991) *For they know not what they do. Enjoyment as a political factor*, London: Verso.

Index